Wynn Wheldon was born in London in 1958. He has worked in cultural exchange, politics, publishing and broadcasting. He is the author of prize-winning short stories, the poetry collection *Private Places* (2015), and several books, including *The Father and Child Companion* (2005) and *Porches* (2003). He is the lyricist for the Jack Rabbit Project and a founding member of the Elbow Room Writers' Collective. He is married, has three adult sons, and lives in North London.

KICKING THE BAR

Huw Wheldon:
A Filial Biography

Wynn Wheldon

unbound

This edition first published in 2016

Unbound
6th Floor Mutual House 70 Conduit Street London W1S 2GF

www.unbound.co.uk

Grateful acknowledgement to the following for the use of images:
BBC; Mark Boxer; S. Morse Brown; Raymond Jackson (JAK); Elsbeth R. Juda with permission from the Victoria and Albert Museum, London; Richard Levin; Willie Rushton and Christopher Booker; Don Smith; Topfoto/John Hedgecoe; Rory Trappe; TV Mirror; Sian Wheldon.

While every effort has been made to trace the owners of copyright material reproduced herein, the publisher would like to apologise for any omissions and will be pleased to incorporate missing acknowledgments in any further editions.

Text Design by PDQ

A CIP record for this book is available from the British Library

ISBN 978-1-78352-220-0 (trade hbk)
ISBN 978-1-78352-221-7 (ebook)
ISBN 978-1-78352-258-3 (limited edition)

Printed in Great Britain by Clays Ltd, St Ives Plc

1 2 3 4 5 6 7 8 9

Dear Reader,

The book you are holding came about in a rather different way to most others. It was funded directly by readers through a new website: Unbound

Unbound is the creation of three writers. We started the company because we believed there had to be a better deal for both writers and readers. On the Unbound website, authors share the ideas for the books they want to write directly with readers. If enough of you support the book by pledging for it in advance, we produce a beautifully bound special subscribers' edition and distribute a regular edition and e-book wherever books are sold, in shops and online.

This new way of publishing is actually a very old idea (Samuel Johnson funded his dictionary this way). We're just using the internet to build each writer a network of patrons. Here, at the back of this book, you'll find the names of all the people who made it happen.

Publishing in this way means readers are no longer just passive consumers of the books they buy, and authors are free to write the books they really want. They get a much fairer return too – half the profits their books generate, rather than a tiny percentage of the cover price.

If you're not yet a subscriber, we hope that you'll want to join our publishing revolution and have your name listed in one of our books in the future. To get you started, here is a £5 discount on your first pledge. Just visit unbound.com, make your pledge and type **barkick** in the promo code box when you check out.

Thank you for your support,

Dan, Justin and John
Founders, Unbound

ACKNOWLEDGEMENTS

I should like to thank the following for their help in the writing of this book:

At the University of Buckingham, under whose auspices it was originally written as a Master's thesis, Victoria Fishburn and Judith Paisner, fellow students who gave great moral support; Frances Wilson and Frances Spalding, who commented so kindly on my original work; and most especially Jane Ridley, my supervisor, who is patience on a monument and an example to us all.

David Attenborough, Melvyn Bragg, Humphrey Burton, and Wynn Rees, for valuable comments on versions of the manuscript; Miranda Arnold, Mike Fairbairn, Mary McCormack, Chrys Salt, Jody Vandenburg, and Sue Whitmore, for constant suggesting, urging, nudging, and tweeting; Mr E.W. Thomas, Archivist, Bangor University; staff at the BBC Archives at Caversham and the ACGB Archives at the V&A; Gwyneth Wheldon; the staff at Unbound, especially Mathew Clayton, Georgia Odd, Philip Connor and DeAndra Lupu; my editor Tamsin Shelton; Peter Palumbo; Norman and Midge *in loco parentis*; my sisters Sian and Megan, who have been staunch, useful, funny, and encouraging; my sons, Thomas, Jacob, and Cal, for their general good-spiritedness.

Most of all, my wife, Debby Mendoza, without whose forbearance, generosity and love this would not have been possible.

All errors are my own.

For Thomas, Jacob, Cal, Cat, Molly, Helena, Merle, Maud, Nat & Johanna, none of whom Dad knew, so that they may know something of him.

And for Sian and Megan, and for Debby.

The problem was not how to tell the story, but how to tell the right story.

Huw Wheldon

There's a fundamental sense in which you did not and cannot make yourself the way you are.

Galen Strawson

Completeness is not merely impossible; it is undesirable.

A.J.A. Symons

Many paragraphs in the story of a man's life are so heavily deleted they cannot even be read by their author. They are like small flames struck by matches. Blown out, where have they gone?

Dannie Abse

Love makes the heart yearn for eloquence.

Jacqueline Wheldon

(

CONTENTS

FOREWORD

DAVID ATTENBOROUGH

Huw Wheldon once dominated BBC Television. From 1965 to 1975 he was, in effect, in charge of it. His title varied, as is the way in bureaucratic organisations, but his presence in Television Centre, where the majority of the BBC's television programmes were then produced, was in those years almost palpable.

It was certainly both audible and visible. His laugh – famously loud and unmistakable – echoed around that huge and labyrinthine building. And he was seen everywhere in it – in the corridors, and in the conference rooms, in the canteen where he chose to eat rather than in the more select senior staff dining room, and, for a few minutes most evenings, in each of its eight studios when he regularly toured the control galleries – just to see how things were going. His approval of a programme was much sought after and his disapproval much feared. And most importantly, his beliefs about the function and responsibilities of broadcasting were widely known and discussed. In short, he was a leader in a way that has not been seen in British television either before or since.

I was his colleague for twenty years. For eight of them I served directly under him, and I heard him say, several times, that he was, fundamentally, a regimental man. And indeed he was, for during the Second World War he had served in the British Army's Airborne Division, winning the Military Cross on D-Day. However, as well as being a doughty fighter, he also, like most successful leaders, needed a cause, an ideal, to fight for and champion. He found it in public service television.

He had first become widely known as the avuncular host of a television programme called *All Your Own* in which he encouraged youngsters to explain their enthusiasms and demonstrate their particular and often extraordinary skills. He then became a producer, responsible for a range of programmes, many of which – perhaps significantly – examined the nature of leadership as seen and assessed by such diverse people as Orson Welles and Sir Brian Horrocks, the distinguished General. But viewers from that time will remember him most vividly as the editor and presenter of the world's first regular arts programme, *Monitor*. After that, he ran the whole television service.

That was, in brief, his professional life. But how did such a powerful, dominant and daunting figure behave privately, within his family? Was his professional persona something that he could switch off when he got home – and switch back on the following morning? Only his family can properly answer that question. And here is the moving and heartfelt answer – from his son.

But this book is much more than that, for the intimacies of childhood have enabled Wynn Wheldon to examine and understand the complex character of his father in a unique way. As a consequence, he has produced a rounded portrait of a great man which will fascinate people far beyond the limited bounds of television.

PREFACE

My father tapped me gently on my upper arm with the back of his hand.

'There you are,' he said. He was pointing to a paragraph in the *Daily Telegraph* in which he was described as 'legendary'. He was clearly chuffed. I've no recollection of what the article was about, just Dad's chuffedness. However, he then asked me whether really one ought to be dead in order to be legendary. I very likely ummed and ahhed, and may have pointed out that he wasn't dead. Still, I have the distinct impression that despite being chuffed he was also a little discomposed. But only a little.

To be a legend in one's own lifetime is usually the hyperbolic lot of sportsmen and pop stars, or occasionally individuals known to select coteries (Patrick Leigh Fermor, for example, and I recently saw Adam Phillips described as 'the legendary psychologist'), but there it was in black and white, ungainsayable.

So what is the legend that my father inhabits?

I would quite like to have called this book *Drunken by the Wine of a Noble Aim*, which is a phrase from one of my great-grandfather's speeches. You will come across it in due course. I acknowledge that it is rather a mouthful, and doesn't chime quite with the times, but it does more or less provide the main theme of this book.

My father was moved by the idea of public service, as his father and his grandfather had been. I think it took the war to properly reveal this motive. The war turned him from a mere thinker into a doer. However, there was no nobility to be found in war, only 'waste'. It was in the BBC that he found the wine, both as a maker of programmes and as an executive.

It all seems very old-fashioned now, but BBC Television of the 1950s and '60s led the climb out of the despond of war. It was a place of tremendous energy and cross-fertilisation, the creative heart of the nation. My father was in no small part responsible for that, and for the programming that made the Corporation 'one of the great institutions of the Western world', as he liked to put it.

Father and son, a long time ago

INTRODUCTION

FATHERS AND SONS

I did not grow up in an ethically stentorian household, but I think I was ever so gently, even unconsciously, persuaded that there is such a thing as the Good Life. What follows is an attempt to describe a life, my father's, lived in this belief.

It is a curious, mongrel piece of work. It is made up of shreds and patches. I have taken what I have found out about my father's existence before me (a kind of shock to discover such a person in the first place) and blended it quite wantonly with my own memories of him. The whole exercise becomes positively chaotic when you consider that I have also drawn on the memories and accounts of others, although I have not formally interviewed anyone. I have spoken with my sisters,

15

Sian and Megan, of course. Our parents continue to fascinate, even haunt us.

Lest the foregoing suggest that this is simply a work of louche appetite, I ought to add that I have wanted to write about my father for a long time, ever since the publication of an earlier, rather baffled biography. However, the present work is not an attempt at reproof or redress but rather an investigation prompted by love and curiosity.

As Milton found, and Blake perceived, the devil has the best lines, and the devil is markedly absent from what follows, other than as part of its wider context. Sons have always written about their fathers. It tends to be a subject on which they feel expert. I'm sure there are some great lost texts: it would be interesting to read Isaac's thoughts on Abraham. Curiously, that particular tale, unlike most of the rest on the subject, is about Abraham's willingness to do anything for his father (God), rather than disobey. Generally, sons are forever throwing off their fathers' laws, codes, rules, conventions, chains, yokes, and of course shackles, and asserting themselves (usually as superior beings). In English the acme of the genre is Edmund Gosse's wonderfully clever *Father and Son*,[1] which Gosse published having already written a formal biography of his father. JR Ackerley's *My Father and Myself* is an altogether more vulgar book. More modern works, such as *And When Did You Last See Your Father?* by Blake Morrison and *Experience* by Martin Amis, maintain the superiority, but are more forgiving. The same could not be said of Auberon Waugh's 1991 book about his father Evelyn, *Will This Do?* In fiction, Samuel Butler's *The Way of All Flesh* was a virulent attack on his father's hypocrisy, not published until after its author's death. Father and son is an old, old subject. It is a major theme even in a story set in a galaxy far, far away, a long time ago.

Published in 1907, *Father and Son* remains attractive because it perfectly balances scorn and tenderness. And the tenderness is from both sides. Gosse is tender about his father because his father was tender to him. It is also a funny book. Until the bitter end, the son in retelling their story seems often amused, and this amusement speaks of love not ridicule.

Father and Son is often held to be the great hammer-blow that did for the Victorian father but Philip Gosse was not such a man in any of the clichéd senses; Edmund was not unhappy, did not feel repressed or abused: 'I had a great difficulty in persuading myself that I could ever be happy away from home'. When he does leave home he feels the oppressiveness of his father's concern for his spiritual welfare much more keenly. At breakfast his father's letters 'lie awaiting me, destroying the taste of the bacon'. The book seems to accelerate in time and meaning as it moves towards its remarkable climax in which the son, 'in the hot house at home, among the gorgeous waxen orchids', loses his temper with the father's 'customary interrogatory. Was I "walking closely with God"? Was my sense of the efficacy of the Atonement clear and sound? Had the Holy Scriptures still their full authority with me?' The son resolves to take the 'human being's privilege to fashion his inner life for himself'. (I'm rather worryingly reminded of my own customary interrogation of my son Jacob's reading habits.)

The 'inner life'. It is a modern note. So where did I learn that there is an 'inner life'?

Well, it was probably in the pages of DH Lawrence, a writer of whom my mother was very fond. I think my mother's inner life was everything to her. However, I'm not sure my father spent a great deal of time fashioning an inner life for himself. The Welsh Methodism he was born into was experiential not theological. Life was for getting on with. Which is not to say that he didn't recognise the worth of or even perhaps envy the more ruminative life: but you had to ruminate properly. There was all the difference in the world between idleness and thoughtfulness.

This book is not about my relationship with my father. It is a story of his life mediated by that relationship. We loved one another; I might even say we knew one another. There was, at least, very little that was difficult between us. I do not have issues to resolve; I do not seek closure, none of that stuff, and while his concerns for me had more to do with character than success, they were not oppressive, at least not most of the time.

Until Lytton Strachey spilled his sarcastic self over the world of biography in *Eminent Victorians*, lives of the great and the good were worthy tomes in which vices were glossed over and virtues highlighted. Well, I have no desire to turn back the clock, but I would suggest that occasionally the great and the good are indeed great and good, and that their lives can be exemplary. I happen to believe this of my father's.

I daresay Dad was assailed by lust from time to time (indeed I know he was, as am I and you); he was occasionally greedy I imagine; gluttonous – no; slothful, well, by his own account, certainly; wrathful – terribly so on occasion; envious – difficult to remember any envy: at golf, he may rather have envied Alasdair Milne the length of his golf drive (though not his accuracy); pride, yes I think he was proud, but not startlingly more so than anyone else. He was, in short, a Good Man, a fairly old-fashioned notion in this relativistic age; but I continue to measure myself against him, and sometimes I find myself wanting, and very occasionally I think myself superior.

My mother, who may very well have been a genius – and I am aware of the hyperbole that so often attaches to this word – died in June 1993, feeling she had wasted an opportunity life had given her. My father, who was not a genius, but was a great and good man, died on my sister Megan's twenty-third birthday in March 1986, I suspect feeling that he had been neither as good nor as great as he ought to have been. I look back at these two lovely parents and, among a myriad other thoughts, wonder why such kind and clever people should have died remotely disappointed. But perhaps we all die disappointed.

'Don't curse life,' was one of my parents' chief commandments. It is odd that I cannot remember which one said it, because they were very different people despite being, for me, in a sense, one enormous thing. I suspect it was my mother, because it is the kind of Lawrentian phrase that would have come easily to her, though she would have found it much harder to obey the command than my father. I think for both of them the temptation into which we ask not to be lead in the Lord's Prayer ('a great poem' according to Dad) was despair.

Although he gave all the indications of enjoying life very much, I don't think Dad enjoyed his own self that much. He very rarely spoke about it. He was a pessimist, always anticipating making a mess of things. He preferred to celebrate others, people and things and institutions – the hornbeams in Richmond Park, Jack Nicklaus, 'peachy' weather, the music of Poulenc, the BBC.

I have tried not to curse life; and indeed I have not had much cause to. I am very happily married. I have three sons of whom I'm very proud. I have odd moments of transcendent joy, usually, like Coleridge or Wordsworth, while walking, or perhaps listening to music or watching my children being happy. Of course, I am given to periods of unhelpful self-loathing in which I feel I have squandered sinfully all the advantages and favours that life has given me. Oddly troubling has been a sense of retreating into the future. So another motive for this book is an attempt to put the past where it belongs, behind me.

Were my parents let down by life? Did they let themselves down? Did they believe in God? Did they lead godly lives? I have neither the space, nor perhaps the intellectual capacity, to answer these questions of my mother's life. She had the most wholly original mind I have ever been close to: she was entirely herself responsible for it. She wrote fiction that is immensely ambitious and difficult, and in the end she was somehow defeated in her attempt to articulate that inner life in the outer world.

Dad on the other hand succeeded in everything he did. He joined the army as a private and ended the war turning down promotion to Colonel and decorated with the Military Cross. He finished his work with the Arts Council with an OBE for his contribution to the Festival of Britain. He became the mentor of a generation of film-makers, including Ken Russell and John Schlesinger and John Boorman. He oversaw what some have called the 'golden age' of British television; he was knighted and was regarded as an outstanding Chairman of the Court of Governors of the London School of Economics. He had six books that I know of dedicated to him, and several poems. Television professionals still employ his maxims and phrases: 'the aim is not to avoid failure – the aim is to give triumph a chance', 'the pursuit of excellence', 'narrowcasting', 'ignore the obvious at your peril', 'the three duties of the broadcaster are to the subject, to the audience and to the craft', 'to make the good popular and the popular good', 'programmes calculated rather than made... are slums of the spirit and slums of the mind'. His memorial service was at Westminster Abbey. Jessye Norman sang Purcell. Several people have said that he was the finest man they ever knew. Beyond all this he was a loving father and husband and a good friend. The only wrong step he took was to die too young.

I have myself failed in almost everything I have attempted. I say this not in a spirit of self-pity, but because the contrast with my father is so stark, and yet I feel him within me, and recognise myself in him, though I don't have his modesty. He was a self-deprecating man, though he had little reason to be. One of his favourite stories of his schooldays ran as follows. The schoolteacher, Mr Roberts, is handing back essays. As each one is handed over Mr Roberts makes a little comment. 'THOMAS, JR, seven out of ten. Good. VAUGHAN, DL, five out of ten. Poor. WHELDON, HP, four out of ten – a great improvement!'

On the whole, I think that fathers try not to show their sons their vulnerabilities; indeed I think they try to disguise them. It is left to the sons to discover them. Hence the tone, in many filial biographies, of barely suppressed superiority: the father who for so long knew best now doesn't even know himself, and the son knows all. I am not at all like that. I don't especially think that my father tried to hide his weaknesses: he was quite clear what they were, and what he disliked in himself he disliked in me.

I no longer aspire to the achievements of either of my parents. For a long time (for far too long, a fatally long time, fatal for any other prospects to make themselves realised) I had in mind for my career only the idea of writing a Great Novel.

If the shadow kills the growth, it was my mother's shadow, not my father's. I was brought up with her broadly Leavisite view of literature – that the sacred works of Western civilisation were by Homer, Dante, Shakespeare, Goethe, Tolstoy, Proust, and that to be a writer was the ultimate status. Writers were holy men. But I might have had a different idea of what was sacred, as we shall see.

There is no particular science or specific craft to biography, other than the writer's: 'the proper study of mankind is man', and if the reader learns a smidgen more about mankind from reading further, then a job will have been done, a thing made. I make no claims for my objectivity, nor even for historical accuracy, although I have certainly not consciously tinkered with chronologies or skewed facts. I have no theory of biography to push, other than this: that a man or a woman is made of many things and it is puerile to ascribe to one source the motive for behaviour. The best one can do is describe action and attempt, when the situation dictates, to find an empathy with one's subject. In this case that includes at some points younger versions of myself, characters as distinct (or indistinct) from my present self as any other. Certainly I have stood in different places to look at my father: from within his own letters, from the point of view of the biographer, in my mother's notes and writings, in the contexts of histories of war and religion. I hope the result is as multi-faceted as this suggests. I do not want to interpret or pin down or explain. I want to show.

'HUGE WELSHMAN, BBC Supreme Commander!'
Caricature drawn by Mark Boxer for Clive James's satirical poem The Fate of Felicity Fark
in the Land of the Media

---

* My father was usually described as 'tall' – David Attenborough, for example, in his autobiography *Life on Air*: 'his tall, slightly hunched figure'. He wasn't tall. He was five feet eleven inches. He just *seemed* tall.

Capel Rhosydd, Cwmorthin, Blaenau Ffestiniog, photograph by Rory Trappe

CHAPTER 1

LAND OF HIS FATHERS

I am sitting on a length of slate, set across a fast running mountain rill, and staring down at my feet. The skin about my toes is becoming more and more translucent until I can almost believe that what I see is bone, the deathly comic phalanges waving loosely in the stream at the end of the metatarsals. The day is hot and my feet were sore. The water has the coldness that water would have in heaven.

I am at the far end of Cwmorthin, a valley outside Blaenau Ffestiniog in North Wales. I have parked my car at the bottom of the valley and walked up through the quarry workings, past the lake and the ruined Capel Rhosydd (also known as Capel Y Gorlan, which means 'chapel of the sheepfold', and one or two sheep graze there now), and I am taking a breather before moving on up over the pass between Moelwyn Mawr and Cnicht from where I will descend into the village of Croesor. And as I look down at my skeletal feet I feel suddenly tremendously alive, above and beyond time, and though the cold of the water is beginning to bite, I am reluctant to withdraw my feet. I don't want to lose this moment. And it turns out that I haven't, or not entirely: *tap, tap, tap* I go at my keyboard.

Cwmorthin is my favourite place in the world. It is beautiful and full of ghosts. My great-grandfather might have preached in the ruined chapel. And Cnicht, the side of which rises away from me when I look up from my feet, was one of the first mountains my father took me up. It was from Cnicht that I learned about false peaks, one following another until at last we reached the summit. There my father told me what to eat at the top of a mountain: a pork pie, an apple and a bar of Bournville chocolate. Cwmorthin is now an abandoned place but in the middle of the nineteenth century it would have been heaving with activity as the slate was wrenched from the hillsides. The evidence of the industrial ravages – the great flanks of discarded slate scaling the hillsides – has about it a melancholy beauty. I have always preferred man-made landscapes to desert wastes. Mountains should have names.

All branches of the Wheldon family have a print of a photograph of the kitchen at Llwyn Celyn, a farmhouse facing the eastern flank of Snowdon bought by rent-collecting ancestor John (or Sion) Wheldon in the early 1840s. It is a modest enough place. The wallpaper, poorly applied, covers the ceiling as well as the walls, in a fashion nowadays only seen in unreconstructed cheap French hotels. But there is a dinner service in the large Welsh dresser, and there are plenty of cluttering knick-knacks. In the corner are larger willow pattern platters. Several pairs of shoes hang from the beams. On the wall, artlessly displayed, are pictures. One looks like Charles Dickens. There is a portrait of the great Methodist preacher Charles Haddon Spurgeon, who could draw crowds of 10,000 and address them all without benefit of amplification. There is a large framed print of Mr Gladstone. My father always referred, in his half ironic way, to 'Mr Gladstone', never merely 'Gladstone'. I do so myself. Prime Ministers who have their pictures hanging on farmhouse walls are not the easy butts of cynical metropolitan world-weariness. They demand respect.

Thomas Jones Wheldon at home at Llwyn Celyn, photographer unknown

Sitting on the settle is my father's grandfather, Thomas (or Tomos) Jones Wheldon (TJ), the very picture of the wise patriarch. Looking out towards the light, he seems confident, wise, at home, energy at rest. He was for a time the Moderator of the Calvinistic Methodist Church of Wales, *Y Gorff* as it was known – 'the body' – or, more familiarly, *Yr Hen Gorff* – 'the old body'. Calvinistic Methodism is not really very Calvinistic at all. Calvinism is usually understood as a particularly cruel form of Protestantism, with its emphasis on the 'elect' (God, who is omniscient, already knows who will be rewarded by heaven and who will go to the other place), but Welsh preachers were warm, witty, and enthusiastic rather than declaiming: 'joy and rejoicing and singing were the great characteristics of Welsh Calvinistic Methodism.'[1] Worship – praise – was to feel, not to think, an act, not a rumination. And while the conviction of sin was absolute, so was the assurance that sin was forgiven. There seems to have been little of the bully in the Calvinistic Methodist Church of Wales. Its congregants wanted to know God personally. They liked Him. (In several letters to me Dad described God's reaction to golfing foibles and – less often, much less often – heroics: 'God spoke', 'God smiled', 'God swore').

Thomas Jones Wheldon, for whom my own first born was named, Thomas Johannes, died when my father was five months old, and so could have had no direct influence on him. Nevertheless, the character and beliefs of the scholarly, though pugnacious, minister ('it is true, I believe, that he once floored a man in the street, in the early days of Ffestiniog, and that with excellent results', wrote his son Wynn proudly[2]) exerted their influence on succeeding generations. I think an understanding of how my father ran BBC Television is to be found partly in the liberal nonconformist determination of my great-grandfather.

TJ was born in Llanberis, in the heart of Snowdonia, on 10 March 1841. (This was the day after the first ever photograph taken in Wales, of Margam Castle, by the Reverend Calvert Richard Jones; *The Times* was urging the Duke of Wellington to re-enter politics). His parents were John and Mary Wheldon. John, or Sion, born about 1815, was the son of Pyrs and Elinor Wheldon, about whom nothing is known. About John we know that he was a quarry worker, a sometime rent-collector, and later a farmer at Llwyn Celyn, near Llanberis. He was possessed of a fiery temper, strong will and independent mind. Mary Jones, his wife, was a devout Calvinistic Methodist, a great-granddaughter of the celebrated Robert Jones, Rhoslan, the author of *Drych yr Amseroedd* ('A Mirror of the Age'), which, according to Emyr Humphreys, is a Welsh classic.[3] (Jones also compiled the first Welsh-language hymnbook, *Grawn-sypian Canaan*.) Mary survived a serious illness, and John was impressed enough by the efficacy of her prayers that he became an enthusiastic member of the church at Capel Coch. In due course he became an elder (a Presbyter). He was well known for his singing.

John and Mary's son Thomas was educated at the British School at Capel Coch and at the Calvinistic Methodist college at Bala. He took a degree by correspondence at the University of London, and then took the examination for the Indian Civil Service. He finished in the top 100 and was offered a job that would have given him a good career and a handsome pension. He turned it down, preferring to stay in Wales. Why did he take the exam? Why turn down the job? And why did neither my father nor I inherit any ability to do well in exams? Dad wasn't a terrific student, and nor was I. In my art A-level I wrote a rather good essay about Bellini's *Ecstasy of St Teresa* without once mentioning the name of the sculptor, the name of the piece, or where it might be found (Rome). And when I say Bellini, I mean of course Bernini.

TJ ran both the English and Welsh churches at Newtown, Montgomery until 1873 when he became pastor of the *tabernacl* and Bethesda chapels in Blaenau Ffestiniog.

Blaenau Ffestiniog, I used to boast to school friends who holidayed in France or Spain or Italy, was the rainiest town in Great Britain. When TJ took up his post there, it was entering its golden age as the world capital of slate. Under the near feudal ownership of the Barons Penrhyn the slate mines of Snowdonia provided slates for the roofs of empire and beyond. 'The roofs of San Francisco are lined with slate from Blaenau,' my father would tell me. The quarries reached their peak of production in 1889,[4] three years before TJ moved from Blaenau to Bangor. They employed 16,000 men. Affluence should have been evident throughout the community, but 'the autocrat of Bethesda' (Penrhyn) and his fellow landowners made sure that the profits slipped almost entirely into their own coffers.

The nonconformist chapels were the social and cultural focal points of Welsh life. Preachers were often poets as well as preachers. TJ was not a poet. *Welsh Outlook*, in its review of his biography in 1925, observed that 'Mr Wheldon was never a popular preacher, for he disdained to cultivate the art of pleasing the crowd.'[5] The same could not be said, perhaps, for his grandson, who could not help himself from pleasing the crowd. The same review insists that 'there never lived a man who so hated shams and sanctimoniousness as Wheldon' – and that could indeed have been said about Dad. *Welsh Outlook*'s view of TJ is contradicted by the view of Reverend George Reith:*

His speech was both impassioned and humorous; it amused while it impressed the assembly. Its matter was spiced with clever and pungent frivolities which were more than half serious – much to the delight of the House.

---

* A Scotsman. It is pleasing to imagine that he might have been related to that 'Wuthering Height' (Churchill's phrase), Lord Reith of the BBC.

In example, referring to his dearly beloved brethren the Welsh bishops, he remarked that they claimed to be descended from the apostles. If so, he added, in a tone whose pitch suggested the Welsh hwyl, if so, the descent was great.[6]

In 'clever and pungent frivolities which were more than half serious' I recognise at once a kinship, to my father, and indeed to myself, although my own pungency and cleverness may be a good deal more frivolous than that of my forebears. The discrepancy between the two accounts is best explained by describing TJ not as a preacher but as a lecturer. There is, in the Wheldon male, an intellectual forever being camouflaged in one way or another.

TJ was also an educationalist. He caused schools to be built, among them the first Higher Grade School – to all intents and purposes the first secondary school – in North Wales, at Blaenau Ffestiniog. Education, naturally, was distrusted by the quarry owners, and the establishment of schools was no straightforward fracas with local bureaucracy. TJ himself described his struggles, which were for both educational and political causes, as 'pitched battles'.[7]

He was much involved in the setting up of the University College of North Wales at Bangor (to which Penrhyn would contribute neither land nor money), and he subsequently sat as a member of its council. TJ also caused to have built (despite the opposition of other church members) a large chapel, a *tabernacl*, on Garth Road in Bangor, completed in 1906, at the height of the famous Welsh Revival of 1904–1906 that had reverberations throughout the world. John Betjeman, I understand, regarded the chapel highly. 'St Wheldon's in the Field'[8] it was known as locally.

The thirty years between about 1870 and 1900 saw a great

change in the structure and functioning of Welsh society. Where there had been no educational establishments to speak of, no cities, by 1900, according to Kenneth O. Morgan, Wales 'possessed the kind of intelligentsia, the kind of literary élite that it had previously lacked. The fact that this élite was so closely enmeshed with the daily concerns of the people, through chapels, *eisteddfodau*, and popular publishing, made its influence all the more lasting.'[9] The foundations had been laid for a grand administrative Wales, and for Lloyd George to take the Welsh language into Downing Street.

'The least pompous great man I have ever met', wrote sculptor Jonah Jones of my father.[10] This absence of pomposity, I believe, was a function of my father's Welshness. He had none of the Englishman's awkward class consciousness. He grew up in a society that was much more of a piece than was (and perhaps still is) English society.

It sounds a little flip to say that TJ's loyalty was to God first and Wales second, but it is probably true. He did a great deal for both, and it is not easy to untwine the two causes. By 1895 there were almost 3,000 Calvinistic Methodist chapels in Wales, over 145,000 communicants and 300,000 adherents. This was out of a population of 500,000 Welsh speakers. Even allowing for inflation (these are the church's own figures) these are impressive numbers.

TJ had a temper, as the pugilistic story suggests, and could be impatient when he saw no reason for delay (my father had a similar irritability, and I think my family will vouch for my own). He would probably have had to be rather stubborn as well. These vices were likely to have been virtues in the conditions in which he had to work: saints do not fight 'pitched battles' (it is the 'pitched' that gives the phrase resonance and suggests he was being only half metaphorical).

During the General Election of 1885 a meeting was held in the Public Hall of Blaenau Ffestiniog, probably a Liberal rally. A mob gathered outside (possibly paid for or goaded into action by quarry owners) and began to smash windows. TJ, who was chairing the meeting, formed a phalanx of able-bodied men and lead them four abreast through the front door. The mob had expected flight by the back door, and was taken aback and quickly dispersed. Nevertheless, TJ was struck on the head by a rock. Hard times. I have no difficulty in asserting that TJ was a man who feared only God.

My father was a tender man, a quality rarely on display in his public life. I suspect the same is true of TJ. Of the few letters I have from TJ to his son Wynn, most are in Welsh and beyond me, but there is one letter written from Dinan in France which struck me as suggesting a tone of voice similar to that of my father's – gently irreverent, slightly ironic and delighting in the natural world. 'You are fortunate,' wrote TJ, 'in being educated in Wales and not here where all are Catholics and Sunday like some other day.'[11] One must naturally assume some degree of aversion to Catholicism,* and understand the unavoidable temptation to make a point to his much-blessed children. On the other hand the tone is very far from sanctimony or indignation, and the sentence is followed by a delicious non sequitur: 'there are apple trees and pears everywhere and all other fruits and plenty of grapes'. So endeth the sermon. It is almost as if, having criticised Catholicism (not France), it is now necessary to report on the abundance of nature. His child is left with an image of bounty not meanness. This is exactly how my father operated.

* Dad was always aware of the Catholics around him: Paul Wright, Cecil McGivern, Ken Russell, Elgar, Charles Curran…

Both men were born to celebrate rather than denigrate; believers not sceptics, and never cynical. (I can't remember Dad being cynical about anything – other than the beliefs of the sanctimonious.)

In 1895, TJ addressed the staff, pupils and gathered notables of the Grove Park Grammar School for Girls, in Wrexham, on the occasion of the school's opening. His speech identified those 'aims and deeds' closest to his heart and mind:

> The school belongs to the whole community. Both act and react upon the other. We are here as citizens, putting one noble stone again in the great building of National Education, which is and must be built in our land. All may gather round this school, Welsh and English, rich and poor, cultured and uncultured, men and women...
>
> What possibilities lie within you? God knows. We believe that there is a richer store in your minds and hearts than in the minds of the whole country. We echo in part today the great creative word 'let us make men'. Men, not money; women, not dress. Men inspired with the ideal of duty, of justice, of undefiled affection, of great aims and great deeds...
>
> In the capacities of your hand, there is an infinite possibility of usefulness, work, art and beauty. What territories unknown, and unsearchable riches lie within the nature of a child!... Be aflame, be as beside yourselves – mad for the truth, drunken by the wine of a noble aim. Be so before you are thirty or forty years of age, or you will never be. No ashes give flame.[12]

I have quoted this at some length because I can hear my

father in it. What TJ is here most concerned with is 'the great building of National Education', and what he does with his subject is to praise it. He speaks of 'the beauty that is to be', certain that this is what National Education will bring, of the 'infinite possibility of usefulness, work, art and beauty'. What National Education will do is 'make men. Men, not money; women, not dress'. National Education, then, is a cause, one that will make people better. It is to be an agent for virtue. It is not too much to say that Dad thought the same of television. How very odd that now seems. Indeed, how very odd both aims now seem.

Where TJ spoke of 'great aims and great deeds', Dad spoke of 'the pursuit of excellence'. Although he may not have believed in 'the temple that is to be', he certainly believed that there was positive, generative good in most individuals, and that the contribution of their best selves could not be anything but desirable and should be encouraged. But I don't think my father was an idealist. Idealism, it is to be imagined, is hard for those who have been in war. My father was at Belsen soon after its liberation. That had been made by men. Men 'aflame... beside themselves', one might say. My father was thirty years old when he came out of the army, getting on for 'ashes'. His generation was particularly impressive, perhaps, because it had witnessed the extremes of human vice and virtue. He was very likely suspicious of anyone 'drunken by the wine of a noble aim'. On the other hand, that 'ideal of unflinching duty' may have even been reinforced. TJ wrote to Wynn: 'duty is all when properly understood'. I think he meant that one should do whatever one was doing as best as one could, that this was the way in which God was most properly served. My father spoke of three duties when it came to the making of television programmes: to the subject, to the audience, and to the medium itself. If one of those three was unfulfilled, then the programme would fail. Duty is all.

In 1907 TJ suffered a stroke, or what the *Manchester Guardian* described as 'one or two seizures', and retired to Rhyl, where he was looked after by his wife Mary until her death in 1915. He died within months, the following year.

TJ's biography, or *cofiant* ('that specialist form of biography propagated throughout the nineteenth century for the edification of the faithful in all denominations'[13]), published in 1925 at the instigation of his son Wynn, was reviewed by *Welsh Outlook*: 'the picture we get in this book is of an intensely virile man, believing in himself and certain great causes, a tremendous worker, a born leader, often rough but always just and merciful, full of faith in God, and believing that God had great purposes in mind for Wales and for the Calvinistic Methodist body'. It further emphasised TJ's belief in free education at primary, secondary and tertiary levels and his desire for some degree of Welsh self-government.

Nor was TJ provincially minded. He went twice to the United States, on preaching tours in Welsh-speaking communities. Whether he did this out of piety, curiosity or the need for financial stability, I don't know. A little of each I dare say. Wheldons, on the whole, have had good relations with America.

I think my great-grandfather's voice was loud in my father's head. Whether it got there by way of the mystery of genes or by way of the mild manners of my grandfather I do not know. Over and again those who worked with or for Dad testify to his ability to bring the best out of them, by insisting on the best. One can see this as a quality of the born teacher, but I believe the imperative was more powerful than that. I think it was moral. I think he felt that it was his duty.

The best self eschews conformity. But in what circumstances may nonconformity flourish? A very particular kind of institution has to be made, cherished and promoted. Diversity requires manners. Manners allow enemies to speak; without manners there is mere black and white. The best institutions are those that promote conversation (in which argument may have its place) rather than confrontation. The BBC was, in my father's opinion, just such an institution. In the BBC there was 'an infinite possibility of usefulness, work, art and beauty'.

There is one other story about TJ that the family likes to remember, or rather that Dad liked to tell. As TJ was returning home one dusk, in pony and trap, from some meeting or other, there was a great kerfuffle above his head, along with a terrible screeching. An object passed over him and landed in a field further ahead. The pony had been startled, and TJ was curious himself, and felt compelled to investigate. Eventually he came upon the object. Two animals: a peacock lay dead, and a weasel, also dead, its teeth buried in the bird's throat.

We endlessly recreate the past. The concerns of the present are immediate, and the past must continuously be brought into line. This is the job of the historian, and the reason why there is always work for him. He has no choice. Imagining Thomas Jones Wheldon is made easier because he is in some sense the beginning of a history that ends with the present piece of writing. I did not know him, my father did not know him; he is, then, to some extent, open to a kind of mythologising process.

I do, however, remember my grandfather. He died in 1961, when I was three years old. My memory of him is completely untrustworthy, memory being one's own historian and having similarly to change with the times. Nevertheless, a memory it is, and whether developed – even created – after the time or not, it tells something of the impression the man made on me. I took something into his bedroom when he, *Taid*, and my grandmother, *Nain*, were staying at our house at 44 Mortlake Road, in Kew. What I recall is a very upright figure sitting in bed, all white whiskeriness, authority and benevolence. And that is all. But it is enough to preserve him from mythology. He was real, and my description of him, or rather of his life, must be limited, more or less, to fact.

Wynn Powell Wheldon was born in 1879 in Blaenau Ffestiniog, and educated there at the Elementary and Higher Grade School (the one founded by his father). Blaenau was still a fairly remote place. The one story that has come down from Wynn's childhood was the appearance one year of a Russian with a dancing bear. The children of the town fed the bear with anything they could find, despite the Russian's requests for them to desist. The following morning the boys woke to find the Russian on the side of the road out of town, weeping over the body of his dead livelihood.

When the family moved to Bangor, Wynn attended Friars School (which flourishes still, and where my cousin Sion Wheldon taught art). He went to Oswestry Grammar School as a boarder. In 1897 he enrolled at the University College of North Wales (now Bangor University), where he read English and Philosophy.* He then attended St John's College, Cambridge, where he read Law, passing with an Upper Second. He was articled with a Liverpool law firm,

---

* My son Thomas teaches Philosophy at the University of Heidelberg.

Lightbound, Owen & MacIver. In 1906, aged twenty-seven, he passed the final exam of the Law Society and became the firm's Managing Clerk. In the following years he worked for Lord John Russell & Co and Lloyd George, Roberts & Co. In 1914 he enlisted in the Inns of Court and in December of the same year he was commissioned into the 14th Battalion of the Royal Welch Fusiliers.

The years 1905–1914 have been described by Kenneth O. Morgan as 'Wales's Antonine age'.[14] This description he borrowed from Gibbon, who saw the age of the Antonines in Rome as the period when its people were most happy, cultivated and prosperous. Morgan writes (of Wales): 'Almost all the literature of the era, the periodicals, the daily press, the memoirs, the social commentaries, the devotional and scholarly works, provide testimony to the golden glow of optimism and hope that characterised this happy generation'.[15]

Good education broadens horizons, encourages curiosity and plants an aspirant seed. Well-educated Welshmen saw and were attracted by a larger world. While TJ had taken his degree at London by correspondence, Wynn went to Cambridge itself. This was very far from any kind of formality. Cambridge was still overwhelmingly dominated by the English landed classes. Wynn must have been a very hard-working man, determined and self-assured. My father had perhaps a filial affection for Cambridge, despite his general antipathy towards Oxbridge. We used to drive there every Whitsun holiday, up over London from Kew, on the North Circular, past the Welsh Harp, up the A10, to stay with the chemist Aaron Klug and his family. Other friends, too, had come out of Cambridge, by way of my mother: the novelist Dan Jacobson, and New York intellectual Norman Podhoretz.

The BBC of course was full of Oxbridge types, administrators, producers and performers alike. My father – Welsh, LSE – was always a bit of an outsider at the BBC. I think he thought it gave him a bit of an edge, as though he had more strings to his bow than the Oxbridge crowd.

In the tight nonconformist world of North Wales, in which religion, education and politics were inextricably linked, it was inconceivable that coming figures such as David Lloyd George would not be well known to a family such as the Wheldons. Law was one of the professions the new highly educated Welsh had taken up enthusiastically. LG occasionally consulted old TJ on pertinent matters. TJ would have mentioned his bright spark of a son, and so when it came to staffing his legal offices in London, LG would have been looking precisely for men like Wynn Wheldon.

Wynn didn't have long in London (though he got to know LG well enough to call him a friend) before war intervened. Wynn had a long, hard war. He must have been lucky, too. He fought in the Ypres Salient from 1916 to 1918, a total of two years and eight months' active service (by contrast my father had to wait over four years between signing up and seeing his first action on D-Day). He led his battalion at the Battle of Pilckem Ridge (31 July–2 August 1917), the first battle of the British offensive of 1917 that ended in the blood-soaked mud of Passchendaele. Among the killed at Pilckem was the poet Ellis Humphrey Evans, or Hedd Wyn as he is better known.[*] Wynn was awarded the Distinguished Service Order and was wounded at the Battle of Mormal Forest in November 1918 at

[*] Astonishing the number of great writers who served with the Royal Welch Fusiliers during the First World War. In addition to Hedd Wyn there was David Jones, Robert Graves, Siegfried Sassoon, Llewelyn Wyn Griffith and Frank Richards.

the very end of the war. In a report prepared earlier that year he was described as 'a solid and conscientious officer. He has confidence in himself and is reliable. He has a sound military knowledge and the ability to impart it to others. He has a cheerful disposition and could get men to follow him. He has a good word of command and can handle troops in the field. An officer above the average. I consider him fit to command a battalion when required.'[16] He had been Officer Commanding the 14th Battalion, Royal Welch Fusiliers for a year.

Three other events marked his war years. In 1915, on 15 July, at the Calvinistic Methodist chapel in Wilton Square in Islington (irretrievably damaged during the Second World War), he married Margaret Edwards, known more familiarly as Megan, the daughter of Hugh Edwards and Annie Parry-Williams. Edwards was an executive of the Royal Liver Assurance Company. According to *The Ladies' Field* it was 'a very pretty wedding... the bride looked charming in a handsome costume of crêpe de soie with white pearl trimming, and orange blossoms with a veil of Brussels lace.'[17] In the photograph that accompanied the article Nain looks very like my father, and even more like my beautiful sylph-like niece Molly Line. There is a photograph of Dad in a school play at Friars in which he is made up like a flapper. There too is Molly. The curious thing is that Molly should be so beautiful, an adjective that could never have been used of my father.

Wynn's parents were present. TJ was by now very ill, and could not speak, although his interest in the world about him was undiminished. It must have taken courage to make the long journey from Rhyl.

The reception was at the Trocadero in Piccadilly Circus (a very different place nowadays) and the couple honeymooned in Leamington Spa, where arithmetic indicates my father was conceived. His birth on 7 May 1916 was the second event of the war years. The third was the death of TJ the following November.

Having begun his family – late by the standards of the day (he was thirty-seven when my father was born; Dad was forty-two when I was born; I was a mere twenty-nine when my son Thomas was born) – been promoted Major and worked for LG, my grandfather was of sufficient standing to be approached by David (later Lord) Davies with a view to contesting a parliamentary seat in the interest of an independent Welsh party 'on the lines of the Irish Party'. This was 1917, and the analogy is surprising given the serious unrest in Ireland at the time, provoked by the imminence of Home Rule. Welsh enthusiasm for the war had been considerable (indeed, proportionally, more Welshmen fought than Englishmen or Scotsmen), and this was due to the notion that the war was being fought, as Lloyd George put it, on behalf of the 'little five-foot-five nations'.*

My grandfather declined.[†]

In May 1916 Woodrow Wilson first proposed a 'league of nations', and this proposal was later enshrined as the last of his 'fourteen points' in his plan for peace two years later. The war finished in November 1918 and in the following year Wynn Wheldon became the League's organiser in Wales.

---

[*] I wrote to Kenneth Morgan seeking clarification of Davies's political position during WW1. He responded: 'David Davies was an extremely erratic member of parliament, whose influence was limited... I suspect that his letter... reflected his disillusion with Lloyd George, who had recently sacked him and with the Welsh Liberal members who supported the government. I should have thought the idea of an independent Welsh Party on the lines of the Irish was a total no-starter in December 1917'.

[†] Richard Rees – my Uncle Dai, who served as Medical Officer in my father's battalion in WW2 – told my sister Sian that Major Wheldon had been ordered to Ireland at one point, but that he had declined to go, at some risk of serious disciplinary action. 'He wasn't prepared to shoot Irishmen,' said Dai.

My father mentioned this many times, which suggests that Wynn was zealous in his responsibilities and proud of his involvement and regretful over the League's eventual inability to prevent a second world war. Wynn's taking on of the role marked him out as a prominent internationalist.[18] Not at all a Davies man. My father, likewise, was unimpressed by shows of extreme Welsh nationalism.

In 1920 Wynn became Registrar at the University College of North Wales, in Bangor, thereby reinstating the family connection with the college. He was to stay in the post until 1933.

Wynn Powell Wheldon, 1929, by S. Morse
Brown (1903–2001)

I have never really been clear what a Registrar was or is. The Shorter Oxford English Dictionary unhelpfully defines the term as 'one whose business it is to keep an official register', which reminds me of a Gladstone crack my father was fond of. Interrupted in the House of Commons while speaking on some Bill that touched upon archdeacons, the grand old man was asked what exactly it was that archdeacons did. Without hesitation Mr Gladstone responded that archdeacons 'carried out archidiachonal functions'. From what I can gather Wynn was more or less the Chief Executive Officer of the college, under the chairmanship of Sir Harry Reichel. Some years ago I went to Bangor promoting an arts exchange programme between Wales and America. I met with representatives of the North West Wales Arts Association. On hearing my name I was asked if I was related to – and of course I expected my father's name – Sir Wynn. I was taken aback. 'He used to virtually run this town', said the arts administrator. Clearly he was recalling a period very much later than the 1920s, the years following his return from London in 1947, when he was the Welsh Church commissioner and Chairman of the National Council of Social Services for Wales. The arts administrator may well have known him as the Welsh representative on the Council for the Festival of Britain.

I wonder why he did not return to London immediately after the war. It would have been an understandable move, given that his working life before the war had been spent there. In 1919 he was forty years old and had a burgeoning family. Maybe he was exhausted by the conflict, or sick of the English, or simply considered Bangor a better place to bring up children. In a memorial speech the biologist Professor R. Alun Roberts said that 'despite his interest in education and culture and the ways to deepen and nurture them... the Presbyterian Church of Wales – *yr hen gorff* – was the nearest to his heart'.[19]

Bangor, which has always seemed a rather austere,

unsatisfactory place to me, hidden from itself by a corrugation of valleys, was a flourishing city. A small city, it is true (the population has never risen above 20,000), but a city nonetheless. It was a centre of education, of industry, of culture. It was even becoming a holiday destination for the wealthy middle classes of Liverpool ('The sanitation is good, and it possesses an abundant supply of excellent water... the air is pure and salubrious, the breezes from the Irish channel being laden with ozone, whilst those from the mountains are invigorating and bracing.'[20]). The mixture of talents then was rich and, if not quite cosmopolitan, perhaps not as provincial as one would imagine.

The Wheldon family lived in what my aunt Nans calls 'the Hampstead of Bangor' above the Menai Straits, in a house called 'Ardwyn' (which means 'the protected'). It isn't a particularly distinguished house, a little less grand and ostentatious than those around it, but a solidly respectable villa. This is where my father grew up.

Lloyd George was an occasional visitor to Ardwyn. Dad told Pom Hoare: 'LG in the early twenties wanted my old man to go into politics, so he came to our house from time to time, and whenever he came to our house everything smiled. My mother pretended she didn't like him, but as soon as he came through the door everything smiled. The trees bent over and smiled, the piano stood up on its hind legs and smiled, the entire house smiled when this extraordinary man walked in... life absolutely ran out of him.'[21]

Although I have met, through both my mother and my father, a number of very distinguished people, we never had an ex-Prime Minister calling at our house on a regular basis (and what an ex-Prime Minister!). The greatness of a person is not of course measured by mere office, but LG was undoubtedly one of the great political figures of the twentieth century, and I often wonder what effect proximity to such 'greatness' had upon my father. Certainly, it must have bred in him confidence when dealing with his superiors, for I think he recognised no one, ever, as superior to LG. He had a great deal of time for Company Sergeant Major William McCutcheon, for Field Marshal Montgomery, for Churchill, for Orson Welles, for Marcel Duchamp, but none of them I think impressed as LG had impressed the small boy in the house above the Menai Straits. My father voted Liberal all his life, with two exceptions. In 1945 he voted for Churchill in a gesture of gratitude, and in 1979 he voted for Margaret Thatcher. In 1983 he reverted to the Liberals ('Don't tell your mother!'). He told me once that of all the party leaders he had met since LG, another Welshman, Neil Kinnock, was the only one with whom he would have been happy to pass the time.

In 1933 Wynn was asked to go to Whitehall, as Permanent Secretary to the Welsh Department of the Board of Education. The Governors of the University College 'rejoiced that he had been so worthily and deservedly recognised and that the appointment at Whitehall was going to be held by a man who was so entirely free of official reserve and of officious formality'.[22] It is (naturally, I suppose) the final phrases I most enjoy. They suggest that my grandfather regarded life as all of a piece, which is a rarer quality than one might think, and one inherited by my father.

I'm afraid I do not know, any more than I know what a Registrar does, what a Permanent Secretary to the Welsh Department of the Board of Education does. What the appointment did mean, of course, was the transplantation of the Wheldon family from Bangor to Ealing, 'The Queen of the London suburbs' as it was then known. In 1957 Wynn spoke to the Honourable Society of Cymmrodorion at a meeting held to celebrate the fiftieth anniversary of the department. In his speech he described the ferment in Welsh national life in the early years of the century in which poets, preachers, philosophers, museums, miners and Mr Lloyd George were all involved. The Board of Education was itself a major Welsh institution. As my father said, Wynn's job was *the* big civil service job in Wales.* The 1944 Education Act (in which Wynn 'was privileged… to have had some share') saw a considerable expansion of education at all levels. In Wales attendance into higher education was the highest in the United Kingdom. It took the introduction of the comprehensive school system to undermine Welsh superiority, which, in its egalitarian way, I suppose is what it was designed to do.

A sprightly column in the *Western Mail* had this to say about the post and Major Wheldon's appointment:

> …the advent of Major Wheldon to the headship of the department has evoked the keenest interest throughout the whole of Wales. He brings to the position a combination of qualifications, both personal and professional, which was unmatched by any of his predecessors. To this advantage he adds the further advantage of a temperamental imperviousness which cannot fail to be an immense asset to him in the exercise of his duties… Unlike either of his predecessors, Major Wheldon cultivates the characteristics of the strong silent man. He can be counted upon to lend a sympathetic ear to the many deputations who love to make the journey

---

* My Aunt Mair remembered her father, during the war, complaining of exhaustion after 'having to talk to Bishops all day'. That has a familiar Wheldonian ring about it.

to Whitehall for the purposes of airing their grievances; but neither emotional appeal not the blackest of frowns will suffice to deflect him from the path he is bent upon pursuing.[23]

Some of the tone of his tenure can be gleaned from a speech he delivered to teachers in Llandudno in 1939:

It is possible to suggest ideals to our youth – but you will agree that it is not possible to impose them, and were it possible imposition is not the right way. There is no obvious course available for you or for me, knowing as we do that what we do casually and even unconsciously may have more influence on the youth in our charge, than all that is done by taking thought.

Whatever the process, our youth does light up and pupils we may have unconsciously influenced will one day know

> *P'le'r enynnodd fy nymuniad*
> *P'le' cadd fy serchiadau dan*
> *P'le death hiraeth im am bethau*
> *Fum yn casau o'r blaen.**

This you, as teachers, alone can do and no committee or Board or Administrator can tell you how to do it, much less do it in your place.

---

* Where my wish was ignited
  Where my passions were fired
  Where longing came to me for things
  That I used to hate.
(Literal translation by Gwyneth Wheldon. We cannot trace the author of the lines.)

Give us, if you can, a few young people who have seen the value of something great and good and have the courage to stick to it, then though much that we value and love may be destroyed, the life of the world will still be somewhere secure and hopeful.

There are many echoes here of his own father's speech to the Grove Park school. There is an emphasis (in the unquoted first part of the speech) on the role of a school within a community, promoting both 'the language and tradition' of that community and 'communal sanity'; and there is the exhortation to follow an ideal ('Be aflame, be as beside yourselves – mad for the truth, drunken by the wine of a noble aim,' TJ had said).

There is – and I find it impossible to qualify usefully – an unsanctimonious goodness at work in these remarks. I find it almost burdensome. The imperative to lead a good life, if not a godly life, was central to my upbringing without ever being explicitly so; obviously it was central, too, to my father's. But short of sainthood it is impossible to satisfy this demand as an individual. One must find a cause or an institution. Ideals are a function of 'communal sanity'.

Unless of course one is an artist. But that is for a later chapter.

My father always insisted he was saved by the war, that he would have remained content to do jobs beneath his ability, and have floated with a certain amount of what he called 'cheery-be' through to the end of his days. It is absurd to speculate about whether this would have happened had he not gone to war; certainly he lacked his father's and grandfather's determination as a young man. Wynn's Llandudno speech was delivered on 6 May 1939, five days after the Conscription Bill had been passed and three weeks after the Nazi occupation of Czechoslovakia.

In January 1940 my father wrote to my grandfather: 'vaguely I feel that the war is not my war... We go in of course, because whatever our doubts about liberalism, it is obviously more acceptable than Naziism. But the feeling is not profound: not moral'. It wasn't, in other words, a cause, a noble wine.

Wynn Wheldon had been born into a time of ferment in North Wales, at the height of Blaenau Ffestiniog's slate-driven glory, when education was expanding and the native culture of Wales being reinvigorated. He grew up in a self-confident, optimistic age, God-fearing and certain of what virtue was and wasn't. His experience in war may well have qualified his certainties, but he never lost hold of the bottle of the noble wine. Professor R. Alun Roberts, in that same memorial essay, wrote that Wynn was 'a man among men – one who was born to lead somehow in all circumstances... an ideal captain on a sailing ship in the hour of distress in the tumult of a storm... He would never... be found in trouble and confusion, and would have time in hand to listen to complaints and reports coming to his door, and that with cheerfulness and a happy face'. Roberts also wrote of 'the kindness shining like a blade of warmth and light through everything', and finished, 'sweet also is the memory of the kindness and charm that characterised him, the cheeriness – yes, the jocular cheeriness in the corner of his eye, and his freshness as of the open air where he would walk with small quick steps; the strength of his convictions and the quiet resolve to back them up and lead them to good results'.

I think Taid may have been a softer man than my father, certainly a quieter one. But my father was kindly, at times wonderfully fond. Certainly he was charming. David Attenborough has remarked that Dad could have charmed anyone. And he was cheerful. Not quietly, chuckly cheerful (though he could be that on occasion) but loudly full of good cheer, life-embracingly cheerful. People often thought he was drunk. I never saw my father drunk, not even tipsy.*

Wynn Wheldon died in November 1961, much honoured (he was knighted twice), and I believe much loved by my father and his sisters, Mair and Nans. His son Tomos, Dad's brother, had died earlier the same year, of leukaemia. In *The Times* a supplementary obituary notice remarked that Sir Wynn would be 'missed for his gaiety' and added that 'The Nonconformist conscience is not what one readily associates with Wynn Wheldon, but he did much to keep it alert and clear in ways that were not always conventional and easily apparent.'

My father, then, grew up in a world in which chapel and learning and cheerfulness played equal parts. His childhood heroes were preachers. In 1980 he told Pom Hoare: 'we went to chapel Sunday morning, and Sunday afternoon to Sunday school – all in Welsh of course – and preaching was a big thing. A preacher was someone you looked forward to listening to very much indeed. People think – the English think – that they were full of rhetoric and sentimentality, but it is absolutely not true. They were very impressive, extremely scholarly people, but they were preaching, not lecturing, so they told these tremendous stories, with immense dignity and verve simultaneously. The stars – Philip Jones, Dr Thomas Charles Williams, RF Davies – were tremendous people and I admired them no end.'[24]

While God was much liked, He was also feared. This fear,

---

* Or rather I don't remember having seen him tipsy. I was extremely young when Dad, pooh-poohing the legendary strength of poteen while in the company of Donagh MacDonagh, the great Irish judge and poet, drank enough to require him to be wrestled into a cab by my mother and the writer. On returning home he leaned over my cot and addressed me as 'Mister Windilow Wheldringham', which subsequently became my mother's pet name for me.

however, was not, I think, the fear of God the punisher, this was the fear of God the disappointed. Personal knowledge of God makes the judgement of mortals fairly unimportant. It allows for courage; the great paradox is that it allows you to be your own man.

But I think my father at some point during his life lost his belief in God.

Shortly after his death his friend the American intellectual Norman Podhoretz wrote: 'That much underrated philosopher, George Santayana, once said: "There is no god and Mary is His mother". My friend would never have said flatly "there is no god" – he would have thought it brazen and crass – but if he ever had, he would certainly have added, "and the Bible is His Word". Raised in a devout Presbyterian family, but finally unable to sustain the literal faith of his father, still he never lost his belief in the spiritual truth of Christianity. Specifically, he never lost his belief in the idea that the reason we are here on earth is to serve God and praise him.'[26]

This is utterly recognizable to me. We went to church in my early childhood to the distinctly maternal eighteenth-century St Anne's on Kew Green (across from which is The Rose and Crown pub where the Marxist art critic and novelist and my parents' friend John Berger first rode into my consciousness on his Triumph Bonneville – or was it a Norton Commando? – at some point in the mid-1960s) and, after we moved to Richmond in 1970, to the equally eighteenth-century church of St Peter in Petersham (in the graveyard of which Captain Vancouver is buried – Dad was always delighted with that fact and we occasionally paid our respects). We sang lustily. At Christmas at St Peter's a church band comically not quite worthy of a Thomas Hardy novel – all brass and fiddle – accompanied what was always a very joyful and friendly service. My father loved the singing, respected the vicar if he was worth respecting (the Venerable Robb, with his very shiny head, no-nonsense sermons and delighting joviality, was certainly this) but certainly not for any show of piety. In fact, I rather think my father disliked piety. I think he thought piety was a pinched virtue, that it was withdrawn, and not of service. I was baptised at St David's Cathedral by the Bishop of Llandaff (very grand), where my godparents apparently included the broadcaster Wynford Vaughan-Thomas (I never met him), and I was confirmed at St Paul's Cathedral by the Bishop of London (grander still), neglecting to inform my parents of the occasion. My mother was upset. I don't remember my father being upset at all. And I too was upset, shamefully, because everyone else got expensive Shaeffer fountain pens and gold watches, and were whizzed off in family saloons while I travelled home alone, empty-handed, on the tube.

After my father died I started searching out places where the Wheldons had been, and I realised he had never shown us Ardwyn or Llwyn Celyn or the *tabernacl* in Bangor that his grandfather had spent years getting built, or the chapels in Blaenau Ffestiniog that TJ might have preached in. The only chapel I remember going to in Wales was one in Tremadoc that had been turned into a craftsman's studio by my father's friend, the man-of-all-arts Jonah Jones.[*] It was later taken over by the sculptor David Nash and its interior turned into a wonderful jungle of wood sculpture. Nash's office seemed to be suspended among branches. My sister has a painting of

---

[*] Dad met Jonah in Palestine in 1946. A Yorkshireman, Jonah married an Israeli novelist, Judith Maro, and they settled in North Wales, where he worked as a mason, sculptor, letterer, painter and novelist. He was among the twelve friends to whom Dad left 'a case of reasonable quality claret' in his will. His son Peter Jones has written an excellent biography.

his, which he gave to my mother in exchange for a copy of her novel *Mrs Bratbe's August Picnic*.

It is odd that Dad, who was immensely proud of his father, never showed us the places of his childhood. We never even visited the little church in Nant Peris on the side of Snowdon, where the Wheldons are buried and remembered. It may be that, unlike me, he had not very much time for the past, did not want to be burdened with the example of his father and grandfather. They were men perhaps as 'big' as he; perhaps his own bigness depended on his not carrying their weight on his shoulders. He was not remotely nostalgic, constantly forward-looking.

My mother accompanied us to church if she got herself dressed in time. She had been brought up an Anglo-Catholic, very far away from the Presbyterianism of my father's childhood. She loved the smell of incense, the swing of the censer. I am not sure exactly from whence this derived. Her father was the son of an Irishman, from Leinster in South East Ireland. The Church of Ireland was 'low' rather than 'high'. It may have been the case that my mother's grandfather had come to London a Catholic but that his son – who married, in Lillie Nunns, a woman of no great religious belief – had chosen the compromise of the high Anglican church. (It was said that the Clarkes had been servants to the Bishop of London, at Fulham Palace.) I do not know. I do know that my mother had an abiding interest in God, or at least the idea of God – to the extent that she was very cross with her friend Norman Podhoretz for the piece quoted above. I think she thought that Norman was making assumptions about Dad that he had no right to make. I will confess that her anger has always baffled me. (Norman was furious because *The Times* had cut, in quite vulgar a fashion, what he had originally published in the *Washington Post*.) It is possible, I suppose, that she thought Norman was presuming, or that he was concerned too much with his own grief or that he was using that grief to make a self-servingly clever observation. For me, it was consoling and continues to be.

Mum used to say that incense reminded her of her childhood, so I imagine her father (who died when she was six) taking her quite regularly to services (he took her everywhere, from the pub to the library, usually on his shoulders).

My mother, I think, lost her faith and then refound it, perhaps in fighting despair, perhaps only intellectually. She had left school before matriculation, and had worked both for the Labour Party and for her local council. This would suggest that while 'bringing... [her]self up' (as she put it) she did not bother with religion. God – the idea of God – was sublimated to the idea of Politics. God – the idea of God – was to re-emerge later on. It fascinated her intellectually. On occasion she wrote prayers (for example, when my father was in hospital, close to death, in the late 1970s). She described God at various times as 'profound experience' and, simply – the gospels meant more to her than they did to Dad – as 'love'.

By 'love' she meant 'loving kindness' or the 'charity' of 'faith, hope and charity'. *Caritas* in Greek, *cariad* in Welsh. This is some distance away from the modern notion of romantic love, which is brutal, selfish and sexually charged (but of course at the same time passionate, self-destructive and devotional). Loving kindness remains, for me, the highest attribute.

The Welsh word *cariad*, although etymologically analogous with 'charity', has none of the pious baggage. '*O cariad*', family members sign their letters. Nain – my father's mother – always called us grandchildren '*cariad*'. My delicious cousin Catrin still calls me '*cariad*'. I absolutely love it. Its three syllables curl around the recipient like a blanket. It is warmer than 'darling', more embracing than 'dearest'.

But my father never taught us Welsh; he never insisted on anything very much in the way of education. Of those three worlds – of learning, of piety, of kindliness – it was the last that was most important to him, I think. And kindliness is impossible to impose.

Agatha Whatcombe uplit

CHAPTER 2

1916–1940: THE CLOUD GATHERS DENSITY

Biography dwells on success, autobiography dwells on youth. If our childhoods are not the happiest times of our lives, then they are the most intense, the best remembered, and at the same time, of course, the most distant. But I do not know very much about my father's childhood. I imagine him happy, because he grew up in a cheerful, loving household; I imagine him 'idle' in the sense of not committing himself very much to anything; I imagine him perhaps in awe of his father, though not fearful; I imagine him delighting in his mother's talent for mimicry; I imagine him somewhat unconcerned at consequences; I imagine him transfixed by the storytelling of the Methodist preachers; I imagine him delighting in street Welsh; most of all I imagine him seeking out cheery-be.

Dad had three siblings. His handsome brother Tomos, who became ICI's agricultural representative for what he called the Kingdom of Gwynedd, then Mair, whose education at the LSE was to be cut short by the war, and finally Nans, who was to become harpist for the ENO. Being the eldest I daresay must have given him at least some sense of responsibility; also a sense of leadership, which is perhaps not so different.

He obviously enjoyed school theatricals, and presumably was not in the least put out to play Agatha Whatcombe in the Friars Dramatic Society's production of *Ambrose Applejohn's Adventure* by Walter Hackett, a work that has inexplicably slid from the canon. It was performed at the County Theatre,

Huw, Tomos, Mair and Nans

Bangor. Dad was twelve. Some years later it was reported that he gave a 'polished performance' as Claudius in the school production of *Hamlet*.

He remembered hanging on to the back of the coal truck as it made its way to Friars School; and in an odd moment of reverie in the company of my sister Sian, he remembered with horror a boy who had become addicted early to alcohol and suffered terribly from the DTs.

He wasn't a very good student. As a ten year old he managed six per cent in a chemistry exam and a thundering nineteen per cent in arithmetic (though a decent seventy-one per cent in Latin). He failed his matriculation three times. When he was sixteen, in 1932, his father had a psychological report written on him. Among other things, the report said:

> He is a very friendly and sociable boy with an unusually cheerful and confident manner. He is, too, moderately independent in his outlook and is obviously fond of argument. Co-operation with him, however, is an easy matter, and his self-confidence is in no way unpleasantly aggressive. He has no marked leadership qualities, but we feel that if a position of leadership were thrust upon him he would rise to the occasion.[1]

The results were above average in almost every respect, and the recommendation was that he look towards law or journalism as a career, even to business (the psychologists thought that 'it is not difficult to imagine him driving a hard bargain'). He obviously buckled down after this, for his school report the following spring adjudged his term's work 'very good', and that July he gained his School Certificate, signed on behalf of the Board of Education by WP Wheldon.

In 1933 he was obviously considered responsible enough to help out at St Athan Boys' Village in the Vale of Glamorgan, a kind of holiday camp for sons of miners. It is reported that he spent the week passing himself off as Hitler's special envoy, Herr von Klomp, sent to study British youth organisations.

In the early summer of 1934 Taid sent him to Germany, to Soest, to stay with a family called the Schottlers, with whom Dad got on very well – 'absolutely charming people'. Soest itself he found beautiful, full of churches: 'Last night I listened to the bells for quite a time from my window. They sound lovely at the dead of night chiming into the dark.'

On the tympanum of one of the doors of the Church of St Petri, the oldest church in Soest, St John is shown being boiled alive, watched by an angel with a beard: Dad asked his mother to send him 'Texts and Explanations of Works of John', along with a Welsh translation of *Faust*. He explained precisely where each was to be found in the bookcases at home.

In May, from Berlin, young Wheldon excitedly reported seeing the new Führer.

YR WYF WEDI GWELD HITLER YN BERLIN!

Whooppee!

But only his back; he was sitting in a car; but nevertheless – it was he.[2]

He was impressed by the Haus Vaterland, where you could drink Turkish coffee in the Turkish café and cocktails in the American bar, and dance in the Viennese hall; also by a 'great Nazi Exhibition'. Back in Soest, in order to canoe and climb and take part in swimming galas I suppose he might have had to join the Hitler Youth, though he never mentioned it; he learned by heart poems by Soest's most famous admirer, Rainer Maria Rilke (he never forgot them – I remember him reciting 'Herbsttag' – 'Autumn Day' – to my son Thomas's mother, Ute Arnold, a German schoolteacher). He liked Germany, though was taken aback by the vast portions of food.

In the autumn he returned to Bangor and enrolled in the University College (the rest of the family was now in London, in Ealing), though to no particular end. After a holiday in Soest the following summer he concentrated again on work and, ensconced now in London, applied to and was accepted by the London School of Economics, to study Sociology.

The LSE at the time boasted some rich names: Hayek was in ferocious battle with Cambridge's Keynes (losing in the short term, winning in the long), and Tawney and Malinowski and Harold Laski were holding forth to packed lecture halls (according to Dad, Laski was 'amusing and incisive, and witty, malevolent and malicious, he was a most engaging chap'[3]). This was just the kind of atmosphere he craved: cafés and talk and debate. He made a number of very good friends, intellectual friends, friends with whom he shared ideas, who read the same books. Chief among these friends were, I believe, Brian Murphy and Desmond Leeper.[*]

Many years later, admitting to a vagueness about his ambitions at the time, he said that he was at least clear that he 'wanted to have read two or three good books... to be able

---

[*] Desmond Leeper (1917–2003) was fluent in German, and served with the Logistics Corps before joining SOE. In later life he became Chairman of LEP Transport Ltd. His wife, Josephine Burrows, was known to all as 'Ben'. The two married in March 1939.

to approach [hard authors] with some enjoyment... I wanted to be in some way educated and I vaguely, I think, wanted something to do with public service.[4]

The Director of the School at that time was William Beveridge, the architect of the welfare state. At a small party for selected students at Beveridge's flat Dad declaimed speeches from *Hamlet* in German.[5] Another story tells of him fooling the upper deck of a London bus into accepting him as a monoglot Italian student who knew no English and needed their help and guidance.

Just as he had liked Germany, he liked London and he liked the LSE. He was Treasurer of the Student Union, in the 1st XV for rugby and a member of the University of London Union Executive and Allied Committees. He graduated with Second Class Honours (Upper Division) in June 1938 and was spoken of by the then Director as 'a young man of much intelligence with genuine interest in social problems'. One of his teachers reported that his style was 'anecdotal', and that he had 'shown no evidence of an ability to reason on paper'.

During the summer vacations Dad returned to the Continent, taking walking tours alone, mainly in the Tyrols of Austria, Germany and Italy, with excursions to Munich, Salzburg, Padua and Venice, 'a lovely shell of beauty'.

Going through my parents' papers after my mother's death in June 1993 was a curious business. Suddenly all this past was mine. No longer were there chests of drawers that should not be rummaged around in.

The immediate shock on beginning to read old letters and clippings and articles was that my parents had lead lives separate from mine, had even lived lives in which I was non-existent. Hitherto I had imagined that I was privy to the entire gamut of their thoughts and emotions, or at least the external expression of such. I had imagined that I knew who their friends were, and how relationships with those friends had worked. I found I had known only an extract of their lives – that extract that contained the self-conscious me. My father died when I was twenty-eight years old. I'd known him properly for about fifteen years.

When I went through his letters I found much that was familiar, in terms of voice and of theme. Nevertheless, I also felt that I was in a new conversation with him. This conversation included surprises and upsets, just as any good conversation will, but of course this was not entirely the man he wanted to show to his son, and so I could not escape a sense that I was cheating on him somehow. I felt like a voyeur.

Those letters I have in my possession were written either to family members – his father, mother, brother, sisters – or to Desmond Leeper and his wife Ben. There are a lot of them. Assuming regular correspondence on a similar scale with his best friend Brian Murphy,* and on a slightly lesser scale with other friends, the average must be at least one a day. They provide an acute and colourful picture of his war. They also describe developments in my father's thinking, even character, that were more profound than any other in his life. The crucible of war indeed.

In the summer of 1938 Dad was in Paris 'fiddling away

---

* Brian Murphy was one of the great figures of my childhood. He seemed enormous. And mysterious. He always wore dark clothes. He had black hair. It was as if he contained an unknown continent inside him. Most impressively, he was wonderfully slow, slow in the way a whale is slow, with no need to be fast. He was very fond of his garden and he was very fond of books and he smoked a pipe. I don't remember any other man having been so obviously, to me, my father's equal.

quite merrily' in the Alliance Française, supposedly learning French. Among other distractions, he attended a performance of *La Bohème*:

> I sat squashed sweating and perfectly content in the last row of the fourth gallery of the Opera Comique while an enormous Italian tenor perspiring copiously throughout hurled his superb notes at his packed audience. The Swiss I was with had brought field glasses with him and through these I could see a drop on the end of the Italian's nose, 'iridescent as a jewel', quivering and trembling as he sang, as if responsive to his emotions and feelings. And every now and then a particularly lovely note would prove too much for it and it would drop gleamingly, falling like stardust onto the footlights.[6]

The Munich crisis was in full swing. 'Paris is in a panic: not wild, shouting fear, but gentle, quick-glancing panic', he wrote to Leeper. He heard 'Brother Adolf' on the radio perorating from Nuremburg, 'in the company of two young Germans' who 'lapped it up. As far as I was concerned it was lunatic talk, but not, so far as I could judge, calculated to start a war tomorrow. A postponement rather.' At the same time he was impressed by the stubbornness of 'an earnest young Nazi with no highbrow pretensions':

> He went on with his drivel about instinct & race-superiority & other regurgitated muck… and although he was surrounded by hostility he still went on, dead loyal to his creed.[7]

No one knew for sure that war would come. Life had to be lived as normal. My father and his friends passed their exams, got their degrees, and began to look for jobs. Brian Murphy went into advertising (his first commercial was for Grape Nuts, which his friend thenceforth ate loyally to the end of his life – I eat them myself, occasionally, as a kind of memorial to their friendship). Dad tried to get into Unilever but was turned down. He wangled an introduction to a merchant bank, but found their staff too snobbish. He worked for a time in Glasgow asking questions in factories on behalf of the National Institute of Industrial Psychology (the same organisation that had conducted an examination of the sixteen-year-old schoolboy). At some point he started reading for the Bar, perhaps at the same time as he found a job with the Kent Education Committee, towards the end of 1938 or beginning of 1939. From his letters there is no telling what this job actually entailed, except that part of it involved helping young people with their career prospects. He was horribly bored ('I have to sit on my bottom in Sandwich two hours every week, in case someone wants to bully me. I never do anything.'[8]).

The work was at first peripatetic, taking him around the boarding houses of Beckenham, Sidcup and Sandwich. Eventually he was posted permanently to Deal ('the roaring metropolis'). He lived in digs with a fastidious landlady (she insisted he use the lavatory sitting down – I don't know how she monitored this), but he obviously grew fond of her and her family as he undertook to look after the house and belongings when invasion fever drove them (as it did many others) north. He also made friends with a chap called Bacon, an oculist, who had a prodigious collection of records (and, according to my uncle, Dai Rees, who was taken to meet the Bacons in Exeter in 1942, 'the biggest trumpet of a horn I have ever seen: it filled the whole of their sitting room.'' Almost fifty years

---

*   Letter to the author, 19 August 1994.

later Norman Podhoretz, also with a prodigious collection of records, had installed a vast hi-fi system that stands – it does still – shrine-like and dominating in his sitting room like the components of some prehistoric temple in which impenetrable rites are carried out. Dad was terrifically amused at what I think he saw as a harmless arrogance expressed in superfluous technology in Norman, and I imagine may have felt the same way about Bacon's prodigious horn.)

Every now and then he got up to London.

> Brian and I saw 'Playboy of the Western World' on Saturday. I liked it & Brian groaned and sulked with disapproval. Also I heard Mozart's 'Cosi van Tutti' on Thursday – this an experience, a plunge into new waters, beyond expression. I have an idea that the big point about Art is its miraculous quality... Mozart & Bach both have it; one feels that they have done the impossible, jumped over the moon, turned water into wine. But novels, on the whole, lack it... Out with the second rate. To the dung heap its rubbish.[9]

One hears in this the sound of a relatively intelligent young man enjoying his own opinions, but the tone should not be allowed to deceive. He never regarded art, in itself, as a superior mode of endeavour or experience, and certainly neither fiction (with the major exception of my mother's writing and Tolstoy) nor visual art played all that important a part in his personal life. He didn't like the indiscriminate use of the word 'creative'. 'Only God creates – man makes', he said to me. He may have made an exception for Bach. He did not like to be without music. We were invariably woken on Sunday mornings by the sound of Radio 3 issuing brassily from the Roberts radio in the kitchen. The war letters touch often on music. It was in Deal that he came to know and love the late Beethoven quartets. He listened and he read – Forster and Montaigne and TE Lawrence and Bergson and Eliot ('good on Thomas a Becket...but better on Charlie Brown').

Writing for lack of anything else to do. E.M. Forster and Roman Law lie at my elbow but do not tempt. The one too spinsterish, the other too dusty: both smelling a bit of antimacassars. I've Eliot and Berdayev and other high-brow knick-knacks upstairs, but none of them draw. And it's raining cold rain, cold water in a wind, outside. So restlessly I'm starting a letter which I hardly think I'll end. Talk would be better, but the landlady has her limitations & the others are out. Beethoven's string quartets would be perfect... Hitler and lodging-house loneliness. I don't know about H. Indecent way he has of doing things. Unenglish. O piffle, more than that to it. Central Europe crumbling, breaking. The cloud gathers density. Heigh-ho.

Title for book: 'Hectoring Locusts'

... Bach's 3rd suite (part of which I played to you on the gramophone, you remember?) last Wednesday played by the BBC orch. O lovely! Still pools, depthless. Then Debussy, smoothing the creases of existence. But after Bach & Debussy, Beethoven's 'Eroica', a great rock hurled into the stillnesses, ice-splintering, harsh echoing, tumultuous. I once swore, after a great bout of reading on the subject, never to put word to thought where music was concerned, and reading this last paragraph I could wish the vow still unbroken. Still.

... the essence of a miracle is not its unbelievableness but its actuality.[10]

The cloud gathers density. It was obvious that something very dark, very large was already at work on the Continent, but 'German aggression finds no answering note whatsoever in me. Just the prim, priggish little Ego: that's me. Up the fringe by all means, and count me in it I suppose; but not yet as part of the answering wave in its surging simplicity; just a detached morsel of spray. This makes me feel as-near-as-dammit-perverted; a grotesque, a goblin, a bit of yesterday irrelevant to today, sunlight on a broken column.' He is here reflecting on the absence of anything to set against the 'wave' of National Socialism (or indeed Communism).

By May his job in Deal had become 'permanent for the Peace', though he claimed not to understand the work: 'I have what I grandiloquently call a Pending File into which I throw everything I don't understand. All this week's post is in it.'

War was declared on 3 September, and there was, within minutes, an air-raid siren in London. Brian Murphy and Dad were together in the Strand. He was impatient to be called up, hoping his father might be able to get him into the Royal Welch Fusiliers, but: '...can't get into the army for love or money; providence is looking after its own perhaps... Foreign Legion?'

So he had instead to keep to his job. Its tedium allowed other thoughts to play in his mind.

Another week of news bulletins fearfully & eagerly awaited: and I am filled with a sense of shame when the list mounts up, apparently so unscrupulously; a rising tide of irrevocable political evil – the shame is personal and curious, perhaps owes itself to my years of political indecision when I argued and yelped with customary dogmatism, but shrank within myself from dubbing Hitlerism evil, really evil. Even now, when the label seems irresistible I feel a withdrawal of judgement in spite of straightforward German bloodiness, in spite of Halifax's Oxford speech. Black cannot be so black; a factor of importance is missing... I was raised in a sufficiently Christian family not to be overawed by a recognition of human indignity; but when the indignity and the sin is so much a monopoly of a certain group of men (or so it seems) it grows fantastic and unbelievable, and, if really so, shameful. I am shamed, and you. Even though, to all appearances, we neither condone nor assist in acts of conquest & cruelty, their occurrence degrades not only the perpetrator but also the victim... The evening is beautiful beyond words; odd how the tranquillity of sunlit evenings cannot be visualised, cannot be recaptured by the imagination during the winter, during a thunderstorm, during August heat, although so often experienced & sometimes intensely.[11]

The lyricism of that final paragraph hints again at Dad's belief that words could not perform the miraculous, but it also reminds me of a familiar but unexpected facet of his character, his wonder at the natural world. In the mid-1970s he took up running and would return from Richmond Park with rich descriptions of how the hornbeams looked in the morning light or how the Isabella Plantation was 'gleaming'. On one occasion, having been into the park at night, he returned in a state of controlled excitement. While running in the middle of the park he had heard a clicking sound coming from a stand of trees nearby. He was intrigued enough by the sound to investigate. He came upon the following scene: two stags, their antlers locked, surrounded by a circle of females. The moon shone. This was as miraculous to him as Bach or Shakespeare, and undoubtedly a good deal more miraculous than, say, the paintings of Derain or the novels of Fielding. He told the story beautifully, clearly moved, and with great tenderness.

The sense of collective shame alluded to in this letter did not leave him. He felt it even more powerfully at the end of the war. There was no sense of triumph.

Life dragged on in Deal until in May 1940 he was informed by the War Office that he was to be posted to an Infantry Training Centre in Canterbury, the following month. He would be attached to the Buffs (the Royal East Kent Regiment). By the end of May Churchill had persuaded his Cabinet, despite Dunkirk, to continue to resist Hitler. There would be no peace. Dad typed and signed his will, and sent his friends the Bacons to stay with his mother at Canonbury, in Prestatyn.

Royal Welch Fusilier

CHAPTER 3

1940–1942: BUFFS AND FUSILIERS

My father was unimpressed by the Infantry Training Centre in Canterbury.

> The general organisation here appears to be incredibly bad: we are kept waiting hours for everything: & when I think of the BEF* being reequipped in this style I am filled with anxiety. This morning the CO gave us a lecture – a one-armed man called Major Wilson. It was unbelievable & all the men quartered in my barrack-room were filled with horror & dismay. He

---

*   British Expeditionary Force, the one that got pushed back to Dunkirk and beyond.

71

told us that Germans were dogs, cowards & villains, that the British army was invincible, and that the bayonet was the most important instrument in modern warfare[1]

His antipathy to the status quo grew as he came face to face with 'English half-men'. For the moment, however, the apocalyptic tone was the prevalent one.

the OCTU[*] people here are very unexpectedly thoughtful, and a great deal of talk between parades & over meals concerns itself with whether the liberal democracies are worth saving. It is impressive, the amount of weight given to the idea that the whole system of Western industrialism is a no go, & that any progressive policies like socialism, because they accept the fundamentals of modernity, are really evading the issue... socialism thinks that leisure is the redeeming clause, & that dignity will come with carefully-used free time, but I am becoming increasingly more & more convinced that this is at best a very dubious proposition. People must be given jobs to do... the only gleam is that the war may see us all blown to bits, and history, so to speak, will do it for us.[2]

'People must be given jobs to do' could have been written by his father, who, according to Professor Roberts, 'set a high price on full and correct use of time. Plenty of space for pleasure and merriment, but it hurt his heart to have to kick one's heels holding an empty bag.'[3]

On 9 July the Luftwaffe began to increase the number of its attacks on Channel convoys, not so much in order to

---

[*] Officer Cadet Training Unit.

damage supply and trade, but to lure British fighters out over the water. Goering, aware that the RAF was short of pilots, thought that shooting down Spitfires over water meant their pilots were very much more likely to be killed. Dad witnessed one of these 9 July attacks:

> Yesterday we were down at the coast, and during the afternoon six of us went onto the cliffs to doze. It was a lovely day, and the sea was green, far below. We were lazily watching a convoy moving diagonally across the sea when suddenly nine black bombing airoplanes [sic] came out of a bank of white cloud. In a single line, like disciplined flying insects, the aircraft flew above the convoy and dropped many bombs around it. This done (although nothing was hit) the formation swung round, still in rigid single file & very black against the blue sky, & crawled deliberately back into the cloud bank. Then another seven appeared, dropped bombs, & retired in the same manner, apparently unruffled by the destroyer accompanying the convoy which was piling up a barrage against them. Nothing was hit, & the whole thing was incredibly beautiful. There were dogfights during the afternoon, directly above us; & lying about in the fields we were excited spectators. Except when a German came hurtling down, & a Spitfire after it, to crash into a field, again the astonishing thing about the whole business was its amazing beauty. Horror & fear were almost entirely absent – in the bombing, especially – as far as we were concerned. The colouring has much to do with it – flashes over the sea, the great pile of water uplifted, foam-white: the deliberate harmonised movements of the planes & the ships. Seeing that nothing was hit, it made remarkable entertainment.[4]

One thinks of Paul Nash's great Battle of Britain painting of dogfights in the blue skies over the Downs.

In September the Luftwaffe turned its attention away from convoys and airfields and onto London. The Battle of Britain gave way to the Blitz. Fear of invasion remained acute, and Dad felt seriously unprepared: 'Hitler would laugh with delight could he see us'.[5] The immediate danger receded. A drunken letter soon afterwards contains this:

Stoneham, an architect in the next bed, & I drink a Guinness. Both pretty drunk. Impossible to write anything sensible. Through the haze & the jangle, a man pounds the piano, incredibly badly.

I like this life, I think; don't want now ever to become an officer, although doubtless this Training company will split up some time & I'll go to an OCTU. God knows when – the further off the better as far as I am concerned.

In khaki men have nothing except faces. Faces over tea & beer with cigarettes stuck into them. A species, like monkeys or sparrows.[6]

This last idea was, for my father, an attractive one. A little later he wrote: 'The men have become human beings with the passage of time; and the uniform & the lack of family ramifications & occupational differences & so forth all serve to annihilate background'.[7]

When I was at the age when school uniform seems restrictive and repressive of one's freedom, and other such blather, Dad told me that he was in favour of uniforms because they allowed the expression of personality ('"Let us make men!" Men, not money; women, not dress,' TJ Wheldon had exhorted fifty years before the end of the war). As a television performer he made sure of always wearing the same 'neutral' suit. On the other hand, he did enjoy buying clothes, especially in America. He would invariably bring back clothes for Mum and for us. I remember in particular a pair of red jeans – unheard of in England, and very thrilling. In Manhattan once he and the opera singer Geraint Evans went shopping for their respective ladies' underwear. They roared up and down Fifth Avenue together speaking Welsh across the camisoles and girdles, and frightening the natives.

The paradox of the uniform – that it released individuality rather than repressing it – was fascinating to me. I saw something in it; it educated me; from then on there were always at least two sides to everything.

In September Dad wangled an invitation to the Deanery in Canterbury.

He [the Dean*] is a socialist of course: but I had expected an old-fashioned liberal in modern dress. Instead I found with delight that this was the real stuff, red Russia indeed... a prominent table [was] covered with periodicals, presumably the Dean's daily light reading. The Daily Worker, Moscow News, Philadelphia Communists & so on & so forth. Lenin & Trotsky & Greenbaum & the rest on the bookshelves. Magnificent... Communism attracts one's sympathies these days: the army doesn't make one delight in the Old British Methods.[8]

---

* The Very Reverend Hewlett Johnson, author of *The Secrets of Soviet Strength* (1943). Apparently, his MI5 file reports that it was judged 'undesirable for the Dean of Canterbury to be allowed to lecture to troops'.

Later in the letter there is a reference to 'Jock, a working class Scotchman, navvy by trade & very Scotch... Astonishing people, the bloody Scotch. He is in the corner talking busily about Anatole France.' Of course, Dad did not become a Communist. What was being developed here was an idea of a society made up of thousands of overlapping circles, and it was to be articulated in a number of speeches and lectures that he made and gave at the BBC.

> In this country... minority does not mean highbrow. And majority does not mean tripe. It means more than a minority. Minority simply means minority. People from Newcastle upon Tyne are a minority; and so are audiences for snooker, or gardening or Shakespeare. And British television, like our political life, is based four-square on this proposition: that we all of us belong both to majorities and minorities. What is more, they all overlap and they are all important. I like string quartets. I also like Match of the Day. I like Morecambe and Wise, I like The Generation Game and I like Macbeth and I am not exceptional.[9]

Early in November 1940 Dad found himself in, of all places, Barmouth, on the west coast of Wales, a small town mantled by the majesty of Snowdonia's southern-most – and perhaps most beautiful – peak, Cader Idris.

It was here, not unsurprisingly, that my father's antipathy to the English officer class rumbled most loudly. It runs like a theme in the bass all through the letters of these months, from November 1940 to February 1941.

> there is the same silly snobbishness about the whole system of officerdom in the British army... Young gents with nonsense-

caps and bad taste & coarse manners & offensive habits & tiresome ways... sparrow-gents... They want a new sort of material, but an old sort of officer... with the result that they pick very largely on Clerk types who say 'endeavour' instead of 'try' and 'require' instead of 'want'... these English semi-people are no good.

When I become an officer I shall probably perish out of pure ill-humour.

... the thought of scores of young gentlemen & not-so-young gentlemen with their backgrounds of Lancing & Kings College* & two months at [?] Weber's & three in Paris & sherry on the table and guns discreetly cased, being in positions of pretty decisive authority in the Diplomatic & Foreign services really makes me very angry. Barmouth is full of their kind: & I distrust & dislike & disapprove of them, the cream of the creamiest universities in the world. If we are to fight a war at all I am in favour of doing it thoroughly and not in a gentlemanly way...

They'll go, of course, inevitably. I think the whole Western bag of tricks is doomed, finished: and so be it – as a civilisation & as individuals we have to endure & suffer deprivation before we finally perish. That worries me not one atom. Let the whole thing blow up, as it will; I am for it; but it is annoying that we can't perish decently, but must be fluffed out for good & all in an atmosphere sultry with stupidity & selfishness & wrong.[10]

---

* Dad maintained that the novels which most closely described his own experience of the war were Lancing- and Oxford-educated Evelyn Waugh's *Sword of Honour* trilogy.

So, not much time for Oxbridge, then. He never did have. When I was informed that I had won a scholarship to New College, Oxford, his reaction was notably muted. I think he would honestly have preferred me to go into the army. The fact that I was to read English, rather than something useful like Law (something that would give me what he described to my dear friend Dr Stephen Graham as 'a fucking profession'), made things worse still. My mother naturally was delighted. When I lost that scholarship at the end of my first year he wrote to me saying that he was 'pleased, because I never much believed in that scholarship. I always thought of it as rather a burden.'

Dad never lost his prejudice against Oxbridge. He always trusted an engineer before a mandarin, even, indeed especially, when he was a BBC nabob. The Royal Television Society, which properly speaking is an association of technicians, not policy makers, was an organisation of which my father was especially fond. In his farewell speech as Chairman he even compared it to *Yr Hen Gorff* itself. He liked makers rather than self-styled creators. I think it is unlikely that he was in the least bit awed by the smooth-talking officer class; more likely, although I admit to the romanticism of the notion, he had his grandfather's regard for the pious craftsman, the selfless worker. I think this because he had tremendous regard for his godson Charles Murphy, for his nephew Sion Wheldon, for chaps who got on and made things – chess boards, houses, that sort of thing – and I have always myself never felt up to the mark in that respect. And this is a feeling of quite specific moral inferiority. While I have hero-worshipped writers from afar, it is the builders of the world who have been the moral markers.

Nor was he anti-intellectual. That Oxbridge ethos that

despises any kind of ostentation, be it intellectual or material, was alien to him. The Scots navvy with the Anatole France obsession was far more familiar a figure.

Being in Wales would obviously have made Dad feel the differences between himself and the Oxbridge crowd even more acutely. There were odd occasions when his Welshness proved especially useful.

> The platoon commanders' week has gone reasonably well. Yesterday morning I had to engineer & take command of a Withdrawal scheme, and the thing worked quite satisfactorily because I met a shepherd in the hills who proved to be an invaluable & tactful person who knew quite well what we were about & who told me the proper routes to take and so forth in Welsh under the pretence of telling me not to worry his sheep. The officers who naturally regarded shepherds as being one with private soldiers & all other unspeakables suspected nothing, listening to our conversation with amusement as if they were being entertained by two clever little budgerigars in a Cheltenham drawing room![11]

And nor was he simply a Welshman, he was a Welshman with a well-known name (John Morgan, a *Manchester Guardian* journalist of the period, said that the Wheldons occupied a position in Wales similar to that of the Governor of the Bank of England). While waiting once for a train in Portmadoc, Dad fell into conversation with a fellow passenger:

> I told him that you were my father. This interested him a good deal, and he related to me the story of his single National Eisteddfod entry. The task (in the Carnarvon eisteddfod of '20) was to write a 'Personal Impression of the Great War', to

be judged by the Rev David Williams. But as things turned out it was you & not DW who judged the competition, and at the bottom of this good man's essay you had written 'Too much Me'. This had tickled him to bits, and while on the one hand he felt that 'Personal Impressions' surely meant 'Me' he admitted on the other that the 'me' part had been worked up to please the Rev DW on the grounds that the Ministry always fell for Y Profiad Personol, and that in this cutting his coat to suit his cloth he had jettisoned most of his intellectual integrity, and damned well deserved what he got... he evidently thought of you, whom he has never actually met, as a genial & warm-hearted scoundrel. For Taid Wheldon [TJ] he had enormous respect: as a youngster he had attended the school in Ffestiniog from his home in Minffordd. He was a fine man, & I enjoyed the hour or so I had of his company.[12]

The story would have found resonance with Dad, because that notion of cutting the coat to suit the cloth was especially inimical to him. The swarms of executive producers that now bedevil much programme-making would have horrified him. For him television was an expressive medium that had little to do with reading the audience. If someone had something funny, entertaining, sad, wistful, shocking or earnest to say, then it was up to them to do so with as much passion and energy as possible. 'There is no such thing as a "good idea for a programme",' he said. 'Ideas are ten a penny; it is the making that counts.' He was an absolute anti-Hamlet.

The training at Barmouth was hard, but it is impossible to escape the impression that Dad was beginning to enjoy himself, the sparrow-men notwithstanding. In December he went

Up Cader Idris – smacking big mountain – and saw two

kestrels, five buzzards & many many herons, dropping lazily into flight as we interrupted their meditations in a way that would have made Arnot Robertson* scream with ecstasy: that lazy, effortless drop into clear air, with its hidden moment of tension.[13]

He went to chapel on Sundays, twice a day when the preacher was good. He read *The Enormous Room*, *The Quest for Corvo*, Orwell (evident from many of his letters), Henry Miller. Above all, and including the most exciting event of the four months, there was music: 'A tall, lanky & very nice lad who was at Canterbury with me, has joined me in a move into these new digs.'[14] This was David (later Sir David) Willcocks who was then the organ-scholar at King's College Chapel in Cambridge, and so by definition one of the very best young organists in the country ('a very fine musician indeed'). Dad wrote full accounts both to his parents and the Leepers (and I daresay to Brian Murphy) about a particular trip to the 'local kirk'. Willcocks was evidently no sparrow-man.

This morning I took [Willcocks] to the local kirk, and after the service, the organist let him play about on the organ, a little unassuming organ, but sweetly toned. Willcocks played beautifully for some time: and the little local organist, properly impressed, asked him to play him a new hymn tune which was to go into the evening service. Willcocks played it through – a simple four-line hymn tune – & then went wandering off on his own, sending running organ sounds along the rafters of the roof, and suddenly the tame little

* Eileen Arbuthnot Robertson (1903–1961) was a British novelist and film critic. She was a regular on the British radio show *My Word*.

theme came creeping back into these irrelevancies & became the basis of a really fine [?] fugal construction, improvised at a pinch, but impeccably done. The organ swept along quietly for eight or nine minutes, and then finished. I was deeply impressed... & the little organist almost went off his head. 'O Mr Willcocks!' he said. 'O Mr Willcocks!' Very exciting.[15]

This story is simply and effectively told (I heard it first when Dad told it to me, though I believe he may have set it in a Welsh chapel on Cambridge Circus, which now houses the Limelight Club). One can almost imagine it as a short *Monitor* film, perhaps by John Schlesinger.

Dad was aware that Willcocks's facility was hard earned. In 1964 he took exception to a review by Anthony Burgess in *The Listener* of two television programmes made under his aegis as Head of Documentary Programmes. These were *The Pilots* and *Ballet Class*. What Dad objected to was that although Burgess had much admired the programmes, he had failed to mention their 'authors', had failed indeed to note that each programme had come 'out of a mind [rather than] delightfully out of a box'. The author of *The Pilots* was Richard Cawston and the author of *Ballet Class* was Margaret Dale. Burgess had written of the latter film: 'Here there was no subtle selection of image and fact... nor was there any need of it. The simply observed actuality of grace and sweat and routine was enough'. My father responded:

Mr Burgess knows that the simple in poetry and in literature is normally an achieved effect. A book praised for simplicity would not suggest to a literary critic a book simply made. Simplicity in literature is rarely artless, and the same is true of television... no one could possibly have made [Ballet

Class] who was not very much at home in the world of ballet, and no one could possibly have made it who was not equally at home in the world of television... the sophistication was visible, to anyone who takes television seriously.[16]

In February 1941, through the good offices of his father, Dad was transferred to the 12th Battalion, Royal Welch Fusiliers in Whitby on the Yorkshire coast ('If Hitler takes Yorkshire, it'll bloody well serve him right'). From thence the battalion moved to Redcar, and in July Dad was sent to the Junior Leaders' Course at Bellerby Camp near Leyburn, also in Yorkshire. He was to stay there, becoming Chief Instructor, until May 1942, when he transferred to the Royal Ulster Rifles in order to be involved in airborne operations.

His preoccupations in Yorkshire were not much different to those of Barmouth and Canterbury. He was one of the few Welsh-speaking officers in the Fusiliers. Music and religion remained central to his enjoyment and understanding of himself.

A fortnight ago I played hell with the Padre because the singing in Church Parade was simply disgraceful – a dirge of dirges. So in a huff he got me detailed to take off the so-called choir on their first practice since our arrival here. I drummed into them the necessity for doubling the pace of the singing, and made a plan of complicated & extensive strategy for last Sunday's parade – little knots of fast singers here & there to influence their lethargic neighbours and the choir at their back where they could be heard, & myself, an unseen (but not unheard by Gosh!) codwr canu** at the organist's elbow.

The result of it all was the singing went like the Scottish express, and most of the officers spent the service in an agony of repressed laughter... still better quick than slow, & I hope to get them doing it reasonably within a month.[17]

As it happens, this was all to the good. Whitby had been musicless; rather plaintively he had written to his mother: 'I'd like to hear a concert sometime. We can't even get a wireless here. I miss it.'[18]

I can imagine his fury at the second-rate singing. His most often-used criticism of me was that I was being 'casual'. This I took to be a combination of carelessness and idleness. Dad would have had no time for Chesterton's witty paradox that if a thing was worth doing 'it was worth doing badly'. He had a genuine contempt not for failure, but for the second rate, the mediocre, whether it was in the climbing of mountains, the making of TV programmes or fighting wars. Of television programmes: 'the aim is not to avoid failure – the aim is to give triumph a chance.'[19]

What he excelled in was seeking the best in people, as he sought the best in himself; and this being one's best self was consonant with the act of praising God. Just as a heron would perform its beautiful airborne ballet, so should men make the best of themselves.

---

* *Literally 'lifter of the singing'. 'He knew the words and the hymn tunes, would strike the key for singing. Very important when there was no organ or piano.' (Letter to author from Richard Rees.)

The CO is a man both intelligent & well-read: so much is evident, and I can't understand, can't conceive, why he chooses to spend his leisure rereading the Tatler & the Sketch. It infuriates me to see him. Why can't he join Boots? [which provided a library service][20]

It is the 'rereading' there that is provoking. Dad was no intellectual snob. ('My mother is under the impression that her favourite programme is *Panorama*, and she goes to quite a lot of trouble to make sure she sees it. Her favourite programme, in fact, is Harry Worth*... she will, in the last resort, miss *Panorama*, but she will not miss Harry Worth, and why should she not like Harry Worth best? There is no reason in the world, but she does not like saying so.'[21]) What he was exercised by was not an intellectual distinction but a moral one.

Grand politics were still a source of trouble to him: what was being fought for? And why? These questions did not cease to be asked, even as the itch to see active service grew stronger. On the contrary, they became more acute and better informed, as my father became a Unit Education Officer, attended training courses organised by the Army Bureau of Current Affairs, and began to teach.

In June 1941, the month in which Germany invaded the Soviet Union, he wrote to his father:

I think education should be derivatory. That is, although not necessarily 'vocational', only 'liberal' in the limited sense that it fits the particular society within which it is at work...

---

* Harry Worth was a bumbling comic actor, best remembered for a trick in which he reflected half of himself in a shopfront window thereby appearing to defeat gravity.

army education fails... in this supreme task. It is irrelevant. To chaps of my age liberalism and democracy of the 1936 non imperial, non advancing type, are, to put it plainly, a mess... One must be pro-something, and we are asked to fight on pro-nothing.[22]

Two months previously he had written to Desmond Leeper:

There are storms brewing in tiny teacups over what is called my Bolshie tendencies. I called Churchill a mountebank (which he certainly is in my opinion) the other day, and horrified many. But I am growing to hate more, as I feel about it the more, the prevailing unanimity of opinions.[23]

Tiny teacups, maybe, but by July he was 'beginning to get haunted by a feeling of helplessness – I despise everything I see that comes from Higher Command'. While the army was growing attractive, its leaders weren't. He liked the men, and he was also doing rather well precisely what he was waiting and itching to do rather well, albeit in more benign circumstances.

The weekend was good. On Saturday I was platoon commander, & we had to do an attack on a reservoir. The CO & the adjutant were watching the scheme, & as I hadn't the remotest idea how to conduct the operation, I had to rely on bluff & vigour... I collected the most terrific kudos... although one's platoon isn't a traditional society, yet it can take the place of roots very easily. My platoon takes up my activities, interests & affections.[24]

However, he was not himself happy with his own performances. The letters are full of self-chastisement. He used to make clear to me all sorts of weaknesses in himself. He described himself to me on any number of occasions as 'an idle chap'. By most standards this was nonsense. The description contains both modesty and arrogance, the latter in the sense that he might have felt in himself some untapped potential. Actually my father wasn't remotely arrogant and he really did regard himself as idle. He did not, I think, mean lazy or slothful, although there was an occasional lapse.

> Last Tuesday morning a friend of mine & I overslept (for the very first time EVER) and had breakfast at 9 (a criminal, unheard-of hour)... O ignominy![25]

I find it almost equally humiliating to admit that this is the most incredible paragraph (to me, at any rate) in all my father's letters. He never overslept. 'Idleness' might very well have included playing cricket ('I have made rather a tour de force at cricket, so there you are', 'still playing brilliant & incredible cricket') or reading contemporary fiction ('*The Enormous Room*'... escapes sentimentality by a hair's breadth because of an inaccessible quality of sincerity in the author' – a second reading of one of the four novels recommended by Dad to my sister Sian years later, along with Lionel Davidson's *Smith's Gazelle*, Samuel Beckett's *Murphy* and Giuseppe di Lampedusa's *The Leopard*[†]) when he might have been reading the Old Testament ('Am reading

---

*   e.e. cummings (1922).

†   In 1992 when my wife and I were looking for a house to buy, we came upon Lionel Davidson in his house in Hampstead. I felt at once that I was in a sacred place, a feeling made more acute by the curious design of the house, which felt more like a boat, with the rooms tucked into places that could be found for them, than a house. There was a lot of clapboard and high windows and whiteness.

the New Testament, & am about halfway through Paul; it is scandalous the little I know... I doubt I can summon up the guts to tackle the Old T.').* One of Dad's few pieces of fatherly advice to me was that I should read 'one difficult book'. He meant something along the lines of Hegel, and by 'read' he meant also understand. By so doing one would know that, if necessary, one could, and this would absolve one from having to read others. I'm not sure I have ever managed to read a 'difficult' book in this sense. Frances Yates on Elizabethan occult philosophy is about as difficult as I have ever allowed myself to get.

At the end of July 1941 Dad went to Bellerby camp, yet another training establishment. Apart from the soldiering there was also political education with his old friend the Army Bureau of Current Affairs. This continued to appal him.

> At the moment I am quite violently prejudiced against any statement of belief or thought that defies translation into actual activity; I call it Wind. On that peg I hang a sincere and even earnest distrust of the Army Bureau of Current Affairs.

> Broadly, 'education' I think should be regarded as training in making judgements – rational deductions from certain given data, either isolated like the xyz of algebra or less distinct like history. Judgements can be moral or technical,

---

* Participating once on Nigel Rees's *Quote...Unquote* radio show, Dad was asked where the phrase 'the skin of our teeth' came from. As he told Frank Gillard in an interview, 'Something told me it came from the Book of Job. "The Old Testament," I said, playing it safe. Could I say which book? I drew my breath in order to say 'the Book of Job' and heard myself say 'Exodus'. The correct answer was of course Job. In my reply I had been looking for an Escape... and that was exactly what I found: Exodus.'

so the educated person must be able to distinguish between good and evil as well as between efficient and inefficient. 'Knowledge' is accidental to the central issue.

Now 'propaganda' is the opposite…

I have to lay on half-hours for various platoons on Libya and the Democratic Machine and China's War and Naziism, and it makes me ashamed of myself & my society.[26]

Thirty-five years later Dad described the kinds of television programmes he deplored as 'pap' and 'propaganda'.

Television is so expensive that it has to be run in many parts of the world either by government or by commerce. And in consequence, a great deal of it is either propaganda or pap.

With situation comedy, for example, it is technically possible to take a plot or a character or a situation, put a group of script writers on to it, add some media men to them, get the team working, develop the stereotypes, work out the permutations, analyse the possibilities and start turning it out. It is the way advertisements are written. Aims and purposes are identified, targets are exact and the work is precise. There is nothing disreputable about advertisement writing: in its place, and its place is advertisements. What it is not is literature, and what it is not is art… what it would not have is the individuality which is part of original creation… what David Croft and Jimmy Perry brought to Dad's Army is exactly what would be missing.[27]

This is why *Fawlty Towers* and *The Office* could not be successfully replicated in American versions. He did not, of course, see the latter, though I have absolutely no doubt that he would have recognised it as something other than 'pap'. I am aware, of course, that the US *Office* has been very successful – it ran for over 200 episodes – but I would suggest that its standing, in cultural terms, is in no way comparable to the heft that Gervais and Merchant's measly fourteen episodes carry. David Brent is an invention of literary genius.

My father's fury at the incompetence and wrong-headedness of the army was undiminished. New Commandants came in for a good deal of criticism. In March 1942 Dad wrote to his father:

> The new commandant [is] another utterly incredible appointment – a pig-eyed lout of a chap with the legs of a mastodon & the thoroughly credible reputation of having the brains of a hen.[28]

A further letter, again to his father, written the following month at the end of the course, and just prior to his transfer to the Royal Ulster Rifles, picks up again on the (missing) quality of leadership in the country as a whole.

> I suggested there was no point in urging indoctrination unless one had a doctrine, and implied that neither Democracy nor patriotism nor Anti-fascism nor Liberalism were satisfactory. Not that they are insufficient as such, goodness knows, but simply that they are technically unworkable in contemporary England as doctrine owing to a multitude of causes... it further grew out of the talk that the only doctrine worth a moment's practical attention is a hell-for-leather bang out Christianity... There was a measure of agreement among us too that Christianity if it's to be any good as what one can

only call a Dynamic must recover its Dogma (although as Wavell[*] pointed out the Dogma once discovered he almost certainly wouldn't believe it himself! We all felt alike!)

The School officially wavers between a hate line and the Democratic Crusade. Neither of these means anything to anybody so far as I can judge.[29]

Fairly desperate stuff, the search still on for something to fight *for*, rather than merely *against*. Given that this was a letter to his father, my father's airy dismissal of Christian dogma (as though his father would understand and share his own feelings) strikes me as surprising. Here was a man who had not ceased to attend services (or at least sermons) and to read the Bible denying the credibility of Christian dogma. Presumably he means Anglican or Catholic dogma. I have always rather suspected that the Calvinistic Methodists were more interested in God than in Christ. This may explain why my father found in Jews such congenial minds and friends.

The search for a creed with which to indoctrinate the troops and thereby improve efficiency was never successful, and it was indeed simple patriotism and Churchill's rhetoric that provided as near to a doctrine as the British got.

In a recorded conversation in 1980, Dad described the effect of good leadership. 'Monty' is, of course, Field Marshal Bernard Montgomery.

Monty really was a heroic figure, in the sense that people

---

[*] Archibald Wavell, son of the Field Marshal. He lost a hand while fighting the Japanese in Burma and his life fighting Mau Mau rebels in Kenya on Christmas Eve 1953.

did project a great many hopes upon him, and a great many expectations, and what is more he didn't let them down. Nowadays it is fashionable to think of him as being very full of bombast and so on – and no doubt he was – but he certainly exercised a great hold over troops. I remember very well the regular officers in my battalion did not care for him... I remember being woken up one morning – at a time when I should not have been woken up – by the adjutant, and I was quite cross and I had another three or four hours sleep to go on my schedule – it was four o'clock or some ridiculous time – and he woke me up and he told me he thought I would be interested to know that this attack we were supposed to do was going to take place the following Tuesday – and I wasn't a bit interested – fancy waking me to tell me that! We had already been defeated three or four times in trying to attack some damned town, and he told me the reason he woke me was that the attack was not only going on on Tuesday, but that Monty was coming over to take personal charge of it, and I said 'He's not!' 'He is,' said the adjutant. 'Personal charge?' I said. 'Monty himself?' Well, then I knew that it could not possibly fail – everything would be properly arranged – and I woke up everybody and they were very cross with me, but within about ten minutes the morale of the company had gone up by about one thousand per cent.[30]

What this search for a doctrine and concern with leadership was about was, of course, morale, and good morale became absolutely central to my father's way of running things, and morale depended not merely on a touch of Harry in the night, but also upon the knowledge that 'everything would be properly arranged'. Confidence and trust are two composites of morale. At the BBC, both as a programme maker and an administrator, he tried to make sure that those who worked for him were confident that those they relied upon were doing their jobs properly and that they were themselves trusted. Imperative to this was the requirement that they do their jobs as well as they possibly could. My father was occasionally described as 'schoolmasterly', the term being used in a mildly pejorative way; but actually, remove the moss of disdain and it is not such a bad thing to be. In order to draw the best out of a pupil the schoolmaster will have to be demanding, even harshly so, from time to time. Sometimes Dad could be a bully. When he was certain of something in his own mind, he needed a lot of shifting. You had to be as certain as he was. However, if you convinced him that you were, then he would quite happily cede a point. The young Nazi who had impressed him in Paris before the war had done so by the strength of his belief, not by the 'regurgitated muck' of his ideology.[31] It wasn't, of course, the ideology that was attractive, it was the belief.

Leaders must set examples. In February 1942 he did that, though he wouldn't have put it that way, of course. He wrote home. He told the story of a death, a 'frightful catastrophe'. He had led his platoon across a river and a young private had fallen in.

> ... he got carried away – nothing, by a miracle, hindered his passage – and thirty yards or so downstream fell right down over a fifteen foot waterfall into a whirlpool at the base of the fall. I saw him crash into the pool, and, being the responsible officer, had no other alternative open to me except to go in after him. The current was much too strong however, and when I had hold of him I could do nothing except go swirling round and round myself. The pool was about the size of an

ordinary dining room I should say, and full of white water. After a bit I lost Oliver, and eventually got out, not without difficulty. We didn't see him after that for some time until he came to the surface once more, and without the slightest effort of decision, I found myself, as if by mechanical reflex, in the pool again. Same bloody business went on: there were hands and walking sticks and goodness knows what within eighteen inches of me every time I came round, but I couldn't draw out of the whirl; and a second time I lost him. This time I was quite convinced on the surface of my mind that I would never get out and I remember giving detached consideration to the futility of the whole business, and being shocked in quite an everyday way with my own lack of fighting spirit which wouldn't get me any nearer salvation. The water was infernally cold (although I didn't notice this at the time) and had so affected my hands that my fingers were entirely immobilised, and this put me in the terrifying situation of being swept past crags and buttresses which were no use to me because I couldn't hold on to them. I have no clear recollection of what happened after this, but presumably my primeval instincts were stronger than my horrifying surface-thinking which was quite prepared to leave it at that and call it a day, because eventually I got out once more and this time, willy nilly, stayed out. An officer called Cutting then went into the pool, but by now Oliver was only appearing very infrequently, and eventually the thing was given up. His body was brought out later. Cutting and I then spent a trembling session in a maze of blankets and whiskey and by now everything is back to normal except that poor Oliver is dead and his wife a widow. It was a rotten show altogether, and although by now the terror and the fright of the thing has vanished from my mind as if it had been tied up in a bag and coughed out, the loss of Oliver is very sad and one can't do anything except be sorry it ever happened. The inquest and the fiddle faddle is over and done with and that's that. It is extraordinary the degree of dispassionate detachment that can arise in one's mind concerning this sort of thing. Assimilation – sympathy – dismissal.[32]

It is indeed extraordinary, the dispassionate detachment that informs this letter. It reads a little like a statement, but then how else could one describe 'the thing'? Dad never spoke to me of the horrors of his war, of which this must have been the first. It is as if such horror was as ineffable as the miraculous beauty of Bach or Beethoven. And although Evil was not present in this event, I am tempted to believe that there was a religious dimension to my father's silence on these matters.[*]
As indeed there was in so much else.

Went to a Salvation Army service this morning. It was conducted by a magnificent ex-naval Petty Officer, a Salvation Major, who amongst other things played the Last Chord for us on the Concertina! He was a first class chap & it was by far the best army service I have ever attended. The C of E has a lot to learn about handling a roomful of chaps from the Salvation Army.[33]

And at Easter 1942, 'a very unreligious Easter, by and large', he reported to his father that he had 'just heard Bach's Oratorio: very lovely performance. And a fine C of E service this morning.' The Church of England had its moments.

---

[*] *Apparently Dad gave a filmed account of the incident for Michael Gill's series *The Commanding Sea*, but its length precluded its use.

As I've already suggested, there are present in these letters seeds that were to bear fruit in the years after the war in a kind of Wheldon doctrine that insisted that the best institutions were those that allowed and encouraged the potential of individual creativity; and that creativity resided not in mere thought or idea but in doing and making.

The letters also describe an increasing loss of youthful cynicism. The student-smartness, even flipness, has drained out of them by May 1942. His letters to the Leepers become less frequent, and it is to his father that most of his letters are directed. It is as if he has, at heart, more in common with his father than with his friends, a kind of seriousness that he was unwilling to betray elsewhere. And yet the correspondence is never solemn, on his side rarely blindingly deferential, on his father's markedly unpatriarchal. They appear to have been friends.* I am ever so slightly envious of that.

In June 1942 he transferred from the Royal Welch Fusiliers. 'He was, obviously, an excellent instructor,' wrote my Uncle Dai, Richard Rees, who my father was very soon to meet. 'That Battle School would have kept him on indefinitely. He told me that he had been there too long, that active service would pass him by: the only way out was to volunteer for Airborne service: they eventually offered him transfer to either the RURs [Royal Ulster Rifles] or the Ox & Bucks [Oxfordshire & Buckinghamshire Light Infantry]. "I chose the Irishmen rather than the Ox and fucking Bucks."'[34]

---

* Paul Wright, Dad's colleague during the Festival of Britain, and subsequent close friend, had occasion to visit Wales to speak to Sir Wynn. Dad gave Paul some words of greeting in Welsh. Paul was suspicious that Dad might have fed him some frightful faux pas. He was never to know for sure: 'You don't think my father would let me down, do you?' asked Dad.

Rees and Wheldon, two Welshmen with the Royal Ulster Rifles

CHAPTER 4

1942–1946: RIFLES

As seems to have been a common experience for servicemen during the Second World War, Dad saw a lot of the country. Within the first five months of his service with the Royal Ulster Rifles his unit was moved from Nottingham, to Kidlington, to Bulford, to Exeter and Ifracombe and back to Bulford.

One of the first letters from the RUR contains an ecclesiastical crack: 'I haven't yet met anyone whom I instantly liked in the sense I like Desmond [Leeper] or Brian [Murphy]: but the Padre seems a good chap; this is the road to Rome!'[1] When I used to accompany my father to Cardiff Arms Park, during the glory days of Welsh rugby in the 1970s, the jokes and quips in the crowd around us often referred to chapel or assumed a knowledge of the Old Testament. Even today, when asked why the roof of the Millennium Stadium is open, a Welshman will tell you that it is in order that God should be able to watch Wales play rugby.

In July the 1st RUR went to Kidlington in Oxfordshire in order to learn to parachute. It was an RAF base, and Dad was struck by the contrast between the services.

> Correctness is everywhere. There is no shambling in to a cosy meal in shirtsleeves... I prefer the army with its added measures of sweat and repression and sudden respites, exasperation, community, baffled anger. The men with their irrelevant names and common attitudes. Dust and Friday night drunkenness.[2]

There is a suggestion here of the profoundly intimate camaraderie felt between army soldiers, even before battle is joined, the idea that soldiers are men first, servicemen when required. This may also be one of the seeds of Dad's club theory of British society.

He used to get very upset with me if I dressed inappropriately. For a long time I thought this was a rather uncharacteristic stuffiness, but after he had explained his club theory, I began to see what he was on about.

The club theory holds that Britain is not a class-bound society at all, but a club-bound society, and while some clubs might be very exclusive (the Club for Royals, the Club for Speakers of Welsh) most required only the appropriate manners for entry. If you wanted to be in the Club for People Who Wanted to be in the RAF you had to be prepared to smarten up for dinner, whereas if you wanted to be in the Army Club a certain degree of slovenliness at mealtimes was called for. So when I went to the Proms I had to wear my velvet jacket, and I certainly couldn't wear my brushed denim bell-bottoms. Whether this had the effect of making me unclubbable – which I certainly am – is unlikely. I believe I simply have my mother's shyness.

Dad continued to see injustices, merit going unrewarded, hierarchies unhelpfully replicating themselves: 'seeing idiots get responsible jobs simply because they are senior infuriates me'. His friend and former landlord in Deal, Bacon, who had moved westwards in fear of invasion, was employed as a clerk in Bristol: '[Bacon] is wasted in this job. It angers me when I think of his fragile, accurate, inquisitive energy being thrown out of the window.'[3] He could not bear the waste. He never could. In a letter to my mother after Dad died, Tony Jay wrote: 'he was one of those precious spirits who judged himself and others not in terms of who they were but of what they did: it was achievement, not status, that provided all his pleasure and fuelled his admiration.'

From Ilfracombe, where the battalion learned to swim, he wrote self-searchingly:

> I am improving – but terribly slowly – as a company commander, although still despairingly lacking in some quality which provides a foundation for discipline. My discipline [he is speaking here presumably of his imposition of discipline on others] has always been appalling, & I have always known this. But I am too feeble to deny myself the pleasures of incessant matiness, & too soft to be serene even when I know beyond a shadow of a doubt that serenity is wanted.[4]

I recognise this same difficulty in myself in my relations with builders, plumbers, gardeners and so forth. I would always rather be their friend than their boss. 'Feeble' was one of Dad's favourite words. More forgiving than 'casual' – at least an effort had been made.

In September 1942 the battalion was appointed a new Medical Orderly, Richard Rees. He was a Welsh-speaking man from Swansea – 'a first rate chap… a fine man'. Dai Rees* was to become my father's brother-in-law, marrying my aunt Mair, and one of his two or three best friends (the others were Brian Murphy, whom Dad had met at LSE, and, to come, through my mother, Norman Podhoretz – a Swansea Baptist, an Irish Catholic and a Brooklyn Jew).

Despite the move to the RUR, in search of more action, he continued to be frustrated, along with his friends Brian Murphy and Desmond Leeper. In November 1942 he wrote to the latter:

> All these beautiful battles go on and Brian goes to his Salisbury office every morning at O Ninehundred hours, you presumably continue your incomprehensible meanderings around the country, and I am turning into an officer's mess article in bloody Bulford. Dicky Desbrow,† I suppose, is in Messa Matruh‡ [sic]

---

* When it was discovered in the officers' mess that he was a Welshman – not hard as he had an accent, while Dad did not – he became the officer-equivalent of Taffy – 'Dai' – and so he remained to RUR comrades and Wheldons.

† LW 'Dicky' Desbrow had been a highly active student at the LSE. In a piece called 'Union Night', written in 1933 for the *Clare Market Review* – the LSE student publication – he had reported: 'The Canadian debating team opposed the motion that "Liberalism, though it yet speaketh, is dead," which Mr West had proposed. No one agreed with anyone else's idea of Liberalism, and few could decide if what they thought was Liberalism was dead, because they could not be certain what was meant by "being dead". People sorted themselves out and decided that it was not dead.' The death (or not) of Liberalism (whatever that was) continued to tax my father until he actually started fighting the Nazis.

‡ Mersa Matruh: battle fought by Auchinleck against Rommel while falling back on El Alamein, at the end of June 1942. A month after Dad's letter to Leeper Montgomery won the Second Battle of El Alamein, breaking Rommel's grasp on North Africa.

I used to hate missing an LSE Hockey Club Dance: remaining true to my herd nature I am furious because I am not allowed the chance of being bored, terrified & outraged in a desert.[5]

The same letter finishes:

Finally, I was brought up in a household & in a community where Equality was the fashion, and I can't take easily to the problems of command. So you see the kind of mess B Company is in. I am not a natural commander, but circumstances here put me in that laughable predicament with the result that I am hopelessly preoccupied day and night with my job, wondering whether it is Yea or Nay, Black or White, inclining always to gray, self-condemned.

This is a reiteration, in the language of friendship rather than filial piety, of Dad's claims of discomfort at being a commander. I'm not sure whether I believe this or not. What I would believe is that he perhaps enjoyed it rather too much, and his enjoyment bothered him. I mean by this that he didn't feel himself worthy of the responsibility given to him, and felt ashamed of the fact that he revelled in it. It is an expression perhaps of conscientiousness. I feel rather superior in writing this and wish I could have put it to him. 'That's what I think,' I might finish. 'Do you?' he might have responded, sucking on the arm of his spectacles, the 'do' starting at a high pitch and held a nano-moment longer than necessary, the inquisition made not only more emphatic but also more companionable. 'Yes.' 'Well, I think you may very well be right.'

Another reason why I don't quite believe this is a letter written soon after, again to Leeper:

I know now why it was I never wrote, why I was cut off from everything. I arrived in this battalion as a captain, but immediately took on command of a company, which is a major's job in this racket, and my command continued until last week when I lost it (very properly) to a man already a major and therefore The Man for the Job. I knew – it was no secret – that this would of course happen, but as the months went by and no one came along to fill the vacancy I grew more and more accustomed to the job, and when this man Warner* eventually took my place I was angry and hurt. Angry because Warner got in on seniority and is certainly not my equal, or the equal of at least eighty percent of the officers in the Battalion, hurt by the sight of my plans & even my small consummations, going astray. I don't know whether this can make sense to you – but the affairs of the company took up so much of my energies that reading writing thinking friends relatives films sex politics religion all became distant and uninteresting. The company was my wife home and family and commanding it literally took everything I had. I had never imagined that such an immolation was possible: and did not know that it was so even, until I lost the job, turning to letters films sex friends and the rest with a warmth that surprised me within two days of losing the job.

The most revealing thing about the whole affair has been the recognition of the attractions of power.[6]

---

* 'This man Warner' was probably the same Tom Warner who had enlisted as a rifleman before being granted a commission in 1940. He missed D-Day, having been wounded when, by accident, a grenade went off in company lines five days before the invasion.

In other words, he found himself possessive of something he hadn't known he wanted.

Later in the year, he was at Naworth Castle, Brampton, at the School of Military Administration, and the battalion was at Chilton Foliat during the spring of 1943, in 'a foggy atmosphere of nonsense, bullshit and inefficiency'. Time lay heavy.

They went to see movies occasionally. *How Green Was My Valley* was 'atrocious', *Casablanca* was 'roaring', *The Arabian Nights* was 'the worst film I have ever known'.

1943 ended in Harlech with yet more special training. Harlech, perhaps because it was Wales, and well-known Wales at that, was 'very good indeed'.

It was like being at LSE again, a plunge into forgotten waters… we worked mornings and evenings: our afternoons our own. I went walking on all five afternoons. The first walk was with a chap called Chambers. I was proud to show him the country, and we spoke to several old chaps by the way, fetching up finally in a tea place in Llanbedr where an old woman gave us tea and her old husband gave us wisdom. It was a hellish session because these two old owls were as miserable a couple as ever wandered in Bosnia. The old boy was all for ending the war – 'drawing it' he said – and his hideous spouse was full of righteous indignation against the English on the grounds that they knew nothing about poetry, quoting as an example of the barbarity the entire ignorance among Englishmen of 1) Shakespeare and 2) Ironside. By Ironside I could only take it that the old fiend meant Longfellow. I kept my end up as best I could, keeping the conversation along neutral lines as much as possible, and striving to hide all discomfiture from the horrified Mr

Chambers who spent most of his tea time drawing whisps of grey hair from the sugar. The tea cost us 2/3 each and wasn't worth tuppence. The next day I took this bull by the horns and practically forced citizen Chambers up a mountain, together with a Wren called Smithers – a singularly delightful girl, engaged of course blast and hell – and we found ourselves in a farm called Gerddi Bluog* where black became white in a twinkling, and we ate honest bread and talked to Mr & Mrs Williams, the couple. They were more than delightful: and seeing them, unspoilt, well-bred, and gentle in their equally beautiful kitchen made my heart ache with a vague sorrow – their English was slow and correct, and their courtesy overwhelming. I returned to Harlech cogitating on the waves of industrialism and vulgarity and shoddiness and the rest that had drowned people like this along our coasts, regretting the whole age like mad.[7]

The day after this letter was written, the Red Army launched offensives against the Germans in the Ukraine. In January they advanced into poor Poland, invaded twice already by the Nazis, and now twice by the Communists. Per head of the population the Poles lost more citizens than any other nation in Europe, other, of course, than the Nation of Israel.

January 1944, and they were back in Bulford on 'the abominable plain' of Salisbury. Preparations for D-Day began to gather apace and the amount of information that Dad was able to communicate became narrower still. Annoyingly, Dai

---

* Gerddi Bluog was a farm with a distinguished history. The poet Edmund Prys is said to have lived there in the sixteenth century. In the 1960s it was renovated by none other than Clough Williams-Ellis, the genius of Portmeirion.

was way ahead in their competition to finish Gibbon: 'His conversation is full of Justinian & Theodosius & the Nicene Creed.' I'm tremendously impressed by this race. I've managed a chapter of Gibbon. Perhaps if I was in a war I would manage more. It is altogether too civilised – too literary to be history, too historical to be fiction; it serves neither as escape nor as knowledge. It is exactly the sort of book that I would thoroughly enjoy did I not live in a world that demands to be either escaped from or known about.

Music remained important:

This afternoon I am taking twenty of my chaps who profess themselves eager and even enthusiastic, to a concert of what is advertised as 'Good Music'. If a cellist starts playing little things by Fauré, they will, of course, stamp and giggle and whistle in their primitive way. And if they do I will punish them with utter vindictiveness. So I plough my cruel rut.

Dai is coming with me.

... I have got a new sergeant major thank goodness instead of the ineffective Mr Bunting – a little snarl of a man called MacGregor.* Short, thin, long-necked, with piercing eyes, and a voice like a pneumatic drill. He reminds me of a corncrake, being bird-like in a fierce, magnetic kind of way.[8]

Whether there was stamping, giggling or whistling, we never find out. It may well be that there was not, and that Dad might have learned something about the nature of audiences.

---

*   Possibly actually CSM McCutcheon, of whom more later.

In March Dad saw *The Merchant of Venice*: 'Shakespeare as usual triumphing over everything. He is always so startlingly good – one thinks: Oh Shakespeare, well, one might as well go – and then, within five minutes of the first line, he has you overwhelmed.'[9] Funnily enough I don't remember seeing very much Shakespeare with Dad. He preferred to take us to music – always to the Proms, where he had a BBC box, and often to Gilbert and Sullivan. I later saw an ageing Robert Eddison as Feste, and Dad said that he too had seen Eddison as Feste, in Alec Guinness's 1948 production. I do remember seeing with him Albert Finney as Hamlet, I think directed by Peter Hall. Finney began 'To be...' off stage, rushing on with a breathless '...or not to be', the whole thing horribly garbled and gabbled. There were one or two seasons, too, when the RSC was at the Aldwych and Alan Howard was in his pomp as everyone from Hal to Coriolanus. Dad also took me to the opening of the Olivier to see *Plunder* by the still-living Ben Travers. Best of all was being taken backstage to meet Kenneth More after a performance of *The Winslow Boy* at the Mermaid. I must have been about twelve years old.* *Reach for the Sky* was one of those war movies schoolboys loved, and More was a charming but down to earth hero. In my first term at Oxford Dad wrote to tell me he had seen 'Ben Jonson's *The Alchemist* at the Aldwych on Wednesday – a simply brilliant production by that chap who followed Peter Hall. I forget his name. He's married to that woman who played Lady Macbeth. I forget her name as well! Something Suzman. *The Alchemist* was the

---

* Actually, best of all was when Dad on the spot (to Mum's horror) invited Jack Charlton home to tea, having bumped into him at Wembley during the 1967 FA Cup Final. Not only did I get to see Tottenham beat Chelsea 2–1, I got to play football in the back garden with a World Cup winner.

RSC at its best. You really should arrange to see it. It is in the Repertoire. A peach.' For the record, Ian McKellen was the star and the director Trevor Nunn (later married to Imogen Stubbs, the brightest, kindest, most beautiful girl of my Oxford days, and sadly no more than an acquaintance).

Easter 1944 was spent at home at Canonbury, in Prestatyn. When Dai wasn't paying court to Dad's sister Mair, the two men went hiking on the hills. To Desmond Leeper Dad wrote:

> Back last night after five days climbing in the hills [with Dai]... Hills magnificent: mist ubiquitous of course, but the rock was nice and hard, & the grass uncomplicated. Wet days, warm evenings, vast meals – strong treacle all this, & very fine.[10]

Correspondence, he reported after returning to Bulford, now had to go 'through devious channels'. About the only information vouchsafed is that he is reading Macaulay rather than Jane Austen.

> One sits in the middle of all this boiling up, these increasingly urgent moves, in a strangely dispassionate mood. There is an unreality about everything, as if the evasive colours and moving distances of early spring were making the very lorries insubstantial, giving a vague and faery quality even to logistics. There is no room in a world full of transient and circumambient grace for the arithmetical, the flat-footed. Daunsinge cometh with the springe.[11]

Ben Leeper gets a similar message:

England indescribably lovely with her parklands and beech trees & little hills; the whole countryside a pressing testimony to the proprieties, and even to the virtues of peace, although no doubt we should be naughty, you & I, altogether to disregard the dog beneath the skin, the forgotten wars, the mysterious wealth... I can only say that my heart and head is full of the beauty of it all: happily full, no aches.[12]

In May, one can feel the tension, the ratcheting up of preparedness. And after a war spent, at home, wondering what it was that was being fought for, my father seems to have come to his own conclusions, resenting attempts on the part of others to think for him:

I had to attend another service, all denoms – earlier in the week... the chaplains entered... and settled about the place like a flock of geese, after which we were gravely dedicated to the 2nd front. I am tired of being dedicated to the 2nd front, especially by a chap who speaks in a Noel Coward way. All this stuff about our crusading spirit is desperately false I think: dishonest in fact. At the best the whole war is a poor thing, but alas necessary – I don't think that any soldier would fight more feebly if he stayed on that level so far as his philosophical basis went. What we fight for is, I am sure, as right as what we fight against is wrong. This fact can be quietly accepted... I feel that chaplains & their like might keep quiet about our so-called determination and our love for this that and the other until such time as the demand for an emotional expression of that sort comes from the men themselves. Still, I suppose it gives comfort to some of the chaps. It made me furious...

Dai has just looked in. He is not, he says, altogether pleased with the Emperor Justinian.[13]

Books remain the chief source of interest. He finds himself using the line 'the dolphin-torn, the gong-tormented sea', and wonders where it has come from – he believes it may have been his own invention, but is not sure – he admits to quoting St Paul and Shakespeare under the impression that their lines are his own. It is, of course, the last line of 'Byzantium' by WB Yeats.

One of the last letters before D-Day rages against the vulgar. It is the same rage and upset that overtook him at the prospect of his chaps giggling at Fauré or the threat to the survival of the old-fashioned grace exemplified by the old farming couple. It is, I think, an uncomplicated love of goodness, for the simplicity of goodness.

Only two things have marred the idyllic last few weeks – a camp fire sing song I arranged, & which went beautifully, with the boys singing sentimentally about Ireland, drawing easily from their vast reservoir of songs, until a newly joined young officer from London elected to change the character of the meeting and struck up what I can only describe as a Rugby Football Club song, after which of course everything deteriorated and the singing dwindled unto the usual run of obscenity in the minor but by no means gentle key. I left them to it, trembling with hideous rage, & presently sent over & stopped it. I also stopped the wretched officer, good, as they say, & proper.[14]

I don't think this is snobbery. I think this is awareness of the fragility of the beautiful, especially when up against the greed and the easiness of the merely fun. The laughter of the spoiler is one of the most horrible sounds in the world. When I was at Oxford I joined one morning a group of people who were going out to sabotage a fox hunt. We tore around the fields of Oxfordshire playing The Clash at full volume. We all thought it was very funny. I don't quite know when my shame kicked in, but I had not expected that people other than the hunters also enjoyed the hunt. I began to feel out of place, small, mean. The electric guitar suddenly seemed like the instrument of the bully. This is not a point about the pros and cons of fox hunting – it is a description of a particular feeling in a particular time in a particular place, where it was easy to be crass.

On 5 June, the day before D-Day, Dad wrote a going-to-war letter to his father.

> I have just finished packing. I wonder whether any major crisis will ever find me ready? The soap I meant to get, the bootlaces I put off buying, the holster which should have been repaired... yesterday's procrastinations are at last bearing fruit! Wheldon goes to war pitifully ragged.

> My recent letters have been very colourless, I fear – I could not help it, hated doing it, the partial deception. We have been in a closed camp for some time, sealed off entirely from everybody, and the tentacles of security have reached into everything. Free at last, at least to tell you that the last few weeks have been very very happy ones, working away at our operation orders (the whole thing has been very like working for an exam) – sunbathing and taking things easily.

> We are off very shortly, and the sounds of whistling and

shouting, odd songs, the gang round the goal posts, reach into this tent. Everyone is amazingly happy. We have studied the whole thing so deeply that the natural apprehensions are submerged in a general feeling of elation based on this great preparation and on the knowledge that the job is well within our capacity. The Staffs have indeed done their jobs well. Our job is one which, if done to any extent whatsoever, will relieve pressure on other large groups of chaps. This too is heartening. The possibilities of service are there to be seen and there is no feeling of futility. We have much to be thankful for. I personally would not like to miss it, and I am going much more firmly based – spiritual values apart – than ever I hoped.

There is nothing else I can say. You know what my feelings are about most things – and you will realise that nothing is being thrown away in this venture. No matter what happens I personally feel that a service (again, on the purely tactical, not to mention any higher plain) will have been rendered. This makes everything worthwhile.

So please don't worry – this, like the note I scribbled to mother, is ludicrously inadequate; but the depths can't be plumbed in a phrase or a letter.

All my love and affection

Huw

Coupons herewith! These will buy socks, etc. I don't fancy they will be much good in France.[15]

It should not be surprising that I find this moving – depths recognised but unplumbed are always moving. There is an emphasis on 'service', and, perhaps with a slight bow to his father's experience of Ypres, its being possible; of there being 'no feeling of futility', a term analogous with 'waste', surely. But the word that makes me catch my breath and pricks my eyes is that 'affection'. In that word is all that mere 'love' cannot hold – it is somehow less abstract. It contains humour and shared experience and familial safety. There is about it the sense of warmth and trust. It is not love that one walks away from into war, it is affection. Loving kindness.

I wonder how long it took him to write the letter, whether it took deliberation, several drafts. I used to envy my father the war. I am a very rare creature in human history, of a generation that has not had to go to fight. I have never had to test myself in the most trying of situations, never been wounded in malice, never seen friends wounded and worse. I pray the same will hold true for my children. Only, of course, I do not pray because I do not have a god to pray to. I wonder if someone was trying to kill me with mortars whether I would suddenly find a way to pray, just as Dad's 'boys' did ('like bloody hell and incessantly') as soon as the shooting started.

Having been 'yanked across the sky as if we were in a very old railway carriage', the Horsa gliders of the 6th Air Landing Brigade, including 1st (Airborne) Battalion, Royal Ulster Rifles, touched down in Normandy at around 9.00 pm on 6 June. Operation Mallard was under way. On board the men had been given tea and water and all ranks had been instructed to drink as much as possible before landing. 'I was conscious,' wrote Dad, 'of bursting out of the glider... the next thing I noticed, and shall never forget, was the sight of the troops, ever sensitive to unexpected opportunity, standing on the quiet grass in the twilight relieving themselves with the absent-minded look that men assume on these occasions.'[16]

The 6th Air Landing Brigade was a part of the 6th Airborne Division (the 2nd, 3rd, 4th and 5th were purely imaginary units, designed for consumption by German intelligence), whose role was to secure the left flank of the Allied landings. This flank was to be the hinge on which the Allies would pivot out of the Normandy bridgehead into France and towards the Rhine. Dad landed by glider near Ranville, about five miles north east of Caen. The following day he won the Military Cross: 'In total disregard to his own safety and under heavy small arms and artillery fire, he moved about from one Platoon to another encouraging the men and making arrangements for the evacuation of the wounded. His fine display of courage and coolness was an outstanding example to his men.' To his father he wrote that it was 'a shameful thing... When bravery has been required I have in most cases shirked it, being miserably frail. Still, there it is.'[17] The casualty list for the battalion that day read: sixteen killed, sixty-nine wounded and forty missing in action. Dad's company had received 'a colossal amount of attention from enemy mortars.'[18]

The fighting around Caen was ferocious following D-Day. German Panzer divisions were fighting for their very lives. You wouldn't think so from the letters: 'Dai is still reading Gibbon.' And after the stupendous English spring and early summer, the weather in France was atrocious. Dad wrote to Desmond Leeper on 19 June, a fortnight after the invasion: 'Today the entire war has stopped for the time being presumably because of the RAIN, which is undoubtedly worse than the war itself'.

Dai was also working:

during that very same bombardment... Huw walked in. I really thought at that time that my flimsy cowshed would disintegrate, but its solid Normandy stone walls saved us.

Huw: 'Dai, give me something for my back.'

Me: 'Why, what's happened?'

Huw: 'Nothing much, but my back hurts.'

Me: 'Well take your shirt off and let me see it.'

Huw: 'No need for that, old boy, just give me some ointment!'

Me: 'You'll get nothing here, not even sympathy, until I see it.'

In fact he had a nasty transverse series of 2nd degree burns across his back associated with much bruising and superficial wounds. He had been struck by the red hot casings of 'Moaning Minnies'. These were Nebelwerfers, a group of six huge Mortars packed with high explosives. When fired they sounded like a very large ratchet. One could hear them a mile off and took cover. This lot had landed in Huw's slit trench. He got his ointment, and refused evacuation in spite of my concern that his ribs might be damaged.[19]

So much for the shirker.

Like his father before him, Dad recommended and secured decorations for several of his men by making up fictional citations, on the grounds that it was fairer to reward consistent bravery than singular flashy acts. And as to a report he had to make about a brave soldier who had died foolishly his father advised him to 'Lie, and, if you lie, tell a whopper'.

What horrified Dad was the 'waste': 'There is waste and devastation everywhere', he wrote to his mother; and to his father: 'The waste is overwhelming to a chap like me, new to it – & a nonconformist conscience to boot.'

It is remarkable the degree to which the tone of these letters is of a piece with those that precede them. Obviously the writer is limited in what he can say, both for operational reasons and because he is writing, on the whole, to his parents – 'as to *The Times*', as he put it to the Leepers. But even with full licence I am not sure how much further he would have gone. The term 'the waste', perhaps borrowed unconsciously from Eliot, is very Wheldonian, suggesting as it does the devastation not only of what is, but also of what might be. That, at any rate, is what I hear in it. I hear the moral imperative to live to the fullest; I hear an echo of my mother's idea of God as being profound experience. War brings, paradoxically, both profound experience and its opposite, waste. The even mildly cynical will probably bridle at this, so it is important to emphasise that what I am describing is something inherited – an intellectual meme or trope. What was meant then perhaps does not mean what it does now; it has been qualified by the passage of time, and by the qualities of thought and understanding that I bring to it. It has evolved. My loyalty to my parents is absolute. I cannot remove to a critical distance. While I may find myself occasionally mystified by mere meanings, I read these letters from inside. I hear my father's voice, I see the ink on the page and know it flowed from a pen held by him. I do not interpret, I receive, as of genetic right.

As is the case of many in desperate straits, the recourse is humour. On 30 June he writes: 'I can't see what God had in mind when he created the moustike [mosquito]. It is all great fun really and not unlike living with Lady Kenyon."* A week later a victory is reported:

> Last night I either killed or severely wounded James Ellis, a large and private mosquito enemy who had hitherto lived with me in my trench and was easily recognisable by his prodigious size and his no less wonderful powers of evasive flight.[20]

In July an odd thing happened. On the 14th he wrote to Ben Leeper: 'Living too soiled a life to read the New Testament'; the following day he learned he had been killed. He wrote to Desmond:

> I firmly believe that we are all in the hands of God – there is consolation here, possibly the only basic consolation there is. Everything else is mystery... My short life in Normandy has been sufficient to prove this to me again and again: that the only peace there is is the peace of God.[21]

This is the most explicitly believing my father ever was. I found it rather shocking, in fact, as though my father's accent had changed or his silhouette become blurred.

Thankfully it was a false report and Ben was alive and well. The letters return to their more jocular tone, no mention of the fact that the six weeks following D-Day had involved a good deal of heavy fighting, that the battalion was in the front line, holding the ridge that ran north to south from Merville to Troarn.

Le Mesnil remained the battalion base until the breakout in the middle of August. Dad made himself at home. He wrote

---

*   Gwladys, widow of Lord Kenyon, Chief Whip in Lloyd George's coalition government and sometime Lord Lieutenant of Denbighshire.

to his mother describing furnishings, and to his father about his reading: 'Isaiah 55 is rotten in English and starts like a cookery book.'*

Nor did he neglect 'the boys'.

> Today has been splendid... working like a Trojan all day on a Rest Room for the boys... I feel like Beethoven... reading Moby Dick – finding it impossible to live with Dai until I have read it. I started yesterday and have read two pages... a swallows nest in some rafters. The young swallows are fed very regularly... and their progress is watched daily by one and all. Mice galore. Mice, gentle little chaps.[22†]

In *Men at Arms*, the first novel of *Sword of Honour*, Evelyn Waugh's great trilogy of the Second World War, Guy Crouchback thinks of 'this strange faculty of the army of putting itself into order. Shake up a colony of ants and for some minutes all seems chaos. The creatures scramble aimlessly, frantically about; then instinct reasserts itself. They find their proper places and proper functions. As ants, so soldiers... Men unnaturally removed from wives and family began at once to build substitute homes, to paint and furnish, to make flower-beds and edge them with white-washed pebbles, to stitch cushion-covers on lonely gun-sites.'[23]

---

* 1 Ho, every one that thirsteth, come ye to the waters, and he that hath no money; come ye, buy, and eat; yea, come, buy wine and milk without money and without price.
2 Wherefore do ye spend money for that which is not bread? and your labour for that which satisfieth not? hearken diligently unto me, and eat ye that which is good, and let your soul delight itself in fatness.

† The following February Dai wrote in his diary: 'Bath tonight. Excellent! A mouse kept me company, gambolling like a lamb – extraordinary!' I find very moving the tenderness of these men in the midst of the horrors of war.

For Dad, the chaos and the waste of those first days had given way to a feat of astonishing organisation:

> The way in which two months (during which there was much hard fighting) has been enough to make the bridgehead into an organised structure with roads and hospitals and repair outfits and rest camps and bridges is tremendously impressive. Everything runs on wheels. The planners did a wonderful job, forgot nothing, and their success is startling.[24]

Bob Sheridan, who was battalion adjutant, wrote the following account of a 'cruel trick' played on himself and Dai sometime in the middle of July while the battalion was in placement around Breville. Enemy mortar shelling continued, and snipers were a constant threat.

> During a lull in activity one day, I suggested to Dai Rees that we might take a walk and visit C Company. He agreed, so after telling one of our signallers to tell C Company on the field telephone that we were on our way, we set off...

> The ground ahead of us was a gentle upward slope, so we could not see what lay on the far side of the field. Away to the left, the countryside was thickly wooded, and I could not help wondering whether that area was held by 'us' or 'them'!

> At the crest of the hill we saw a cluster of solid but dilapidated farm buildings; when we reached them we found a rifleman standing over a horse trough with a towel wrapped round his neck, busily shaving. I asked, 'Where is Company HQ?' He pointed over his shoulder with a soapy razor to a stable-like building on the far side of the courtyard. As we walked

across, 'Killer' Johnson, the CO, came out to greet us. 'Hello', he said, 'how nice to see you. You are just in time for elevenses'. 'We didn't come up here for elevenses', replied Dai in his lilting Welsh voice. 'We came to see what you buggers are doing about winning the war'. Just then Huw Wheldon (2 i/c) appeared in the doorway, unshaven, with battle-dress jacket flapping open. It occurred to me that we had woken him up from sleep. However, Huw wasn't the sort to be put out. He held his arms out in a gesture of welcome and said with an air of exaggerated surprise: 'Two gentlemen from the War Office, I presume. You would like to know how the War is progressing? Do come in to our operational HQ', and stood aside, and, with a mock bow, gestured us to enter...

'Now', said Huw, as if welcoming us to a cocktail party, 'what would you gentlemen like to drink?' 'I don't suppose you have any champagne', I replied, 'but I don't think Calvados would do us any harm'. Killer's batman had appeared on the scene with four enamel mugs, and also pushed up to the table an inverted wooden tub and a milking stool. Huw carefully poured out four small measures of Calvados and with mock solemnity Dai and I toasted the continued success of C Company. Killer's batman, an 'old soldier', enquired innocently, 'Will Capt. Sheridan and Capt. Rees be staying to lunch, Sorr?' 'Yes, of course', replied Killer, 'and bring it along as soon as it is ready'...

After a few minutes back came Killer's batman, carrying four china plates on each of which were two pork chops, boiled potatoes and carrots. Both Dai and I looked at this in amazement. I realized the pork had certainly originated with the pigs killed at Battn. HQ, but the thought of sitting down to eat these chops, well-cooked and with fresh vegetables, in a cowshed two hundred yards from where the enemy was undoubtedly scheming to blow us all to smithereens, was difficult to appreciate. However, there were more surprises to come!

Halfway through our meal, the large frame of Mike Gann, platoon commander, appeared in the doorway. He saluted Killer and said, 'Just to let you know, Sir, the Germans are reinforcing their forward positions, which would suggest they are going to put in an attack.' Killer finished eating and asked, 'Where about, Mike?'

'In front of 14 and 15 platoons areas.'

'OK, thanks for letting me know,' and Killer went on eating. I looked at Dai and Dai looked at me.

Neither Killer nor Huw made any reference to the impending threat of German attack, and carried on the conversation as if we had been sitting in a Piccadilly hotel. We had all finished our food when Mike appeared in the doorway once again, saluting as before. 'The Germans are forming up in front of 14 platoon, Sir,' he said, 'and it is pretty obvious they are going to attack pretty soon.' Killer looked up at him and paused a few moments. 'Thank you, Mike,' he said. 'Keep me informed, if you would.' Mike saluted and disappeared. I looked again at Dai and Dai looked at me while Huw remarked how well the pork had been cooked. I was sure the same things were going through Dai's mind as were going through mine. If a German attack was imminent, our place was back in Battn. HQ. On the other hand, with Killer and Huw showing such composure in the face of what seemed imminent danger, how could we withdraw without creating an impression of cowardice in the face of the enemy?...

At that moment there was a sudden burst of machine-gun fire immediately outside the door... Dai and I stood up, certainly startled, whilst Killer and Huw burst out laughing. Looking out of the door we saw Mike Gann still standing with a Sten gun in his hands pumping bullets into the heavy plasterwork of the adjoining building...

Highly exaggerated versions of the affair soon spread through the Battalion. These were not entirely unkind. It was considered that, for Battn. HQ officers, we had conducted ourselves reasonably well.[25]

Dai regarded this as a 'performance' and Dad did indeed enjoy performing, but he wasn't an actor (Stanley Kubrick, who had wanted Dad to narrate his movie of *Barry Lyndon*, was disappointed to find that Dad was not a member of Equity – not that Dad would have done it anyway*). He was a Master of Ceremonies. He performed that role at a twenty-fifth anniversary performance of *Under Milk Wood* at the Duke of York's theatre. As much of the original cast as could be brought together appeared in a semi-circle of chairs on the stage, most significantly Richard Burton as the Narrator. The show went well, and there was an interval. Towards the end of the break, as people were trailing back into the auditorium,

---

* Later David Puttnam wanted Dad to play a College Master in *Chariots of Fire*, opposite Sir John Gielgud. Again Peter Plouvier, that master of the closed shop, objected on behalf of Equity, and Lindsay Anderson – whom Dad detested – got the part. Much to Dad's dismay, 'he was EXACTLY like me'.

my father walked onto the stage, calling for 'Lights!' He was pulling someone by the wrist. As the lights finally came on, he said: 'Look who I found skulking about backstage.' Wearing a white man's shirt and tapering blue jeans, and looking very sheepish and very beautiful, it was Elizabeth Taylor. We all went for a meal at the Garrick afterwards, Dad and Burton swapping anecdotes and roaring.

In the middle of August the battalion began its advance along the northern coast of France (Operation Paddle it was called). The weather had improved markedly.

> We have been very busy, traversing Europe, marching through the orchards and the fields, seeing, for the first time, the genuine delight of villages properly liberated... we have been virtually strolling along unmolested through new country, rich in grain, in sunshine and in smiles.[26]

In October he was under Uncle Dai's authority again, with tonsillitis, the battalion having arrived back in England at the beginning of September. Recovering, he stayed a couple of nights in London before moving to the West Country for manoeuvres on Dartmoor and at Netheravon, staying briefly with the Bacons at Exeter ('went to a sung Compline at Buckfast Abbey last night. Fine.'). Seven days' leave in early December saw him in Prestatyn and then with the Leepers at Claygate before returning to 'bloody Bulford' on the 15th. On 20 December, according to Dai, 'aircraft of 38th Wing from Netheravon left for N. Ireland to get special Christmas turkeys for the Brigade and the RAF – "forward planning" by astute Ulster Quartermasters.'[27] Unfortunately, that evening the battalion was ordered to proceed immediately to Belgium. 'It was a twelve hours performance,' wrote Dad to his mother, regretting not having been able to say goodbye to his father. On 23 December the battalion was back at war. The Germans had launched an enormous counter-offensive in the Ardennes: the Battle of the Bulge.

They arrived too late to have a significant bearing on the engagement; the American 101st Airborne had done their stuff. But the Rifles didn't go home. They made for Holland.

Dad wasn't very impressed by the war or by himself. In January he wrote to the Leepers:

> This piddling war, bloody awful reluctant performance that it is to such as haven't the fire and zeal of heroes and Germans (no doubt) and in whose ranks Wheldon stands uncompromisingly, his feeble performance is a smooth and dull lake [?] in comparison, a humdrum business. Life is unexpected, and there are hateful powers everywhere. All cheer. H.[28]

To his father:

> Not a good day today – my organising capacity is good in its conception. My orders are lucid, always. But the direction of affairs finds me lacking single-mindedness and drive, and most of all, discipline. So things get lost, and meals go wrong. A shambles occurs, as they say. Tomorrow may be better. Enspere.[29]

And the new chaplain made things no better:

> Intractably high-church, our new C of E padre has just finished outraging the low church souls of the Irish Protestants, scandalising one and all by placing two sorry

candles on the makeshift altar, making the sign of the cross during the final blessing, so that even Dai is suddenly transfigured by Baptismic fires, and nonconformity is obvious in his very tread.[30]

On the whole it was a dismal time. From Maas, in Holland, Dad wrote home.

> Food is my great concern: a dirty cookhouse & a habitually dirty cook my worry. The men (and I myself) complain quietly all the lifelong day about the food – I plan meals, arrange rations, personally supervise the cleaning of dishes and floors; but the meals continue obstinately cool gritty small & tasteless.

> It was cold when the hard continuing frost held us, and men in outposts were occasionally stiffened with cold so that they had to be assisted in. Personally I suffered neither discomfort nor harm, my position and employment giving me an advantage. But petrified or not, I would gladly swop this rain, for any cold provided the cold came clean and dry. What was white and frozen under bitter blue skies, has become black and soggy like the sky itself. We live in mud. It is a peculiarly hateful existence. Busy of course, busy as hell. Ten men soaking wet return from a fatigue. Drying them is a job which will take the full extension of any time, any faculty available. For what cover there is is derelict and dirty: fuel is absent, stores few, wood soaking and useless. It becomes a problem of the greatest practical difficulty.

There is no enchantment here.*

Nevertheless, we survive happily enough: don't mistake my attitude for depression. One finds what one finds.

Statesman & Guardians & Cymros come pouring in, all higgledy piggledy because the whole postal system has gone to the devil, but nevertheless as welcome as sunshine.

My love to everyone.[31]

A food story comes down: a recce party that had gone scavenging for food had returned with a meagre number of eggs, certainly not enough for every man in the unit. There was, however, enough meat to make scotch eggs, which could then be divided, thereby allowing each of the men at least a morsel of egg. Dad was pleased with himself for having thought of so equitable a way of distributing rations. His men did not agree and were furious. They felt that lots should have been drawn. It suggests a kind of fatalism among them that the surviving Calvinist in their leader ought perhaps to have anticipated.

The battalion returned home at the end of February. A month before, Dad had received a letter from his father about the possibility of standing as a Liberal candidate. He replied:

Your letter about the liberal candidature to hand this morning. Alas, it is beyond my scope! With my shop-window character & general salesmanship qualities I have no doubt

---

* Dai wrote, describing battalion movements a fortnight before: 'We continued to move slowly from village to village in the Ardennes, snow everywhere, and the forests formidable, with no real sunshine to lend a little enchantment.'

that I should revel in the electioneering, and, as they say, knock them silly! I am sufficiently small in character to let my imagination run complacently in that direction. I would make vast promises, be gentle to children, charming to women, sell myself in fact, with the utmost composure. No doubt one is expected to do rather more than election antics, and there vanity must stoop to the hard fact – God knows I have no pretensions in that direction! A further handicap to a budding politician is the fact that I am quite without political passion.[32]

Refusal to be a Liberal candidate was becoming a habit in the Wheldon line. I am still waiting for the approach. (I was a founder member of the SDP but that is as far as my party political loyalties have stretched – belief in liberal democracy is all I'll now admit to.)

On 24 March the battalion was off again from a Transit Camp in East Anglia, to their airfield at Ravenhall, near Colchester, and thence for Germany, which Dad insisted would be 'a welcome change from Bloody B'. It wasn't, though. It was Operation Varsity, the largest single airborne operation in history, and its aim was to cross the Rhine into Germany.

Dad wrote home with a vivid account of the landing:

The flight was itself highly unpleasant, my glider pilot being a poor hand at the job, and having his difficulties immeasurably increased by a sky full of slipstreams and air disturbances from aircraft ahead. The whole firmament was spotted and crossed with aircraft. We swung about, and long before we reached the Rhine apprehension was crawling into every man's brain. As we approached the Rhine, a pall of smoke from Montgomery's screen became evident. The Rhine could be seen through it, a silver ribbon shining through the uniform grey. Ahead the other aircraft were still going on, and by now we could see bombers who had released their paratroop loads or gliders returning low on our flanks. The smoke underneath grew thicker, and I could see very little. Ahead we suddenly saw the silent flak explosions. Knowing we had another six minutes to go, and hating the thought like hell, I got into my seat and strapped myself in. A moment later the pilot cast off from the tug. I knew quite well he had cast off too early, but I welcomed the snapping-sound as the tow rope swung loose. Cowardly, as ever, I was only too pleased to be coming down. For me, strapped in, the descent was blind. We bumped a bit, and I recognised this as flak. After some little time I saw the ground through the little window and knew we were within fifty feet of our landing. Simultaneously, there was a methodical impersonal crackle, and machine gun bullets tore little holes in the fabric, missing everyone. Then we landed in a splintering crash and then sudden quiet. No more wind was passing through the fuselage. The machine gun fired more briskly and everyone unstrapped like mad and made for the exits. The crash had buckled my seat, and my equipment had got stuck between the seat and the side. I was consequently trapped. This seemed to me at the time ludicrous, and I grinned happily at my musical comedy situation, the bullets doing nothing to disturb the peace of mind almost ineffable which possessed me, as soon as we were landed. I took off my jacket and in this way extricated myself. Nipping about I found the boys all unhurt in a ditch alongside the smashed glider. Beyond the glider, hidden to us, was a farmhouse, some seventy yards away, and in this farm was the machine gun. I decided to leave it to someone else,* and led off in dead ground to a little wood. The sky was still full of aircraft in astonishing numbers, and on the ground all over the place were gliders and parachutes; my own chaps, paratroops, chaps feverishly unloading guns, hundreds of Yanks, miles from their objective, and far away, above the pendant smoke, the quiet sun. I found out where we were, and two hours later after a rum journey I found the battalion, all objectives taken, Dai alive, but many gone, including my C.S.M., old McCutcheon, the loyalest and most devotest soldier I ever saw, and a very great personal loss.† There were hundreds and hundreds of prisoners, all digging away like mad on our positions, while our chaps stood happily by smoking cigars like Lords of Creation.

On my way in to the position, moving along the edge of a wood, I suddenly stumbled on three Boche, not five yards away. I was unarmed, the magazine having dropped out of my pistol some time before, and all I had in my hand was a Ration Pack taken from a discarded haversack to make up for my own, left in the glider. I was naturally petrified with horror. As soon as they saw me the three Boche dropped to their knees and begged me not to shoot. With superb magnanimity I showed mercy, forbearing to throw my ration pack at them, and wheeled them in, now grist to the mill.

---

*   This farmhouse was taken by Robin Rigby's company and became Uncle Dai's Regimental Aid Post. It was Dai who came upon the body of CSM McCutcheon.

†   William McCutcheon, awarded the Military Medal in August 1944, wasn't 'old'. He was 28. He came from Harpenden in Hertfordshire. Known for his imperturbability, he once, on a particularly hot day, removed a packet of cigarettes from my father as Dad was about to light up: 'Sor! Never smoke your own sweat!' On another occasion McCutcheon brought the entire company to a halt, and pointed into a field: 'Look Sor!' Two hares were boxing. He was killed, hit in the head by a sniper shot, while escorting a group of German prisoners.

My own company did magnificently, storming a position, killing many and taking over a hundred prisoners. I was away at the time and did not share this action. Possibly fortunately. Under me, it might have been a more academic advance and far less deadly. No casualties there.[33]

The letter was written from a military hospital in Brussels. The initial, furious fighting was over and the battalion had spent two or three days being rained on before being ordered to move on to the town of Coesfeld, defended by five 88mm anti-tank guns. Bomber Command's raids on German towns provided German snipers with excellent cover. Dad fell victim to one such. Dai wrote:

It was in Coesfelt that Huw was shot. As a railway town and junction, Coesfelt had received more than passing attention by the RAF. He had been shot by a sniper and for years afterwards we pulled his leg for having been shot by German Home Guard! But his wound was serious, a through and through wound of the buttock. Fortunately it had missed bone, artery, and sciatic nerve. He was evacuated immediately, and with Penicillin then available in Military Hospitals I knew he would soon be OK again.[34]

Dad left the hospital – 'the lovely house with its gardens made achingly beautiful by cherry blossom and magnolias and innumerable little border-flowers, all flourishing in still sunshine' – on 17 April. On his way to rejoin his unit he passed through Belsen, which had been liberated five days earlier. He never mentioned this to me, or indeed to anyone, not to Norman Podhoretz, perhaps not even to Mum, other than in a letter to his father written a week before VE Day, and here only obliquely, oddly, the syntax clumsy, as though words wouldn't do.

I am just arrived into my thousandth billet in Europe. Or so it seems. It is the usual experience. A twenty-mile march along knobbly cobbled roads reveals nothing much except well-tilled fields, and a spacious husbandry. Villages seem deserted. The Germans are working or fled – liberated workers loaf around in their various and astonishing garments and we plod on. There are no young men: no men under sixty. Where they all are, God alone knows. Our harbour for the night is a village, taken over. Mercifully, the civilians are gone. I am in a nice house, and, as usual, we have crockery and tablecloths and beds. When we go, we simply leave them. The men are similarly situated. Do what you will you can't stop the occasional ransacking. When we left our last place this morning three civilian women approached me, and showed me a cellar broken into, three trunks smashed open, contents spilled and spoiled. Furious with this hooliganism, what could I do? Furious too with the three querulous bourgeois women with their windy complainings. A bottle had been stolen, a tablecloth, a lamp-bracket broken. They understand the etiquette of defeat: May I speak? Could I make so bold as to ask? May I go out to see my sister? – at the same time there is no clear impression of guilt, no question of doing us anything but favours when they give us, willy-nilly, the use of their houses. No room here, they say – I have seven Eastern workers living here, two Polish girls there. The notion of doing anything but taking the propriety of this for granted is not entertained.

I have seen stick-thin children of five, born to an unspeakable world, playing King of the Castle on a heap of naked and rotting dead women.

Four days ago I entered a farm, taken over. It was beautiful; and its centre room a joy in itself. Well proportioned, it had three fine pictures, lovely pieces of furniture, a row of bookshelves which included Emerson as well as Schiller; Goethe, Sinclair Lewis, Wells, Voltaire, Plato, T.W. [sic] Lawrence, Tolstoy. One wondered helplessly at the mind of the tenant, and his present attitude. Later we heard that the tenant was a widow, forlorn at her loss and living only for the farm and her children. She was gone – we had taken it over, and she asked no questions, made no demands. Her husband, who must have been liberal and cultivated, as well as able, had died, a private soldier, in Stalingrad. The burgomaster in the last village was old and rigid. Puffing unemotionally at a stump of a pipe he professed to understand none of my, or anyone else's, German. He was utterly unhelpful, and I respected him at every turn. Odd people came up from time to time asking deferentially would I stop my men taking eggs. (Eggs are so plentiful that my stomach turns at the sight of one.) They were only small people, they explained, but not Nazis. A week previously they had stoned a column of British prisoners marching through, and spat on the R.A.F. In that particular village they were, on the whole, against Hitler, on the single and sufficient ground that he had denied them comforts during the War in order to send stockings and scents and good foods to France and curry Gallic favour. This, like food rationing, was a matter of hard digested fact, and not open to argument. Pleasant faced women walk the streets of rubble, with a Lutheran church untouched in an open square, and a Prisoner of War camp full of unutterable emaciation behind the railway. Emaciation of the mind. Single men, daft after five years of utter emptiness squat down by themselves and, crooning, cook billycans of rubbishy tea. They are helplessly mad, and starved of everything. This, of course, is pleasant and normal compared with the Concentration Camps, which honestly are beyond all imaginable horror.

This gives no accurate picture. When I arrived in this evening there was a wireless prepared. With my ear to the loudspeaker, I listened to what fragments of English news that could filter in usual urbane neutrality through a crashing of electrical disturbance; somewhere close, and cutting irregularly across the already muffled news is a crashing brass band, Boche, playing like mad. There is also, somewhere, odd and fugitive swellings which sound like Mozart. This is Europe broadcasting. Our closest station, German, plays smooth jazz, bringing secure hotels and clean bar parlours to mind: just as if nothing was happening. This, in its crude way, symbolises the chaos all round. The chaos which was a town is, in the long run, less terrifying than the chaos which was a nation. We walk on a world of quicksands, and there is only one solid, undeniable fact, and that is that the one constant thing underlying and implicit in all turns and corners of this fantastic world is that this thing, whatever else it may be, is tragic; tragic in the sense that puts tragedy above sadness and apart from a human thing like pity or pathos. It is a gigantic and uncompassable tragedy.

God only knows what conclusions one can draw from this jumble – no set of things point in one direction; and daily one sees and feels something all the way from indication of depravity to signal goodness. There is construction and clarity, destruction and might, and behaviour in this world is compound, what with the difficulties implicit in occupation, difficulties with these overrun people of all sorts and types; and difficulties on the other side, of one's own behaviour, becomes a hand to mouth compromise. I allow my chaps their fist of booty, I live in someone's house; I condemn all sorts of things, and walk a tightrope, falling off pretty often.

One thing emerges, to me, pretty clearly: and that is that despite all evil, we are all bound up in a tragedy which is to a large extent commonly shared, and that sitting back and blandly condemning Germans is as idiotic as it is reprehensible. Raising pious thanks to God because Berlin is now just about annihilated as human habitation is ludicrously irrelevant. War, like peace, is indivisible. Punishment, God knows, lies like a sword across all items of military news. No more is made without the cutting blade. Let it rest at that. The inchaste mass of humanity left over is outside moral judgment – and no simple opinion will fit the structure of defeat. The only principle of sense which will lie at all comfortably on this fragmentary and million-sided tragedy is that the place has got to be got going again, moral and political judgments apart.

Hitler has a cerebral haemorrhage. This is just another facet to a lunatic world.

A sediment of opinion may sometime drop onto the floor of my mind. Until that happens I can only write such helpless accounts as this. The boys, thank goodness, a normal and recognisable gang, are in superb form, and I am well blessed all round. Dai is fit – so are we all for that matter.

My love to all. It is a tiring business living twenty-four hours a day in a Hamlet Act V atmosphere. This letter has been hard work![35]

Having rejoined the battalion at Lüneberg Heath, the war now over, he found Dai, and they went on an exploratory excursion, during the course of which they came upon a Russian checkpoint, with a tank and crew nearby. Dad and Dai were invited into a commandeered villa and given fried eggs and bread. Dad produced a bottle of Johnnie Walker. The Russian Captain, according to Dai's memoir, 'was a little fat fellow who smelled of Chanel No. 5. He and his sergeants were soon singing us Red Army songs… Huw and I gave them a duet of "Sosban Fach" in return.'

> Sosban fach yn berwi ar y tân,
> Sosban fawr yn berwi ar y llawr,
> A'r gath wedi sgrapo Joni bach.
>
> [A little saucepan is boiling on the fire,
> A big saucepan is boiling on the floor,
> And the cat has scratched little Johnny.]

Dad wasn't to sleep in peace quite yet. The 6th Airborne Division was going to the Far East to fight the Japanese. They were going to be dropped on Singapore racecourse. Hiroshima and Nagasaki made that plan unnecessary. Instead the Division was sent to Palestine, where the Irgun and the Stern Gang were causing havoc for the British forces policing Jewish immigration.

Dad – with pipe – and fellow officers in front of a grand house used as the Officers' Mess. It was apparently the home of a German General, under house arrest with his family in the upstairs rooms. One afternoon the General appeared among the officers, bought them drinks and thanked them for their civility, before returning upstairs to his family, whom he shot before shooting himself. Where he got the gun from is not recorded.

It was not entirely grim. Before it was bombed so devastatingly in July the King David Hotel was a popular officers' meeting place (the south wing of the hotel housed the secretariat of the British Mandatory Administration). One evening a group including Dad was asked to stop singing as it was disturbing the guests. The grand piano around which they had been gathered was on the first floor. The singing must go on, so the piano would have to be moved. And move it the officers of the RUR did, to the ground floor. They were subsequently informed that their further patronage would be welcome only under certain conditions (no moving of grand pianos being one).

Dad hated being a policeman, and the battalion was used to warfare. Frustration at not being allowed to retaliate in a militarily robust fashion, and a knowledge, having seen Belsen, that the behaviour of the Jewish militants was understandable made the posting very difficult. Attlee's Labour Party, which had professed itself enthusiastically Zionist, continued to um and ah about the number of Jews allowed into Palestine. 1946 saw 73 British soldiers killed and 130 wounded; over 300 civilians, British, Jewish and Arab, were also killed or wounded that year. And of all the British army units (totalling over 100,000 men) the 6th Airborne Division was probably the most hated.

Dad found his way, then, to the Mount Carmel Army Education facility, where he became a teacher. This he enjoyed, teaching political philosophy to likely university candidates. He had to become an expert on Aristotle, Plato, Hobbes, Hegel and the rest in double-quick time – or at least appear to be an expert. This, I think, is how he liked to learn. It is how I operate best too. Foxes not hedgehogs. I have at different times been asked to become an authority on nineteenth-century American painting, on American postwar culture, on Pissarro, on the Dutch barn, on Wolfe's victory at Quebec, on mongrel dogs, on the differences between the male and female brain, and so on and so forth. For a very short period I have been such an expert. The expertise drains away rapidly as the next subject approaches. However, it all rather depends on the quality of the work being studied. While I have no doubt that Dad dispensed with the flowery detail, he certainly ingested the kernels. He was a success, and earned the nickname 'Bash On' for the invigorating nature of his sermons. (Did I say sermons?)

It was at Mount Carmel that Dad sealed his friendship with Jonah Jones, a 6th Airborne stretcher bearer (he was a pacifist) and subesquently a colleague in the Educational Corps, which was based in Jonah's soon-to-be-wife, novelist Judith Maro's old Reali School. Jonah wrote that 'in some ways I would place that particular Army initiative as one of the sources of the subsequent Open University', and indeed

I think it is likely that Dad found a filial satisfaction in both. Jones goes on to say that Carmel 'was also great fun, not least because of the inimitable laughter of the great man himself, for even then he was distinguished in the crowded Mess… he was the cynosure, with intermittent gales of laughter radiating outwards like a tidal wave'.[37]

The army was sad to see him go, offering him a Colonelcy to stay on, but after almost eight years in uniform it seems likely that he wanted to re-enter the civilian swim. The stirring up of the intellectual waters at Mount Carmel must have contributed to this.

Dad had been twenty-three years old when war was declared. It finished – in Europe – the day after his twenty-ninth birthday. These are often regarded as being the best years of your life. The life I lead from 1981 to 1987 was marred only by my father's death. His was the first corpse I ever saw. What my father had begun in callow confusion – 'vaguely I feel the war is not my war' – ended with a recognition that 'we are all bound up in a tragedy which is to a large extent commonly shared'. The sense one has is not that of a war won, but of a horror survived. While Dad was not as downcast as Waugh's Guy Crouchback – who had taken up the sword against 'the Modern Age in arms' (and lost) – he certainly never exalted in the Allied triumph. The one rather muted story that reflected his feelings about Germany concerned some big television bash in New York. He was seated next to a German broadcaster who bewailed the German image abroad. Dad's response was that it wasn't the Germans' image that was the difficulty, it was their reputation.

Practically, what Dad brought out of his experiences in war was a belief in a regimental approach – although I think actually it was the Company (around 150 men) rather than the Regiment that counted with him. A natural leader, one of his talents was to attract talent. He surrounded himself with first class talent at *Monitor* and as Managing Director of BBC TV he again assembled a management team of the talents – David Attenborough, Paul Fox, Michael Peacock, Stephen Hearst, Aubrey Singer, Sydney Newman, Richard Cawston among others.

I think he also learned the importance of morale, in the raising and maintaining of which trust is vital. You must speak to people as equals, especially when in a position of command. This meant being honest.

Intellectually, he brought the idea that everyone belongs both to minorities and majorities, that every audience is different. Morally, I believe he saw the imperative in drawing the best out of people, that this might have to be done ruthlessly sometimes. Melvyn Bragg has said that he could be 'very, very cruel' in the editing suite. He had grown to demand not the best, but the best that one could give.

I believe this is Dad and Dai and a Focke-Wulf

Festival of Britain group, including Paul Wright and Dad, and also Osbert Lancaster, Malcolm Sargent, Feliks Topolski, among others. Interesting also as being on the cusp of hats and no hats. Photograph by Elsbeth R. Juda

CHAPTER 5

1946–1952: HERBIVORE

By the end of 1946 Dad was back in Wales. Quite what he got up to before, through the further good offices of his father, securing a job running the newly established Arts Council in Wales is open to question. I did find a fragile slip of officialese among his papers: '28 Feb 1947: Convicted of causing unnecessary obstruction. Ordered to pay the sum of £2.'[1] There was a story that, in the company of one of my godfathers, former RAF pilot Mason Lewis, they had driven into and demolished a gentlemen's convenience while under the influence of alcohol. I suppose such a thing might be regarded as causing an unnecessary obstruction. I don't know. Many years later I was myself ordered to pay £3 for disturbing the peace one New Year's Eve (I had been attempting to gain entry to Bow Street police station to retrieve a cardboard tube that had been confiscated from me).

I say 'running the Arts Council' but I think in truth it was just him. Occasionally, after funnelling some government money into local drama, he would also direct it. One such exercise was *Macbeth* with Leo McKern. It was a production in which Dad had great trouble convincing the pious Welshman playing King Duncan to say, at the appearance of 'a bleeding Captain', the line 'What bloody man is that?'; he objected on the grounds that the word 'bloody' was an oath and not a straightforward description. On the first night my father had still not prevailed and the King, depositing Shakespeare on the cutting room floor, demanded instead, 'Who's that bugger?'

One of his friends at that period was Charles Landstone, then working for the Arts Council, but known also as a dramatist and novelist, and theatre critic of the *Jewish Chronicle*.

Landstone, who had arrived in the UK with his parents from Vienna in 1904, was considerably older than my father, who appears to have been no respecter of the older man's ideas about safe motoring.

To visit Huw in his Welsh region whilst he was Arts Council director for the principality was an adventure. The miners' halls where the companies played were in the Valleys, and the roads to and from Cardiff necessarily ran across a series of hills. He would drive me down to the performance, and then back to Cardiff at night, along the empty but winding roads. I look upon myself as a very good passenger – after all, I had years of training with Cook's, travelling in private cars and coaches all over Britain and parts of Northern France! In that sort of job it is sine qua non that you have an unquestioning confidence in your driver and remain mute whatever happens. Such behaviour becomes, in course of time, second nature. However, one clear moonlit night, coming back from a miners' hall with Huw, I did venture the mild remark: 'You do know, don't you, that you have taken the last two curves at sixty miles an hour on the wrong side of the road?' He replied: 'That's right. That's the only way to drive on these hills.' I felt that any further protest would be useless, and as both he and I have survived, perhaps he was right.[2]

This would have amused and surprised Dad's BBC driver, Roy Daniels. 'Mr Daniels' (to us) was a lovely, cheerful man, who wore many rings and mutton chop sideburns and told jokes about his obviously much-adored wife. He held the Corporation in high esteem, and his view that its integrity had been lost by the 1990s carried more weight with me than any *Observer* or *Telegraph* leader. As Corporation cars, Ford Executives (the marque that Dad had insisted on in place of stuffy 'establishment' Bentleys) were to be replaced by Ford Granadas. Dad was not having that, Granada being one of the BBC's great independent rivals. Therefore, for him, a rather special Australian model was acquired. What was special about it, so far as Mr Daniels was concerned, was its engine, which was the same as that used by the Ford Mustang. However, Dad, despite his younger self (and although enjoying 'a bit of a scorch' in the Mini up the usually empty North Road in Kew – home to both the Pinters and the Patrick Troughtons), probably with a mind to us, his children, did not like Mr Daniels driving fast. So on long journeys Mr Daniels had to wait until Dad fell asleep. On one particular occasion we had been overtaken on the motorway by a Lotus Elite (I had the Matchbox model).

Even from the back seat I could tell Mr Daniels was not happy. I remember him looking over, noticing that Dad was snoozing, putting his foot down, catching and then overtaking the presumptuous Lotus. I seem to recall a look of astonishment on the driver's face as I looked down on him as we swished by.

Since the end of the war Gerald Barry, editor of the *News Chronicle*, had been chivvying anyone he could find into recognising the need for a 'tonic for the nation', as he famously put it, and in June 1947 the Labour government, in the form of Herbert Morrison, Lord President of the Council, declared that 'The centenary of the Great Exhibition should be marked by some national display illustrating the British contribution to civilisation past, present and future, in the arts, in science and technology and in industrial design'.[3]

Barry, made Director-General of what was to be known as the Festival of Britain, began to gather a team around him: the bright, bird-like Hugh Casson was, in Festival historian Barry Turner's phrase, his Chief of Staff, but responsible above all for the architecture; Ralph Tubbs was to design the Dome of Discovery; Misha Black, an exhibition designer, was invited in. Others included Ian Cox (Director of Science and Technology), Cecil Cooke (Exhibitions), James Gardner (Battersea Pleasure Gardens) and James Holland. Almost all these people were friends of Barry.

Paul Wright had recently resigned from the Coal Board in disgust at its failure to treat miners properly. Paul had known Barry – who much admired Mrs Wright, MP – during the war, and he was a Sussex neighbour. He was appointed Director of Public Relations. This group was joined in early 1949 by an ebullient chap from the Arts Council.

Weekends were spent brainstorming at Barry's home,

Forge Cottage, in West Sussex. Casson, Wright and Dad were to become close friends walking on the Downs and 'at Savoy Court, our dingy offices just off the Strand' and in the years ahead. All would distinguish themselves, first at the Festival and afterwards in their respective careers. The Festival, wrote Wright, 'provided just the springboard from which so many leapt into subsequent fame and distinction.'[4] Another member of the executive was Denis Forman, then Director of the British Film Institute and later grand panjandrum of Granada Television.

Work on the Festival was devolved to six agencies: the Arts Council, the Council of Industrial Design, the Central Office of Information, the British Film Institute, the Council for Science and Technology and a Council for Architecture, Town Planning and Building Research. There was also a Scottish Committee and a Committee for Wales (of which my grandfather, Sir Wynn, was Chairman).

The Arts Council was itself a fairly new institution, and as soon as arts organisations were aware of it and the Festival, the requests for funds started to pour in, from all sorts of places, for all sorts of reasons: from Whitworth, Hull, St Ives, Slough, Lewes, Coventry, Bury St Edmunds, Harrogate, Leamington Spa, Preston, Shrewsbury, Truro – everywhere. The requests came from art galleries, architects, arts clubs, local councils, arts societies; for equipment, for premises, for catalogues, for commissions, for repairs. Some were rewarded, most were not. Hull Arts Club got £100, but the Market Harborough Festival of Boats and Barges got not a penny.

There were existing festivals that had to be cajoled into shifting their dates in order to be included as part of the national festival. Sometimes they refused. Sometimes they needed bribes. Grants were made, or events were guaranteed against loss. All in all there were twenty-three arts festivals, wholly or partly funded by the Festival and mounted by the Arts Council. Concert halls that had been damaged in the war reopened. These acts of civic regeneration were one of the unsung benefits of the Festival (which naturally had come in for criticism from all sides).

Occasionally the Festival, in the form of Barry, and the Arts Council, in the form of Secretary-General Mary Glasgow, disagreed. It was a complicated set up: who had the final say as to who might be funded? Dad was even commended (by Glasgow) for 'acting with admirable discretion' during these rows. The arts budget was between £400,000 and £500,000. The total cost of the Festival was around £12 million.

As far as the arts were concerned, music was the clear winner. The conservative tastes of the culturati dominated in the fine arts; there was nothing remarkable to shout about. Pedestrian work by Epstein and Moore was outshone by the fabulous architecture on the South Bank. The Festival Hall went up on the east side of the Charing Cross railway bridge, while the main site, dominated by the Dome of Discovery and the long-lamented Skylon, was on the west side, where the London Eye now revolves.

The wonderful Paul Wright (whose wife, the formidable Babs, was the first sitting MP to give birth, an American to boot; she was also my very dutiful godmother) wrote of Dad during the Festival:

It was through his ebullient energy that the resources in music, theatre and the visual arts were gathered together and spread across the country in a series of regional festivals. He pinched and pulled to make the money go round and took Gerald [Barry] on a series of pep-talking tours to galvanise the local authorities. I often went with them and remember Huw briefing Gerald before a session with some city's fathers which promised to be awkward because they had been left out, or perhaps because they did not want to be included. 'Money for old rope, DG,' he would say cheerfully. 'You can't go wrong.' And between them they seldom did. They made a fine pair, tossing jokes between them like cricket balls and acting as lightning conductors for each other's ideas.[5]

In a private letter to my mother Paul admitted to occasional jealousy of 'his certainties, and the ease with which he expressed them; and of his terrific, creative energy which was, even then, so fundamental a part of his personality'. That sense of certainty was what had to be overcome later on by Humphrey Burton and Ken Russell and the team at *Monitor*.

I have inherited the certainty but not, I'm afraid, the authority or the ease of expressing it that he had. I think my sons would testify to that being the case.

Paul recalled one of many stories that the trio brought back from their travels. They were staying at a hotel in Cheltenham, and a meeting with local councillors had dragged on late. They returned to find a meeting of the regional Magic Circle just finishing. 'When we asked for some late supper, we were reluctantly offered cold rabbit.'*

In his funny but somewhat mean essay 'Festival', Michael Frayn divided opinion makers of the early 1950s into two classes: the Herbivores and the Carnivores, and wrote as follows:

---

* Gerald Barry, quoted in Barry Turner's book *Beacon for Change* (p. 111), remembered 'well polished mahogany tables in Mayoral Parlours or Council Rooms at which the purposes of the Festival were expounded and sharp local questions answered. One learned a great deal about the sturdy independence of the provinces'.

Festival Britain was the Britain of the radical middle-classes – the do-gooders; the readers of the News Chronicle, the Guardian, and the Observer; the signers of petitions; the backbone of the BBC. In short, the Herbivores, or gentle ruminants, who look out from the lush pastures which are their natural station in life with eyes full of sorrow for less fortunate creatures, guiltily conscious of their advantages, though not usually ceasing to eat the grass. And in making the Festival they earned the contempt of the Carnivores – the readers of the Daily Express; the Evelyn Waughs; the cast of the Directory of Directors – the members of the upper- and middle-classes who believe that if God had not wished them to prey on all smaller and weaker creatures without scruple he would not have made them as they are... not even the most Herbivorous of men, in our age of more highly sophisticated class consciousness and guilt, could stand up in public and announce that a committee consisting of a former newspaper editor, two senior civil servants, an architect, a theatre-manager, a cineaste, a palaeontologist, a public relations officer, and Huw Wheldon, was the People.[6]*

I'm not at all sure that Dad could ever be counted as a gentle ruminant, even if he was living at Toynbee Hall, but he was undoubtedly always more comfortable with liberals than conservatives.

One final anecdote from Paul Wright: 'On New Year's Eve 1950, we had a party in the country; Huw dressed up in a ballet skirt, bra, etc, and was driven into the drawing room on top of a small car as the Spirit of 1951, ringing a large bell

---

* The distinction between carnivore and herbivore was used, without attribution, by Hugh Casson in his 1975 BBC series about architecture, *Spirit of the Age*.

and throwing confetti on everyone.'[7] Or perhaps the return of Agatha Whatcomb. I never saw Dad in drag, but he was never afraid to look foolish unless he was proselytising on behalf of the BBC or Richmond Arts Council or the LSE or even the Halifax Building Society (for whom he made a promotional film). He would have regarded it as a disservice to the institution he was lauding. Still, it is hard to imagine his being allowed such innocent enjoyment in our own prurient, puritanical and prejudicious age.

It is said that those who were begonged for their work on the Festival of Britain (a number of OBEs, including one for Dad, a KCB for Gerald Barry) received their medals and their redundancies on the same day.

For my father one thing was certain: London was now unquestionably his home. It was the big world, full of opportunities, surely, to drink of the wine of a noble aim.

Laurence Olivier looking bored, Dad looking anxious, Malcolm Sargent looking on, and Gerald Barry looking at the map

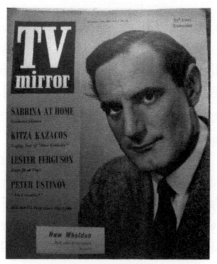

Huw Wheldon... both sides of the camera

CHAPTER 6

1952–1958: 'WE WERE THE COWBOYS'

Television had returned after the war, to Alexandra Palace – Ally Pally – in a fairly inaccessible part of north London. It was a long way from Broadcasting House, London W1. Radio remained the senior service. John Grist, a former Editor of *Panorama* and biographer of Grace Wyndham Goldie, puts the problem succinctly: 'In 1948 the Director-General did not like television.'[1] The post-holder Sir William Haley was a journalist of distinction (he left the BBC to become editor of *The Times*) but he and his confederates saw television as expensive and nasty. They were right about the expense. At this time the BBC depended entirely for its budget on the radio licence. Television, in comparison with wireless (as Dad called it to the end of his days), was a sink hole. As for the nasty, well, the idea was that television was essentially trivial, that it depended on pictures, and that it would somehow degrade the BBC's reputation, so hard-won during the war. The BBC's integrity has always been its most cherished if not its most practised virtue.

Grist again: 'Ally Pally had more than a touch of war-time Britain: youthful, short of money, resources rationed, and the ex-serviceman's suspicion of authority. Whatever Alexandra Palace was, it was not Oxbridge; its roots were theatre, film and show business, grammar schools and the provinces.'[2] Or, as the great arts documentary maker John Read, son of Herbert, put it: 'We were television, we were the cowboys. There was somewhere something called BH and the BBC Charter but the mission centre was at AP. The staff were already thought of in departmental units... but we all ate in the same canteen. There was one place to get a drink, a shed in the car park called the Dive Bar.'[3] One of those departmental units was 'Talks', and, according to David Attenborough, 'Talks Department producers had no identifiable qualifications for their jobs'.

Dad joined the BBC as its Publicity Officer, on 4 January 1952. Television was still a relatively new thing. The war had interrupted developments, but Britain was still one of only two nations in the world to have daily programmes on any scale, the other of course being the United States. I ought, I suppose, to attempt to imagine what that must have been like, but the truth is I struggle with what the present is like. I continue to be baffled by the mystery of how pictures and sounds scuttle through the air. Suffice to say that television must have been seen by young people as at the cutting edge.

However, although the television service had covered the Festival of Britain fairly comprehensively (sacrificing various sporting events in doing so), Kenneth Baily,[*] writing as editor of *The Television Annual for 1952*, thought television was 'having a tough time of it'. He bemoaned the lack of plays made specifically for television. He criticised the 'slavish imitation of sound-radio traditions'. As for light entertainment Baily had little time for its 'lack of imagination, its banality and its shoddy production', especially when set against what was happening in the USA. And again Baily blamed the lingering effects of radio. He pulled no punches, did Mr Baily: 'It is the attitude of the amateur.' Outside broadcasts, especially sport, fared far better, but the BBC was attacked for the slothful provision of new technical equipment. Baily's editorial finished:

> Television is a revolutionary challenge. But, so far, Britain has not discovered the man, let alone the committee or corporation, strong enough to accept the challenge in an open-minded spirit of uninhibited enterprise.

That year, 1952, saw Director-General Sir William Haley succeeded by Lieutenant-General Ian Jacob, and things did begin to change. Radio had started the year as the dominating half of the BBC, but eighteen months later, soon after the Coronation of Elizabeth II had been televised, the BBC's new Publicity Officer was able to confirm that for the first time the television audience (twenty million) outnumbered the radio audience (twelve million). And what was more, ninety-eight

---

[*] Baily was the broadcasting critic for *The People*, and always a trenchant and intelligent critic of the BBC.

per cent of viewers had enjoyed the broadcast. The *Daily Express* wanted to know what it was that the remaining two per cent didn't like. The Publicity Officer replied, paraphrasing Hilaire Belloc, 'Well, you must remember that if Our Lord came back to earth tomorrow, two per cent of people would complain, "There he goes again, always walking on the water".[4] The Publicity Officer received a special bonus for 'lively and intelligent handling of the corporation's needs' during the Coronation.[5] Peter Black, the *Daily Mail*'s distinguished television critic, was at the press conference, and was convinced that he had seen a future Director-General.

'I wanted to be one of the people the Arts Council was talking about, not one of the talkers',[6] Dad told Frank Gillard in an interview about the history of the BBC, conducted in the 1980s. It would happen, but not quite yet: 'I got a job on the press side, with the publicity people, which I didn't want at all'.[7] (I am told his portrait, by William Thomson, RA – not a very good one, though Bill's portrait of my mother is excellent – now hangs in the BBC Press Office.)

The BBC had already featured in Dad's life. His father had made radio broadcasts, and a distant relation, Eleanor Powell, had married Gladstone Murray, who had been Assistant Controller of BBC Television in 1935. The Murrays had lived in a 'great house' in Wimbledon, to which the transplanted Wheldon family occasionally went for tea. Dad said he had been brought up to think of the BBC as being 'an extremely impressive, resonant, many-sided organisation run by great people... with the same sort of weight as Cambridge University or the Cunard Line'.[8] His father may have had some influence on Dad's getting the job at the BBC, but Sir Wynn's friend WE Williams, Director of the Arts Council, was sufficiently impressed by Dad's work on the Festival to make his own recommendation to George Barnes, who ran the television service.

> In some ways he is now too good for the Arts Council... I don't ever try to sell pups, nor, indeed, to sell anything; but this chap strikes me as so extraordinarily good that I could not refrain from asking you whether he might be of any use to you?[9]

As far as I can tell, my father first actually appeared on television as the presenter and adjudicator of a national conker competition. It had been his own idea, thought up while trying to manoeuvre his way out of the Publicity Department. It was phenomenally successful. A single announcement produced 86,000 responses. Conkers had to be sent back, letters replied to. One letter came from 'somewhere in Kent... it was just like Chaucer. It read "I have a conker it is a 52er, it has a crak in it but it will not brak". And it had this marvellous feeling of strength.'[10]

Dad made up the rules: 'The cry "I collyconker my first smack" starts proceedings. String-ums allowed, but stamp-ums on the floor or squash-ums with boot barred.'[11] The winner was an Ian Lyons, of Highgate, whose conker became a 7,351-er when he defeated Tim Pollock, in October 1952. The winner, reported one newspaper, had been given his conker by his cousin Basil.

Dad stuck it out in Publicity until in 1954 the post of senior producer in the Television Talks department fell vacant. The salary was lower than he was receiving as Publicity Officer, but he had not joined the BBC to josh with the press. He had no experience of directing programmes, but he had been presenting a much-loved children's programme called *All Your Own*, on which talented children performed and were brought out 'in interviews of irresistible sympathy and delight'.[12] Several of these children went on to genuine success: most notably Jacqueline du Pré, but also pianist John Ogdon and skiffle guitarist James Page, who was to become better known as Jimmy, the lead guitarist of Led Zeppelin.* *All Your Own* was extremely popular, 'remarkable', wrote Lia Low in *Look and Listen* ('Britain's Independent Journal of Audio-Visual Education'), 'mainly because Huw Wheldon is one of the few people who regard a child as a perfectly reasonable human being who happens to be still young. No facetiousness, no avuncularity, no condescension.'[13] The *Liverpool Daily Post* commented that 'the merit of this programme is that it is genuine stuff... it owes a great deal to Huw Wheldon... he appears to perform his task with perfect ease though actually he is doing a difficult job with great skill'. Even *Tribune*, house journal of the Labour Left, reported that 'Mr Wheldon is the fortunate possessor of a quite remarkable degree of charm'.[14]

Dad also did the odd interview for *Panorama*, most famously with Mike Todd, Elizabeth Taylor's third husband. One television critic described it as like watching someone who had taken three Benzedrine tablets interview someone who had taken five.[15]

Four men were gazetted to Television Talks on the same day in August 1954: David Attenborough, Michael Peacock,

---

* Dad's interview with Page is available on YouTube. From their comments it would appear that Jimmy Page's hard rock fans are not too impressed by the keen, tall, beaky presence towering over their diminutive hero, but HPW was much liked at the time (as late as the 1980s cab drivers remembered him for the show).

Donald Baverstock and Huw Wheldon (preferred to other likely candidates, despite his lack of experience, 'on the score of his considerable potentialities'). All were to have a major impact on British television, and all were to rise high in the BBC's management structure. Nominally they worked under the command of Leonard Miall, who had been the BBC's correspondent in Washington DC during the war;* in truth they were the ducklings of Grace Wyndham Goldie, 'a small, vivacious, bird-like lady – though with perhaps rather more of the eagle than the wren', as David Attenborough was to put it.[16] Miall himself wrote that she 'was not a natural deputy'. She might have made a very good Director-General.

Wyndham Goldie was the 'earth mother' of many programmes, in particular four ground-breaking television programmes: *Tonight, Panorama, Monitor* and *That Was The Week That Was* (*TW3*). At Ally Pally, and, from 1954, at Lime Grove in Shepherd's Bush, around the corner from Television Centre, she assembled teams of programme makers, encouraged young producers, and generally ruled the Talks Department with what some wag (Dad) described as 'a whim of iron'. But this is to be flip about a personality whose influence on British television has perhaps never been fully recognised. John Grist wrote:

> She believed in accuracy, fairness, impartiality, accountability.
> She knew that the quality of television depended on the
> integrity of those who made the programmes and their sense
> of responsibility to the audience.[17]

---

* 'He was very wise. He was very good, Leonard Miall, and I don't think he's had the credit he deserves,' Dad told Frank Gillard (BBC WAC R143/133/2).

Dad was blooded on a programme called *Facts and Figures*, which Wyndham Goldie had devised. She used it as a nursery slope for many of her young (and in Dad's case not-so-young – he was now in his late thirties) producers. Originally narrated by Miall, Dad eventually took over. He also produced *Press Conference*, in which influential figures were interviewed by three or four journalists. These figures were more often than not politicians. But not always. It was on *Press Conference* that Dad first met Orson Welles: 'A really outstanding man, a singular & a great person, whose stature would not respond to the twittering tempo of what I had set up', he wrote to his father, full of chagrin. 'I was doing... a shoddy injustice to one of the most remarkable people I have ever met'.[18] They were to work together several times over the next few years. In *Orson Welles' Sketch Book*, Welles spoke entrancingly into a locked-off camera, telling stories from his career that he illustrated with his own sketches. When the series ended Welles gave these drawings to my father. I found them, after my mother died, in a sheaf of papers wrapped up in plastic in a bottom drawer of my father's desk. They now hang in pride of place on a staircase wall in my own home, seeing me to bed each night. Dad once told us that being in a room with Welles was 'like being in a room with a cathedral'. Mum had a story about how Welles had told her how to leave a room without anyone noticing.

Welles urged Dad to become his European manager, an urge Dad found easy to resist, because although he hero-worshipped him, he knew also that Welles was 'a liar'. According to Melvyn Bragg, Dad feared that Welles would have 'eaten me up'. Another witness, however, remarked that 'I'd seen Welles *crush* people who were theoretically employing him, yet here was this novice paying Welles a mere £75 a programme and making him eat out of his hand.'

In the November before *Orson Welles' Sketch Book*, Dad had been the producer in Downing Street for a special programme celebrating Sir Winston Churchill's eightieth birthday. Donald Baverstock, another inspiring Welshman in Talks, who was producing a news programme called *Highlight* and who would go on to become Editor of *Tonight* and eventually Controller of BBC1, suggested that the programme take the form of a party. Grace Wyndham Goldie, the overall producer, agreed. The great and the good from around the world would make toasts. The hope was that Churchill would respond. No one knew whether he would or not. Dad, General Lord Ismay (then Secretary-General of NATO) and Wyndham Goldie planned for three endings to the programme. Years later my father told his own version of the Churchill story to Frank Gillard.

Now Churchill had to be there of course watching in Downing Street [but] there wasn't a television set there in those days... Grace asked me to go down there. Anyway, I went down there, and presently his family turned up... but no sign of the great man. And then, just before the programme was due to begin, he came in with his wife. I'd been told that he looked old, but I had simply not been prepared for the sight of this pterodactyl coming very, very slowly into the room. I mean, he looked about eight thousand years old... and his skin was like yellow leather. He shuffled to his chair, sat in the wrong one I need hardly say; anyway, there it was; and paid no attention to his children, all of whom said 'Hello', and paid no attention to them at all. Still less to me – he didn't see me.

The News was on, and there was a camera, looking at him. He looked at the News and in a very, very broken, switched-off, childish voice, he said, 'Is this the programme?'

And in a reverential bellow – because it was clear to me that you had to speak very loudly to get at the old thing at all – in a reverential bellow I said, 'No. This is the News. The Programme,' I said, 'will follow in a minute, and Lord Ismay will be there in Shepherd's Bush talking to you.' He said 'Ismay is in Paris.' And I said, 'No, Ismay has come over especially for the programme, and he will be talking to you in a minute or two.' Then I said, 'You'll be here watching the programme, and when at the end they... wish you God speed and best wishes... if you want to respond in any way, all you have to do is look into this camera over here, and you can speak directly to them, and I will give you a signal for doing that if you like.' To which he paid no attention, none. So I was very apprehensive. I went round the back of the chair to Clemmie [Lady Churchill] and said, 'Do you think he'll say anything?' And she said, 'It's very difficult to say. He's very tired.'

... I rang Grace up in the studio and said I had no idea what was going to happen. He looked like an old tortoise – and it wasn't at all clear to me that he would speak.[19]

Cut to Grace Wyndham Goldie at Lime Grove (from her own memoir):

It was impossible to believe that he knew in the least what was happening. But when Lady Violet Bonham-Carter, at the end of her message, said 'Courage, that is your greatest gift to those who know you', I watched, unbelieving, on my gallery monitor the ancient head move slowly from side to side in a gesture of negation and tears rolling slowly down the leathery cheeks. Only we in the gallery saw this incredibly moving spectacle. And we were filled also with professional relief. He was registering something after all.[20]

Back to Dad:

Anyway, the programme took place, and he betrayed no emotion of any kind, of pleasure or displeasure – except that whenever Clemmie was mentioned he looked slightly in her direction, but whether to say 'How nice', or alternatively 'Why should that be said?', it was impossible to draw any conclusion.

The programme came to an end, and I heard Ismay give his final speech, so I was alert and I was just preparing to signal Churchill towards the camera, Ismay having said 'So best wishes for the future, dear Winston', or words to that effect, when I looked towards the great man. He was sitting up in his chair and his eyes were fixed on me, and it was exactly as if I'd come round a little bend in a Pembrokeshire hedgerow in 1934 in one of those little Austins, and run into a gigantic red lorry. It was like running into searchlights head on. In some curious way he appeared to have switched on. I nervously signalled him towards the camera, and he then moved his entire chair so that he was facing it, and instantly spoke in this enormous diapason, 'I have been delighted' and so on, 'This remarkable...' And a great sonorous sentence came out, Gibbonesque, very, very good, very much to the point, extremely rounded, very masculine, very virile, very

Churchillian. So he came to the end of his peroration and looked away from the camera to me, glared at me and said 'Good night!'

Then I heard the trumpets blowing, so I knew we were off old Churchill. I rushed up to him, and so did his family, and everybody said, 'You were wonderful', 'You were marvellous', all that sort of thing, but he paid no attention, he'd switched off again. He said to his wife, 'I hadn't had time to prepare', and she said, 'You were very good, Winston'. He said, 'But I hadn't had time'. He shuffled to the door, and then he did look round for a moment at his family – not at me, he never paid any attention to me from beginning to end – and he switched on for a minute. 'I'm going to have a bath', he said, and pushed off. It was a memorable programme, beautifully done by Grace.[21]

Men in Battle was a series of programmes made with General Sir Brian Horrocks, one of Montgomery's most able deputies during the war. Initially unsure of 'Jorrocks', thinking him a bit of a 'prep-school boy', Dad changed his mind when he found that the General, as Black Rod, kept Pools Coupons in his red despatch boxes at the House of Lords. Horrocks claimed to have made £82 during his four-year stint. Like Welles, like Dad, Horrocks was a natural raconteur ('he was wonderful, he invented himself', said my father), and the programme was an immediate success. So was *Portraits of Power*, made with the LSE's Professor Robert McKenzie (the first episode, on Hitler, with contributions from Alan Bullock and Hugh Trevor-Roper, won the Prix Italia in 1957). McKenzie became a TV immortal with his invention of the 'swingometer' used in BBC General Election broadcasts. My father's eulogy at McKenzie's funeral credited the Canadian as having been 'a major voice and major practitioner' in bringing broadcasting 'out of its Reithian constraints to take its proper and responsible part in the public discussion of politics'.

Dad also produced Harold Macmillan speaking from Downing Street shortly after having been elected Prime Minister in 1957. Macmillan was starchy, to say the least; but he was prepared to take guidance from the producer. In an internal BBC memorandum, Dad wrote: 'I held out very strongly that the Prime Minister's script as written was totally inadequate. I pointed out that it could not be spoken by one human being to another without embarrassment to both parties.'[22] Dad spent an evening with Macmillan, attempting to tutor him. Macmillan was grateful, but the results were not entirely successful. Dad remarked afterwards that although the teleprompter 'undoubtedly worked' it would eventually seriously compromise those who wanted to appear sincere. He himself always memorised his introductory speech to camera at the beginning of *Monitor*, while walking from home, off Ladbroke Grove, down to Lime Grove. Almost sixty years later David Cameron showed how effective can be the eschewing of the device.

There were other programmes: *Harding Finds Out*, with Gilbert Harding (one of the first stars of television), which was a failure (Dad knew this because on the mornings following the airing 'all I could hear was the programme not being mentioned'), and *Is This Your Problem?* This, too, did not go down well. I can imagine Dad not at all enjoying this, as it involved the exposing of private, personal problems. Not only was this likely to have annoyed him as encouraging self-indulgence, it was also veering close to public humiliation, something he was to loathe in later years in programmes even as seemingly innocent as *It's a Knockout*.

In 1957 Sir Arthur fforde, formerly headmaster of Rugby School, became Chairman of the BBC. Towards the end of his stint he produced a paper entitled 'What is Broadcasting About?' It is a wise, odd document, a kind of Christian apologia for the BBC, full of poetry, from Shakespeare to Housman by way of Dante, Blake and Coleridge. It asserts that the BBC has a moral responsibility towards its public, and that this responsibility requires programme makers to always seek the 'courage and *élan*' to make programmes 'that speak the word YES' – that being the answer to the question 'Is human life to be respected and valued?' I rather think fforde, like Dad, would have taken a fairly dim view of *It's a Knockout*, and certainly of the programmes that celebrate humiliation, such as *Big Brother* and its spawn. fforde wrote too of the 'freedom, independence, and *élan* without which the arts do not flourish' and which had to be allowed to 'creative members of the BBC staff'. At the same time 'these things should not be used lightly or ill-advisedly'. I hear echoes of my father in what fforde wrote, but Dad had no Christian dogma to push. It was the shoddy he despised, the 'so what?' or 'who cares?', rather than the absolute NO: 'programmes calculated rather than made... are slums of the spirit and slums of the mind'.

On the night on which Dad did a piece on Lord Baden-Powell's centenary, for *Panorama*, another great Wyndham Goldie programme was launched. *Tonight* was edited by the brilliant Donald Baverstock, with assistance from Alasdair Milne. Milne had joined the BBC at the same time as Michael Peacock, the Editor of *Panorama* (who was to be succeeded by Paul Fox). The teams were forming under powerful Editors. They were little platoons, whose first loyalty was to their programme. *Tonight* featured luminaries such as Tony Jay (later to become famous as the writer of *Yes, Minister*), Bernard Levin and Ned Sherrin* (later editor of yet another legendary Talks programme, *That Was The Week That Was*). Cliff Michelmore was the presenter (he was also the producer of *All Your Own*). Reporters included names that were to resonate in television history: Fyfe Robertson, Alan Whicker, Kenneth Allsop. Directors included Jack Gold and Kevin Billington. And, to begin with, John Schlesinger, though he was soon to be poached by another, equally glittering team.

In March 1957, impressed with the success of *Panorama* and *Tonight*, BBC executives began discussing the possibility of a similar magazine programme, to be aired late at night. The idea that it should be dedicated to the arts came from below. Catherine Dove was a young producer on *Panorama*, who had been badgering Grace Wyndham Goldie about the BBC's need for an arts programme, and when word came down from on high that just such a project was required, she was chosen to oversee it. However, in the light of Dove's inexperience, Wyndham Goldie decided that she required a senior producer to keep an eye on things. And she wanted the same person to present it.

---

* I met Sherrin once, in the BBC box at Lord's in 1972. I remember him complaining that the English captain, Tony Greig, really ought to wear flared whites. It was quite an occasion: other guests included Kingsley Amis, Caryl Brahms, Robert Conquest, Harold Evans, Anthony Howard and Alan Ross. We were in the Tavern stand, above the Tavern Bar, which then faced onto the pitch. Next to us was a box including some young women who invited banter from the largely Australian fans standing below. One thing led to another and banter turned into 'spilt' wine. The *Daily Mail*, getting things wrong, called the incident a 'Beer v. Beaujolais Battle' between the Australians and 'an intellectual mélange of novelist Kingsley Amis, *New Statesman* editor Anthony Howard and super-wit Ned Sherrin'. Australia won by 8 wickets.

At the end of 1957, Wyndham Goldie wrote a confidential report on Dad:

> It is a great pleasure to have anyone of Mr Wheldon's stamp in the Department. His gaiety, good sense and adult outlook on life are of great value in a Department which contains many young people who are full of enterprise but somehow a little over-serious in their outlook. Mr Wheldon shows day-by-day that it is possible to combine high seriousness with wit.

Perhaps Catherine Dove was one of those young people whom Wyndham Goldie thought 'a little over-serious'.

My mother during her egalitarian phase

CHAPTER 7

LILAC TREE

Catherine Dove, in a previous biography of my father, maintained that he was 'not keen on women as equals at work... and... not intellectual at all'.[1] I don't recognise either of those assertions. Were I a cynical sort of chap, I'd say that in the first place Dad wasn't keen on either sex as an equal at work, but he had a high regard for Grace Wyndham Goldie (who was genuinely unimpressed by most of her female colleagues), and women such as Nancy Thomas, Ann Turner,

Julia Matheson and Anne James* flourished at *Monitor*.[†‡] I think it is much more likely the case that he was not keen on recent Oxbridge graduates (which Catherine Dove was). He almost certainly knew more than Dove about music. He would have admitted not knowing as much about the visual arts.

> I hate all picture galleries, without exception. They are too big. I don't like big theatres either; or big cinemas, or big bathing pools. The only big things I like are big opera houses and big elephants.

> This afternoon I went to the Louvre. I loathed it.

> Next week I am going to choose three pictures to look at… tell me which three pictures. Not that it matters much because I won't like them. I don't like any artists. None at all. Late extra: Except Rembrandt.[2§]

He was later to add Augustus John to this very short roll-call of acceptable painters. The above is from a letter written to

---

* Anne James wrote to Dad on her retirement in 1984: 'You gave me, and others, such invaluable things… Like most of us – the ones who came under you – I quote you, and measure things by the values you imparted to us. Programme values. Television values. Let alone the knowledge & memory of being one of a small group of people with a recognisable purpose.'

† Of the twelve people Dad acknowledged as being responsible for the success of the programme in the book *Monitor*, five were women.

‡ Melvyn Bragg remembered 'someone in the BBC bar in Lime Grove referring to a woman who worked on *Monitor* as "a good secretary". Wheldon drew himself up to his full Welsh height and barked: She's a good *woman*. A remarkable *woman*!' (*The Times*, 30 March 1998.)

§ I came to my own conclusion about Rembrandt, identical to my father's. The self-portrait at Kenwood House, is, in my emphatically non-expert opinion, the greatest painting in the world (*pace* Huxley on Piero della Francesca).

Desmond Leeper, before the war, from Paris. It is obviously facetious; he liked to downplay his learning. He probably would not have minded being called 'not at all intellectual' or even 'something of a philistine', but the truth is that he had read Boswell and Montaigne, knew poems by Rilke by heart (in German), was musically literate, had taught Plato and Locke, directed Shakespeare, had worked for the Arts Council for six years and interviewed Jacqueline du Pré. His friends were not unintellectual – Brian Murphy was a seriously bookish chap – and the company he kept could hardly have been said to be anything other than fairly highbrow, from Harold Pinter to Aaron Klug, from Norman Podhoretz to John Berger. Most highbrow of all, and a woman to boot, was my mother.

Jacqueline Mary Clarke was born on 20 May 1924 in Fulham, west London, the first child of Hugh Clarke (1892–1930), a Hammersmith-Irish toolmaker, and Lillie Nunns (1890–1980) – 'Nanny' to us, 'Madam' to my father – a woman who worked in various trades for most of her life (she was the daughter of a railway guard, Harry Nunns, and his wife Elizabeth). Mum had one, younger, brother, my Uncle Ken, born in 1927.

Her father, whom she remembered devotedly despite his death when she was six years old, told her 'with absolute certainty' that she would be a writer. He liked to perch her on the mantelpiece during evenings with friends, inducing in her a lifelong habit of very late retirement, as well as vertigo. She remembered him as a great storyteller. He took her regularly to the library. She also retained strong recollections of being walked into the pubs of Fulham on his shoulders. They went as far as The Queens Elm on the Fulham Road, watering place of the aforementioned Augustus John, where she was petted. The Queens Elm is now sadly some sort of boutique, emphatically Chelsea rather than Fulham. Family history maintains that her paternal grandfather emigrated from Longford Town in Leinster in Ireland to become butler at Fulham Palace, home of the Bishop of London, and there met his wife, who was the housekeeper.

On the death of her father the family moved from Clonmel Road, Fulham, to Fulham Broadway, where they lived with Mum's maternal grandmother, Elizabeth Nunns. Nunns, whose husband had died in 1926, had taken over his job as caretaker of a building housing Cornwall's, a coal merchants. There were solicitors' offices in the floors above and she had a flat on the top storey (sixty-nine steps up, exactly matching her age at the time of counting, according to Uncle Ken). On Sundays Elizabeth Nunns would open up one of the solicitors' offices and they would eat Sunday lunch off one of the desks. Next door was the Granville Theatre of Varieties (demolished in the early 1970s). Mum said she had often been kept awake at night by the screams coming from the grand guignol performances being played next door.

She was educated at Carlyle School, Chelsea, but when the school was evacuated to Windsor at the beginning of the Second World War she chose to abscond back to London by bicycle on several occasions and was eventually expelled.

Throughout the rest of the war she lived in Ealing with her mother, the pair of them working for the Trepur Paper Tube Company (which among other items, such as Smartie tubes, manufactured auxiliary fittings for Spitfires and Hurricanes). Mum then started working for the local council. She joined the Labour Party and in 1945 was the East Ealing Labour Party delegate to the party conference.

In a letter written shortly before her death she wrote that her life 'started with an arrival, inauspicious, at the LSE.'[3] She had been discovered by Professor Harold Laski, Chairman of the Labour Party, after having invited him to talk at the Ealing branch of the Labour League of Youth of which she was chairwoman (or 'charwoman' as Laski pronounced it). Laski, a hugely influential professor of Political Science, invited her to come and work at the School in order to go to lectures and to study for the entrance examination. She worked for two years in the Machine Room as a secretary to the Statistics Department (where Claus Moser was her boss, and to be her lifelong friend) and in 1948 she was summoned before Laski and admitted to the School under the tutorship of Professor Kingsley Smellie. She was by then assistant secretary of the Ealing Labour Party.

With the death of my father I had had a slightly isolated childhood in difficult circumstances. I was always half-deaf and short-sighted and never a great mixer. I liked the company of my familiars. I had unfortunately been asked to leave school at an early age. Somewhere I had developed a 'resistant' state of mind, a barbarous tendency not to want to agree with any generally-accepted opinion from the exhilaration of testing my powers and my vocabulary and giving myself a bit of character. On all the familiar 'questions' I had tackled I had achieved opinions. They were not other people's opinions, I considered. They were mine, and I worked at them, a straw from here, a wisp from there, like a bird at a nest. That was the beauty of them. They made me feel safe. I liked them to be as subtle as possible, surprising, paradoxical. Shy but confident, I was not afraid to speak up with my familiars. I had been content with all that until the night of the Laski meeting. I tell all this because it is important to know that I was an unusually ill-educated person to have arrived at the London School of Economics and Political Science.[4]

Now, studying part-time, it was work during the day, lectures in the evening and the Labour Party on the side. She received high marks for an essay on economic history and was encouraged to expand it and put it in for a State Scholarship for Mature Students, which she duly received. She became a full time student at the age of twenty-six.

Following Laski's death in 1950, his successor – controversially, for he was of a very different political stripe – was Michael Oakeshott. Oakeshott had a profound influence on Mum's politics, which expressed itself very gradually over the years (she 'crossed over' at roughly the same time – the late 1960s – as her American friends Midge Decter and Norman Podhoretz, famously described as being 'Democrats who had been mugged by reality'). While Laski's desire 'to share what is most dignified in human nature'[5] was the reason Mum had arrived at the LSE, one of her own observations once there was that 'it is not the case that the elite possess the works, but that the works possess the elite... The elite as I met it at LSE was at my service; there would have been no "beauties" of Plato, Rousseau, Hobbes for me to have "a sight" of, if generations of individuals whom these writers had come to "possess" had not submitted to serve and to keep these works intact and ever re-creative and re-created.'[6] This is an Oakeshottian notion.

She enjoyed being at the LSE, one of a 'special incestuous race' and in the heart of London, halfway between Whitehall and Fleet Street with the Law Courts and Drury Lane around opposite corners. There were the bombsites, too, which fascinated her, providing the backdrop for her play *Tiger! Tiger!* Finally, there were great lecturers and teachers – Morris Jones,

William Pickles, RGD Allen, Karl Popper. It was written of her that 'Jackie Clarke... is one of [the School's] brightest ornaments and actresses... she has numberless pale characters in thrall'.[7]

Michael Oakeshott undertook the whole course on the history of political thought, and Mum at last felt that her lack of education was going to be made up. She had found what she had been seeking: an intellectual beginning. She later wrote that 'the first book I really read in my life, ignoring all introductions, prefaces, commentaries, was Cornford's translation of *The Republic*'.[8]

She gained an Upper Second (her Economics and Statistics compromising her 'first class' Politics and Philosophy[9]) and, after beginning work on a PhD on Comparative Method, left the LSE temporarily in 1954 to start research at the Nuffield Foundation with Dr Hilde Himmelweit (of the LSE) on the book *Television and the Child*.*

In the summer of 1951 Mum took a budget flight to Athens, and found herself sitting next to an excited young American from Brooklyn. They ended up touring Athens together. He, younger by five years, talked incessantly. 'Why don't you stop talking and *look*?' Mum asked. 'More than just interesting', Norman Podhoretz later said of her, she 'had a certain genius'. Norman went on to become the distinguished and controversial editor of *Commentary* magazine; co-founder, with Irving Kristol, of neoconservatism; a recipient of the Presidential Medal of Freedom. He was to call the lifelong liberal Huw Wheldon his best friend.

---

* Dad's programme *All Your Own* was found to be 'third in popularity among the older children, especially the brighter girls' although 'its "ordinary" quality... may make it uninteresting... particularly to boys'. Hilde T Himmelweit et al, *Television and the Child* (London: Oxford University Press, 1958), pp. 118–20.

If Oakeshott provided the philosophy, Podhoretz provided literature. He was a postgraduate student at Clare College, Cambridge, on a Fulbright scholarship, studying English Literature and in semi-thrall to FR Leavis, who was holding court at Downing (Podhoretz's first published article was in Leavis's extremely highbrow journal *Scrutiny*, an essay about Lionel Trilling, Norman's professor and mentor at Columbia). Mum went to Cambridge at weekends, and was introduced to The Novel. She 'read enormously... came alive in a curious kind of way'.[10]

Through Norman she met the young literary critic Steven Marcus, Aaron Klug and novelist Dan Jacobson, all of whom became family friends (we used to spend every Whitsun with the Klugs – I was much taken with their half-timbered Morris Minor estate). Aaron was to become a world famous chemist, heading the Cavendish Laboratory, becoming a Knight in 1988, and then President of the Royal Society. Oh, and in 1982 he was awarded the Nobel Prize. Aaron was a lovely man, interested in everything, with a quiet voice which would rise in timbre either in outrage or towards a laugh. Dan, too, had a very distinctive manner of speech, slow and sardonic and wise.

The relationship between Norman and Mum, had circumstances been different, might have ended differently. In November 1953 Norman wrote to her from New York: 'The Jews have a prayer that ends: "Next Year Jerusalem." From now on, I'm praying, "Next Easter (No! *Passover*) in London with my darling." You pray too. I love you.' Some time during 1954, though, with Norman doing army service and Mum reaching her thirtieth birthday, it must have become clear to both of them that marriage was not a likelihood.

In his biography of Podhoretz, Thomas L. Jeffers quotes a

passage from a letter written by Norman to Mum, probably in
May 1954:

> We were sitting together in a café somewhere one night a
> long time ago, discussing something or other. We were on
> high stools at a bar (as a matter of fact, I think we were eating
> sandwiches at a pub not far from LSE). You were dressed in
> blue (it was the first time I saw your coat after you had it
> dyed), and your make-up looked very beautiful in the light
> of the room. You had a cigarette in your hand (and the tip
> was red from lipstick), your legs were crossed, and you were
> turned toward me, but not looking at me, holding your
> arm out, and there was that miraculous smile of incipient
> discovery (I think we were groping toward some new idea)
> that transfigured your face and made you look beautiful
> and more than beautiful. I remember my main feeling at
> that moment. It wasn't tenderness or anything like that. It
> was pride.[11]

In the same year Mum met Norman, she met Dad, in very
different circumstances. He had been courting her friend,
Ruth Mansur, an Anglicised Turkish Jew and a fellow student
of Mum's at the LSE. Dad had proposed marriage to Ruth
and then withdrawn his proposal, according to family lore, at
least twice and very possibly three times. Mum thought Dad's
behaviour to her friend was despicable, and told him so. She
enclosed with her letter a copy of *Middlemarch*, suggesting
Dad read it. Dad returned the book and told Mum that if he
wanted advice from anyone she would be 'the last person in
the world' he would come to. She came to be the first.

Nevertheless, something must have been triggered. The
earliest letters I have date from December of that same

year, 1951. They are from him to her and were written on succeeding days. He was very keen to communicate, though what it was he was keen to communicate isn't very clear, except that he was eager to thank her for her 'generosity'. He was very impressed by it.

The first letter whose tone I thoroughly recognise I here reproduce in its entirety. It was written in March 1955:

Fragment of Conversation

'...I thought she had a mole on her shoulder until I saw it move...'

Dear Jacklin

I hope you are in the Pink I am although the snow

Harold

Memorandum for Himmelsitz

All children have mothers even priests and sometimes Nuns.

Note: sex is no worse than poetry.[12]

Reads like love to me: all code. Dad regularly left Mum notes about the place, usually on delicate slips of paper, and often when she was sleeping and he leaving. They were always cheerful. To the manager of the Co-operative Bank in Leman Street, London E1, he wrote, in March 1955, in recommendation of Mum as a potential account holder: 'In my opinion Miss Clarke is a woman of singular talents; and certainly there are aspects of her personality and character which would endear her to many people.'[13]

During the course of 1955 Mum applied first for a post in the Cabinet Office, for which she was accepted, and at the same time succeeded in a competition to become an officer in the Joint Intelligence Bureau at the Ministry of Defence. She turned down both these positions, probably because she had accepted a proposal of marriage from Dad.

I'm not sure Dad wrote Mum love letters. He was forty years old after all, and she thirty-two, perhaps rather getting on for the platitudes of romantic love. Mum told my sister Sian how Dad had proposed:

> Mum turned up one night at, I think, the Savile Club. She had argued with Dad and wanted to see him. His car was there, outside, and, being open (a convertible in my mind's eye) she decided to wait in it and fell asleep. He arrived (whether returning to or leaving the Club, I don't know) in the early hours of the morning and found her there. They ended up outside the car, sitting on the pavement. After talking for some time, Dad asked Mum, to her intense surprise, if she would marry him; taken aback, she was unable to speak at all at first, which prompted him to say, rather sharply, that he thought it was the kind of question that deserved an answer. She said Yes, and almost as soon as she had, he said that they should walk to Fleet St. and make the announcement in The Times NOW, which they did.[14]

It was my mother's belief that he was keen to stop himself changing his mind, hence the haste to publicise the news.

Paul Wright wrote to Mum after Dad died, remembering the first time he and Babs had met her:

It was at a small cocktail party we were giving at Tufton Court, I can't recall exactly what year. Huw arrived late and, as usual, noisily, and in that highly charged pocket of energy that seemed to precede him like a bow wave, was a small, very pretty girl with fair hair, wearing a black velvet suit. 'This is Jackson,' said Huw, glaring at me with that semi-fierce, semi-protective expression which said, unmistakably, 'you'd better take this one seriously'. We did!

The first straight letter comes in October 1956, when he wrote to her from Washington DC:

I hope I will not be impossible to live with. What I want is for you to be happy & well-occupied: & it seems to me that I mean big and important things with both those words. It would be nice to reflect that I had provided someone in the world with something real. Not that anybody can provide these things.

Another, a few days later, having been to New York and now back in DC:

A scrawl – a cab is on the way. Last night a very silly evening: exchanging facetious cracks with unbelievably-out-of-the-question English knowalls from 'The Economist'. Lahdida is the only word. Bored, boring, trite comments on the lousy Americans: tired, idiotic, sneering languor.

Church this morning, you will be glad to hear. Text from Deuteronomy; theme: the ageing Moses. All exactly like Presbyterian temple, Barmouth, in, say, 1893. I prefer sermons from the Old Testament, for all that. They assume and create an enormous myth which gives life to the proceedings. Once sunk into Old Testamentitis, you enter into a tremendous world, & giants walk across your horizons, the true disturbing mythos or whatever the word is.

Still no letters – vaguely randy this morning out of pure tedium. However, off to the Serpells to eat vast meals & drive in the convertible. You are just getting up at the moment. Wake Up!

He was not keen that she should work; it may also be that she was, anyway, keen to start writing. They were married at St John's Church, Fulham on 2 April 1956. It was to be a marriage of intense mutual dependence and uninterrupted loving kindness. Perhaps, at times, each was too keen for the other's success. Dad's career was, by and large, successful; Mum's failure to join the canon of English novelists was due in part to her devotion to him, but in no way due to his lack of devotion to her.

In June 1957, back at the LSE, she resumed a PhD on nineteenth-century political thought. It was excitingly entitled 'The role of comparison in political studies, with special reference to certain writers of the nineteenth century'. The paper was never finished and perhaps hardly truly begun, for by July she was pregnant with me. It was probably this development that ended what might have been a fruitful and probably distinguished career as an academic. For the rest of her life she was to feel herself pulled between duty to her talent and duty to her family, and in the end felt she had failed both. She was wrong about the latter.

She was contributing articles on television to such journals as *Truth* and *Context*, but, even before the births of my sisters, Sian and Megan, she had begun to think about and make notes on a novel that was to grow by 1964 to well over 400,000 words. Eventually reduced to a mere 220,000 *Mrs Bratbe's August Picnic* was published in 1965. It was the most expensive novel that the publisher, Gollancz, had ever produced. It earned plaudits from, among others, Richard Church in *Country Life* ('the most astonishing first novel I have ever read'), Penelope Mortimer in the *New Statesman* and Anthony Burgess in *The Listener* who called Mrs Bratbe, the eponymous anti-heroine, 'as outrageous a prodigy as we have had this side of the war'.* It was well received, too, in the United States.

Mrs Bratbe's August Picnic is a retelling of the Oedipus story, with the sexes reversed. Alexandra Bratbe, daughter of the media magnate Hytha Bratbe, is brought up in France, falls in love (unknowingly) with her father, causes the death

---

* In the mid-1980s I was browsing in Waterstone's in Richmond when I heard a sonorous, distinguished voice asking an assistant if the store had a copy of *David Copperfield*. I looked over and saw Anthony Burgess in the company of his tiny Italian wife, the translator Liliana (Liana) Macellari. Alas, no *David Copperfield*. Burgess, without complaint, was led out of the shop by his wife, and I followed them. Famous authors have always been to me as celebrities are to others. I like seeing Julian Barnes marching about Dartmouth Park; my dog once sniffed Doris Lessing, no less, on a bench on Hampstead Heath. She was very nice about it. So Burgess – this was shortly after *Earthly Powers* had been pipped to the Booker Prize by Golding's *Rites of Passage* – was an exciting beast. And indeed he trailed after the black-clad little Liana like a bear on a lead. He was shambolic, with that absurd Bobby Charlton sweep of hair over the forehead. Eventually I followed them into a pub in a lane off the high street. I was reading at the time Hildesheimer's idiosyncratic biography of Mozart. I knew that Burgess was a composer as well as an author, and so I thought it would not be inappropriate to ask him to sign my book. Nervously, I approached him; he was very nice, told me he wrote music too, and signed the book. I said thank you, and left. When I got home I told my mother. 'Did you ask him about *Mrs Bratbe*?' she asked. My heart sank. Burgess, I knew, had written a glowing review of her novel. I had not remembered. I felt horribly that I had let Mum down. I feel that more and more strongly as the years go by. It is one of the specific regrets of my life.

of her monstrous mother and blinds herself in remorse. The writing was considered (in the *Times Literary Supplement*) to owe much to the 'shadow' of Iris Murdoch and the 'ghosts' of Aldous Huxley and Virginia Woolf. Other influences suggested elsewhere included Noël Coward, Jane Austen and Toulouse-Lautrec (!). In fact, I think Mum looked very much more to the 'great tradition' for her masters (and mistresses) and in particular to Henry James and DH Lawrence. Perhaps the single greatest influence was Proust, which she read (Proust being both a man and a work) at least three times.

Before *Mrs Bratbe's August Picnic* had been published Mum was at work on a new novel, *Daughters of the Flood*. From this she extracted a play, *Tiger! Tiger!*, which she submitted to the Royal Court. Bill Bryden was keen to produce it but asked for revisions that Mum for one reason or another was unwilling to make.

Daughters of the Flood was never published. A conservative estimate of two million words made it quite unpublishable as a single work (for comparison: *A la recherche du temps perdu* is around a million words). Mum would never consent to the piecemeal publication that her publishers urged on her, and eventually, as she wrote to the novelist Dan Jacobson, the book 'shattered' in her hands. It is hardly surprising. Set nominally in London (and Korea) in the years around the Korean War, it is, it has been said, 'about everything', though to Norman Podhoretz she said it was 'about running'. Mum and her own mother – Nanny – had both been much better than average sprinters in their youths. The remark was unhelpful to Norman but I think she meant that it was about living to your very utmost limit, as a sprinter runs to her limit. Mum stopped writing the book when Nanny died, and never went back to it. She wrote that she was never more alive than when she was writing; her inability to finish it was perhaps in some ways the source of as much grief as the death of my grandmother. She certainly believed that each had suffered on account of the other and both at her hand.

In his obituary of Mum Dan Jacobson wrote that the book was 'perhaps deficient in the ordinary narrative continuity readers expect',[15] but the expectations of readers were very likely the last thing on her mind.

Mum suffered all her life from partial deafness (she was completely deaf in one ear and half deaf in the other, the result of a botched middle ear operation in her youth). This made her unhappy in large groups as she could not hear or share in conversation, a tragedy for such an acknowledged conversationalist. This wasn't helped by what is now called bipolar disorder and was then called manic depression. Whether her obsessive writing fed or starved this condition is hard to determine. Probably both.

In 1980 she was asked by Midge Decter to take on the job of Director of the UK branch of the Committee for the Free World. This was an organisation of intellectuals unified by a desire to stiffen the sinews of Western resistance to Communism, and in particular to argue the case against unilateral nuclear disarmament by the West, and for the introduction of cruise missiles in response to the Communist deployment of SS-20s in Eastern Europe. Alun Chalfont was the Chairman and the committee included intellectuals such as Raymond Aron, Sybille Bedford, Max Beloff, Milovan Djilas, Joachim Fest, Lord Harris, Anthony Quinton and Tom Stoppard. Its activities culminated in the conference 'Beyond 1984', which addressed the continuing threat of Communism throughout the world. It was addressed by Jeane Kirkpatrick and Richard Perle among others. Mum herself carried on the struggle against

EP Thompson and other literate supporters of the Campaign for Nuclear Disarmament (CND) in the letters pages of the newspapers, writing long and ferociously intelligent missives.

Her final battle in a life that came to seem like a series of conflicts – against her own perceived ignorance, her deafness, her mental fragility, her literary ambition – was with the author of her husband's biography. Not me. Another, in a story that I am not inclined to tell, other than to say it was a battle she felt she lost, and by so doing felt she had betrayed her husband. It broke her heart.

That biography was published in 1990. She struggled with attempts to write her own memoir, but found that her characteristic need to know everything bogged her down. After three years of deteriorating health Mum died of cancer – Non-Hodgkin's Lymphoma (how misleading that negative is) – at Charing Cross Hospital, Hammersmith, not far from her childhood home, on 21 June 1993. Among her final words to me were: 'I shall have such a lot to write about when I get out of here.' Seven years before, we had spread Dad's ashes around a tree in Kew Gardens. Now we spread hers there too. She had chosen the tree originally because it was not an oak, as many might have expected it to be, but something rather delicate and different, a Liquidambar, sometimes known as a Sweet Gum. Her husband had not been an ordinary man. She was very emphatically not an ordinary woman.

Her very last work had been a literary anthology based on the seasons, addressed to 'relations and friends'. It is a highly personal collection, but vast and surprising, a 'wandering, of discovery' and 'a conversation between poets'.[16] Like so much else of what Mum did it remains a private joy from which the wider world would have derived much pleasure and illumination.

Mum was known as 'Jay' to all but a few very old friends who knew her as 'Jacq' or 'Jackie' (Norman Podhoretz addressed her, in the early 1950s, as 'Clarke'. Dad had a whole lexicon of names. 'Jemima' was I think his favourite.). She was short, blonde, blue-eyed, attractive. Her deafness gave her a kind of physical grace. There was no attempt at snatching conversation. She, willy nilly, observed. She made intelligent friends easily, and with a few notable exceptions, such as Midge Decter, Joan Murphy, Klary Friedl, these friends were male. Not a social animal herself, she enjoyed the company of intelligent men of the world, and they enjoyed hers. An intense correspondence with the writer John Berger was maintained for some years. So too with her husband's friend the sculptor and novelist Jonah Jones. After Dad died Kingsley Amis made rare trips out of London to take tea in Richmond. The political broadcaster Michael Charlton was often in her company. The philosophers Roger Scruton and Kenneth Minogue were regular correspondents, as was the distinguished international lawyer Robert Glynn. John Mansfield, Emeritus Professor of Jurisprudence at Harvard University, read 1 Corinthians 13 at her funeral.

Paul Wright wrote that 'It was perhaps her constant desire for perfection that was responsible for leaving us so small a literary legacy.'[17] She once helped me write a school history project on Cardinal Wolsey. I was awarded 35 marks out of 30. By that kind of mark she was almost satisfied.

She was also a virtuous woman, concerned to live a good life. 'I'm very interested in what God is,' she once said, 'interested in the idea that God is profound experience. I couldn't say that I'm a believer or even that I'd like to be one. But I'd like to know how I feel.'[18] By 1976 she had faith enough to write a prayer for Dad during a dire illness (cancer of the bowel). She equated

God and love. Constance, the chief character in *Daughters of the Flood*, writes that 'love makes the heart yearn for eloquence'. It is a thought that serves as a fitting epitaph.

Dan Jacobson wrote that 'she had a gift for friendship';[19] Melvyn Bragg used precisely the same words, adding that 'she was one of the very few clever people who was also good'.[20] And Norman Podhoretz wrote: 'I have known a few people of genius... but of them all, she was the most luminous'.[21]

Dad once told me that after about three or four days abroad without Mum's company he started to feel edgy and uncomfortable. The following is a letter written from San Francisco at the end of September 1959. He had been away for a month.

Yesterday, somehow, was a lost day. I left myself free to enjoy leisure, but freedom is not my friend, and it was a dirty wasted day. I must tell you this, & disgust & disappoint you, and bore and bewilder you, but how else to share my life? And how else to share the burden? So nothing happened, except that I padded around, like a G.I. Joe in Tottenham Court Rd, reading the pulp in the drug stores, eyeing the 'Fun with Nudists' film ads, longing for some unimaginable circumstance in which I would be snatched from the streets by some virago bent upon seduction, bent upon exposing my risen flesh to the fascinated gaze of her cohorts. This kind of thing can waste a whole day, a total day committed to waste & shame – can and does. Mercifully some dull party took me up in the evening, and the spell of blank-eyed, somnambulist lusting was over, and I came back into a real world, no matter how footling, & drank beer, & chatted...

Tomorrow I spend the day in the TV station, tomorrow night dine with a barrister who has clearly made a fortune out of being sardonic. Thursday I go to an Actors Studio, and I <u>must</u> write to these Los Angeles places so that I am not left there to my own devices, because that only means doing absolutely nothing in a waste of shame. This must have been a tedious letter for you to read, and even as you narrow your eyes to criticize or shake your head in bewilderment or feel your stomach turning at the problem of being married to such a half-man; even as you say to yourself how self-pitying and dismal a letter this is, please grin and snap your fingers at the same time, because I just can't spill my life over in this way unless you are kind and cheerful, & because you are the lilac tree in the middle of my mucky back yard, and how could I smile and beam ever again if the lilac withered at a touch? You said you missed my sense around the place, & I hope you do – but it is not your sense I miss or depend on, it is your whole totality, your breathing, womanly being, no less, and I am living on the assumption that you are THERE, confident & cheerful & lively & to hell with all morbidities.

While I am sure that her devotion to him was greater (do I mean greater? – wider, perhaps, is a better word) than his to her, I believe that his need for her was equally powerful. She gave him intellectual ballast, but I think more importantly she gave him moral courage and comfort. Like Othello, to a little extent perhaps, and Desdemona, he loved her because she loved him. For her he was a warrior poet. (In that unfinished, unpublishable novel *Daughters of the Flood*, the character of the poet Philip Harisson, who fights for the Glorious Glosters at the Battle of the Imjin River in Korea, is based on Dad.'*) It seems like a pat balancing of affections, yet I think this is broadly right. I also, unfashionably, think this is very often the case, and – even more unfashionably – believe that this balance between need and devotion, when properly managed, makes for good marriages. I think Mum and Dad had a good marriage. They argued loudly from time to time, but I cannot remember what about. I have been told that Dad found Mum's troubles very difficult, but then so did she, of course. 'Your Mother is a remarkable woman,' he would tell us, frequently. Often this was after she had managed to fix the tuning on the TV set or tie up a black bin liner with its four corners (this impressed Dad very much indeed – he called it 'an invention', which suggests the extent of his practicality), but I think what he meant was that not only was she a prodigious thinker, but she could do these other things as well. There were aspects of her behaviour that infuriated him: 'Going for a walk with your mother is exactly like going for a walk with a dog. You have to stop every twenty yards for her to examine something.' She was like this in her thought, too. Steven Marcus told Dad that Mum's 'attitude to knowledge and her temperament as a metaphysician require the intellect and staying power of Bacon'.[22] Mum liked to go into things.

But, like Dad, she was also capable of great cheerfulness, of lightness. And, again like Dad, she was much loved, not least for the way in which she encouraged people to see the possibilities of their lives.

---

* The heroine of the book, Constance Yokeham, may marry Philip and 'their marriage will be as it was once said: Married couples resemble a pair of scissors, often moving in opposite directions, yet always punishing anyone who comes between them' (from JMW's synopsis for the novel).

It is tempting to see the pair of them as eros and agape, body and soul, Old Testament and New, but the truth is that they did not complement each other, they melded. There was a large part of each that belonged equally to the other. I don't know how else to put it.

It is my own belief, and I think it was my father's too, that the reward of virtue is not itself but is happiness. I do not of course mean *ha ha* happiness – I mean what Aristotle called *eudaimonia*, often translated rather clunkily as 'human flourishing'. *Eudaimonia* is what we struggle towards, is what we seek – to make the best of ourselves. To do that we must live as fully as possible. It is my mother's 'profound experience' – it is God in other words. Many people admired my father, but those who knew him well loved him. I think he was loved because he encouraged, even engendered, *eudaimonia* in those close to him. It was his purpose.

There is a tragic irony, then, in the fact that he was unable to help my mother to the full flourishing of her own prodigious talent.

Mum's book was the absolutely dominant non-human feature of my own growing up. I think of it now as an enormous black obelisk – think *2001: A Space Odyssey* – at the hub of our lives, into which Mum would disappear for hours, days at a time. Genius is egocentric, not selfish. Mum was not a selfish woman, quite the reverse (remember the 'generosity' that Dad had noted, a quality that extended not only to her family but to anyone who came within her ambit), but she had to attend to this great work. Dad never did anything to resist Mum's need to write. Indeed, the reverse was the case. He offered to edit the book for her. She later on regretted not having let him, because his own great talent as a programme maker was never to lose sight of the story – of the things that made a subject interesting. But she wanted it to be all her own work.

Not that she was not supportive of her husband in his professional life. On the occasion of a preliminary showing to its subjects of the famous 1969 *Royal Family* documentary, the 'royals' were so delighted with it that they kept insisting on clips being re-shown. The night grew long. Mum, tiring, eventually approached Dad and Tony Jay (who had written the script): 'Don't these people have palaces to go to?'

Before Mum became a mother, and after Brian Murphy's first wife, Bill, died, Dad would accompany his friend and his children, Caroline and Charles, on holiday. Later on, when we three children were just old enough Dad would take us to our Rees cousins in Nantgaredig in Carmarthenshire or to the Neptune Guest House in Criccieth, leaving Mum to write. There was even a code for ringing her, which was kept by the public telephone in the Neptune's reception. She wouldn't answer unless we rang three times, then twice and so on. I never got the impression that Dad was jealous or resentful of the obsessive work that Mum put into writing. Like most husbands, what he was most concerned about was that she should be happy. I have been told that he struggled with her bipolar disorder. I was never told of this problem. I have subsequently learned that she was finally diagnosed in the 1970s, and was terrifically angry that it had taken so long. She was put on some kind of medication, though I do not know precisely what. I know she had thought seriously about suicide; I know too that she was horrified by Sylvia Plath's suicide, and by the suicide of her friend the novelist Lisa Roche, Melvyn Bragg's first wife and the mother of Mum's god-daughter, Marie Elsa (now an Anglican priest and herself a novelist). The discovery that her problems were the result of an imbalance of chemicals was a relief to her; it removed the problem from her character.

Other than continuing to love her wholly, thoroughly, and to miss her both on my own behalf and on behalf of her grandchildren, who would have loved her as much as I, I remain immensely proud of her, and do not at all resent the black hub. Were I clever enough I could create a metaphysics that would demonstrate that the black hub was the place of Profound Experience. Of God.

Mum reading the first volume of Richard Holmes's biography of Coleridge in the garden at 120 Richmond Hill, 1990. Photograph by the author

Russell on pictures, Wheldon on words

CHAPTER 8

1958–1963: *MONITOR*

February 1958 saw the birth of the arts magazine programme *Monitor.* And in April: 'WPW docked, arrived,' Dad wrote in his diary. That was me.

All I really remember of *Monitor*, which ran for seven years, is the title music. It was a serenade for strings by Dag Wiren. (Dad went to see the composer with a view to doing a *Monitor* filmed profile, but found him a rather underwhelming character.) To hear it is to be transported into my very early childhood, and it is odd when it is not followed by Dad's voice introducing the programme.

There are bits and pieces of *Monitor* available on YouTube and the BBC website, but much of what was best is lost.

Nevertheless, there was enough, and enough interest, for the British Film Institute to run a short retrospective some years ago inappropriately featuring Spike Milligan on the poster, a vulgarity that gave the impression that *Monitor* was somehow trendy. *Monitor* was never trendy. That was one of its strengths. It was, rather, *modern*.

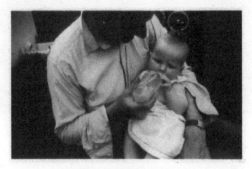

Post-christening bottle

A great deal has been written and spoken about *Monitor*. It has been said that no programme before or since has had so talented a team producing it. Those involved in one way or another included John Berger, Melvyn Bragg, Humphrey Burton, John Drummond, Patrick Garland, Anne James, David Jones, Natasha Kroll, Karl Miller, Peter Newington, Simon Raven, Ken Russell, John Schlesinger, Nancy Thomas, Ann Turner and Allan Tyrer: names (certainly in broadcasting terms) to conjure with. Louis MacNeice sat in on a few early planning meetings. Equally, rarely has a magazine programme ever been so heavily stamped with the personality of its Editor.*

---

* The idea of a programme-making team – 'a force of all arms' in Dad's characteristic military metaphor – under its own Editor, in Dad's opinion came first from Outside Broadcasts – 'the name of the change was *Sportsview*', under the editorship of Peter Dimmock, and including the talents of Paul Fox, Bryan Cowgill and Ronnie Noble. 'It had panache,' said Dad. It was an idea taken up by Talks, and then by Drama, *Z Cars* being the great example.

At a party the BBC gave to celebrate the fiftieth anniversary of the programme, in 2008, several distinguished speakers were asked to give short reminiscences. They all, to a man (and it may have been true of the women, too, had they been invited to contribute), told anecdotes about Dad. Director David Jones recalled being upbraided for not having 'fucked the story' on some film or other. Several years later Jones directed a magnificent *Lower Depths* for the RSC. 'Now that,' said Dad to Jones afterwards, *sotto voce*, 'is what I call fucking the story.' Humphrey Burton told how his first job had been given to him as follows: 'Burton! You know about music. You look after Madame Callas.' Madame Callas subsequently refused to be interviewed by my father and asked for David Webster instead. Webster was the Director of the Royal Opera House, a good man, but not known for his television interviewing abilities. Webster's bland questions infuriated Dad and, unable to contain himself, he walked onto the set – this was live television – and stood between a bemused Webster and Madame Callas and demanded to know why she had wanted to be interviewed by Webster: 'Because Sir David is a gentleman,' was her reply.

Ken Russell finished his little piece (the story of his recruitment by Dad, told also in the form of a dialogue in Russell's engaging autobiography, *A British Picture*,[1] which was dedicated to Dad) with a 'three cheers for Huw'.

In March 1957 Kenneth Adam, Controller of Programmes at the BBC, asked the Talks Department for a new magazine programme: 'a highly sophisticated type of magazine without necessarily appealing only to Third Programme types.'[2]*

---

* The Third Programme, according to Dad, dealt 'esoterically with the esoteric for the esoteric', which may have been a little harsh (BBC WAC R143/133/2).

Catherine Dove, as described above, would produce. Dad would present. By late October the proposed programme had been extended to forty-five minutes. And at some point between then and January Catherine Dove apparently broke her leg, or rather had it broken by her first husband, journalist Charles Wheeler, as he jumped back into bed with the Sunday papers.

Monitor was the third flagship programme to be launched by the Talks Department under the Vice-Admiralship of Grace Wyndham Goldie, following *Tonight* and *Panorama*. She oversaw what Dad described as an 'extraordinary generation of restless and committed people who... took television by the scruff of the neck'.[3] Many of the younger members of these teams were first generation university graduates from working class backgrounds. Lime Grove was vibrant with ambition, ego, a lust for the new, with more than an inkling of what television could be. From Talks emerged a generation of programme makers who became managers during what many consider to have been the Golden Age of the Television Service: Donald Baverstock (Controller BBC1), David Attenborough (Controller of Programmes), Paul Fox (Managing Director, Television), Michael Peacock (Controller BBC2), Alasdair Milne (Director-General) and Ian Trethowan (Director-General).

The original idea for the new programme, as envisaged by Dove and Wyndham Goldie, was for *Monitor* to be a current affairs programme of the arts. Dad was no journalist, however, nor was he taken particularly by politics. He wasn't interested in trends; he was interested in the work that goes into making art.

The whole intention of the programme is to demonstrate how artists are men of vigour and invention and patience, and not in any sense a group of rather curious creatures less real than the plumber or the greengrocer who lives round the corner.[4]

This is from a letter from Dad to the French playwright Jean Anouilh, and seems to me perfectly to express my father's approach to the arts, and in fact to life generally. Just as there was good plumbing and bad plumbing, so there was good art and there was bad art, and there were good television programmes and bad. One mode of employment or application was not superior to another. What mattered was the quality of the work. In order to do good work it was necessary to respect the work to be done, to respect one's own abilities and to respect the customer, consumer or viewer. And in some sense we are back to that enthusiastic young Nazi in Paris, and Dad's admiration for him. It so happened that the ideas – the creed – the boy espoused were beyond the pale, but his energy was not to be faulted.* Further back one might go, to TJ Wheldon's demand that one be 'drunken on the wine of a noble aim'. *Monitor* film-makers had to be fully engaged by their subjects. Everyone on the team made films, they all brought different skills and interests to the programme.

Monitor, described in one condescending early memorandum as a 'culture corner', was first broadcast on Sunday, 2

---

* There were subjects beyond the pale for Dad too. *Monitor* went out in the evening on Sunday – a day still thought of then as having a certain sabbatical value – and Dad once pulled an item by Richard Hoggart 'about Fellini's new film, *Nights of Cabiria*, when he realised that the theme of the film was prostitution' (Anne James, quoted in Sutton, p.165). And an anonymous source told Dominic Sandbrook that he refused to have ostentatious gays on the programme (although, for example, EM Forster's and Benjamin Britten's homosexuality was well known).

February 1958. The first 'team' comprised Producer Peter Newington, already an experienced TV hand, Jack Ashley (later a Labour MP and peer), Karl Miller (later editor of the *London Review of Books*), Ted Scott, Margaret Dale (a dancer who was to make many first rate films about ballet, including *Ballet Class*, mentioned previously), Ann Brown, film editor Allan Tyrer (who, like Newington, would serve the full seven years), Stephen Hearst (later Controller of Radio 3 and 'a leading intellectual in the BBC'[5] – he was a regular at the Wheldon Christmas Party, and always rather frightened me*), Anne James (Dad's secretary, and later herself a producer), and John Read, art-philosopher Herbert's son, and a highly regarded producer of films about the arts.

'I didn't believe much in a programme on the arts,' Dad told Frank Gillard years later. 'I didn't think that it would work. Popularisation I was bothered about,'[6] and indeed the first edition of *Monitor* was not a great success.[†] I do wonder if Dad had regrets at that point about turning down Sir Miles Thomas's invitation to apply for a new post running the Development Council for Wales. Good money was being offered, and the job included both Wales and public service. I can't imagine him giving up the sheer energy of the BBC for

---

* In an email to the author, Leslie Megahey, sometime Editor of both *Arena* and *Omnibus*, wrote that Hearst 'had a moral authority that made us all feel like guilty fourth-formers, but he was affectionate underneath, most loveable. And yes, one of those remarkable European intellectuals who found refuge in the BBC and brought their formidable minds to talks dept. and drama, often in radio – Martin Esslin was my first boss, Hans Keller and others were all still active there. I said at Stephen's memorial that we younger ones who hadn't lived through such "interesting times" – the rise of Nazism and trauma of exile – always felt a touch callow in the presence of that generation.'

† The audience reaction index was 51, 'far below the average (69) for all magazine programmes televised during 1957' (VR/58/68). *All Your Own* tended to get figures in the mid-70s.

such a post, even if Mum was pregnant and a family – me – on the way.

That first *Monitor* contained too many items: Peter Brooke talking about *musique concrète*, with an extract from his *Tempest*, an inexplicably dull interview of Kingsley Amis conducted by Simon Raven, Jacob Epstein talking about sculpture, and Alan Brien chatting to Peter Hall and Gore Vidal about a new Tennessee Williams play, *Cat on a Hot Tin Roof*. There was, however, one jewel, a short film by a film-maker discarded by *Tonight*. 'In truth,' John Schlesinger said, 'I wasn't very happy on the programme [*Tonight*]. In the end they gave me the push. Donald Baverstock… said, "When it works, *boy*, we are happy to have you. But when it doesn't you're not worth it."'[7]

Dad signed Schlesinger on a six month contract. He was to be associated with *Monitor*, in one way and another, for the next five years. He both learned from *Monitor* and taught – 'extended our ideas of what could be done', according to Dad. He made films about Italian opera, about Benjamin Britten, about Brighton Pier, about Oldham Rep, about Georges Simenon, and a film called *The Innocent Eye*, a study of children's imagination, which won the Edinburgh International Film Festival Award.

His film *Hi-Fi-Fo-Fum*, about the new miracle sound of High Fidelity recording, was an example of the way in which *Monitor*'s ideas were extended. Schlesinger showed the famous BBC radiophonic workshop team and various other interested parties marvelling at the quality of the sound rather than the quality of the music, revealing the technological revolution that hi-fi was having. Schlesinger worked as a freelance, however, and he wanted to make a feature film, which he did: *A Kind of Loving*, the first of many, including *Midnight Cowboy* and *Far From the Madding Crowd*.

Other subjects or guests covered or participating in that first hectic year included the Sagan Ballet, Hugh Casson, the New York opening of John Osborne's *The Entertainer*, Korean ballet, buskers, the Rive Gauche, Richard Hoggart, Italian opera, John Wain, Breughel, Coventry theatre, Yehudi Menuhin, John Berger, Sir Arthur Bliss, Moscow Art Theatre, Léger, Ukrainian ballet, the Cannes Film Festival, Masaccio, Charles Laughton, Dutch medieval sculpture, Van Cliburn, Michael Redgrave, Maria Callas, Britten, Fra Angelico, Bernard Kops, Pre-Columbian art, St Ives, Duke Ellington, Simenon, Auschwitz, Jackson Pollock, Chinese calligraphy, Eisenstein and Stravinsky. The Communist Party paper, the *Daily Worker*, reckoned *Monitor* was 'Programme of the Year'.

Among the possibles to replace John Schlesinger as the principal contracted film-maker for *Monitor* was Karel Reisz, who in 1960 made *Saturday Night and Sunday Morning*, but the job was to go elsewhere. Norman Swallow, Head of the BBC Film Unit at Ealing, had received two films from a young film-maker, *Amelia and the Angel* and *Lourdes*, by which he was impressed, and suggested that Dad view them and meet the director. Dad watched the films, agreed, and chose The Red Lion, a famous Ealing pub also known as 'Stage 6', opposite Ealing Studios, for the rendezvous.

Dad liked Ken Russell:

He was shy and quiet... A little watchful, but silent and extremely modest... I liked him for being so quiet, and somehow latent. It seemed to me he was also a very nice man – which indeed he was, and is – and in addition to being nice was, and this was the crux, the director of this film [Amelia and the Angel] which was at least unpredictable and free of clichés.[8]

And Ken Russell liked Dad:

> *Monitor* was and still remains the one and only experimental
> film school ever, and Huw Wheldon was its presiding genius.[9]

Ken Russell's first film for *Monitor* was about John Betjeman and
London architecture. It was made with the help of Nancy Thomas
and Humphrey Burton and Dad's own secretary, Anne James. It
was brought in on time and within budget. One shot, of Betjeman
stepping into a shot of the female nude sculpture at Henlys
Corner in Finchley (or the Naked Lady, as we north Londoners
refer to it), was paid homage to in Michael Gill's famous shot
for *Civilisation*, in which Kenneth Clark emerged from behind
Michelangelo's *David* (*Monitor* hands Nancy Thomas and Allan
Tyrer both worked on *Civilisation*).

Russell's first film went out on the twenty-fifth *Monitor*,
and followed a filmed interview with Pablo Casals, a live
interview with the abstract artist Adrian Heath and a film
about portraits of Elizabeth I. The Betjeman film – *A Poet's
London* – was an instant hit, not least with its subject, who
wrote to Nancy Thomas:

> I watched the film with Graham Sutherland – we all thought
> the Ken Russell film FIRST CLASS. It really could not have
> been better… Tell Huw Wheldon how charmed I was with his
> intro, and with that Ely White stuff which preceded the Ken
> Russell. What fun 'Monitor' is. You must be very happy.[10]

Dad wrote to Betjeman: 'It seems to have gone down very well
all over the place.'[11]

A Poet's London must have tremendously excited Dad,
because it conformed to his idea of what made for good

television, or perhaps because it helped him to understand his own idea. In the introduction to *Monitor*, the book of interviews published two days before the first transmission of *Elgar* (the celebrated hundredth edition of the programme), Dad wrote (having described Russell as 'the most original, unpredictable mind among us'):

> The kind of television we wanted rested first on the knowledge that there is no such thing as 'a good idea for a programme' but only people willing and moved and able to make programmes out of ideas that interest them. It rested on the knowledge that such people do not grow on trees. It rested on the belief that there is no such thing, in documentary television, as 'background filming', for example, or 'incidental music'. Everything contributes or distracts in its degree, including the chair in which the speaker sits; and everything – pace, setting, rhythm, sound, as well as words and shifting images – must not only combine in a single statement but be harnessed to powerful and daring ideas informing the programme as a whole if it is to be more than a piece of scissors and paste anthologizing or so much talk with 'visual aids' tacked on. Television, a conviction no less strong for eluding us so often in practice, resides in the imagination.[12]

Monitor had its detractors. Like television critic Philip Purser, they were put off by Dad's mannerisms – or what Purser called 'conceits'; but mostly the dissenting voices came from those in 'the superior corners'[13] of society, who denigrated television as a whole – Oxbridge grandees like Maurice Bowra, AJP Taylor and Tom Driberg.* Other highbrows – 'Third Programme types' – could not imagine an intelligent person not being *au fait* with the contemporary arts scene. Derek Hart in *Sight and Sound* spoke of Dad 'sliding apologetically on to the screen, attempting to project an image of the common man and looking instead like the personification of the BBC'. Those who did like *Monitor* ascribed much of its success to the same thing. Jeremy Brooks in *The Spectator* wrote:

> There can't be a million people in this country who had even heard of such artists as Elisabeth Frink, Ossip Zadkine, Paul Tortelier, Friso Ten Holt, let alone a million who would, in cold blood, have welcomed a programme about one of them. There can seldom have been such a clear-cut example of television 'creating' an audience in a field where a cool counting of heads would have indicated that one didn't exist.

> Much of the credit for this must go to Huw Wheldon, whose astringent urbanity and flair for original angles of approach is stamped on the programme even when his own hatchet-jawed grin is absent.[14]

In the *Sunday Times* Oscar Turnill wrote that 'the straight interviews... usually get their flavour from the presence of the Great Panjandrum himself, with his hesitations,

---

* Driberg (Lancing, Oxford and High Anglican) bizarrely compared HPW (Friars School Bangor, LSE and Welsh Presbyterian) to the disc jockey Pete Murray (quoted in Kynaston, *Modernity Britain*, p. 274). My mother had her own view of Driberg's TV appearance on Election night 1959: she thought he was 'pretending to be a TV star... more excited about television performance than about the election'.

his emphases, his repetitions, and his almost audible punctuation.'[15]*

The snobs and the highbrows and the irritated were outnumbered both by a growing number of viewers and by television critics. The *Guardian*'s Mary Crozier called *Monitor* 'adult television' and was impressed by there being 'no hint of talking down', *The Times* called the programme 'incisive', *Punch* said it should be cherished and repeated 'two or three times a week', the *Daily Worker* reckoned it was 'consistently intelligent and revealing', and the novelist Monica Furlong thought *Monitor* was 'without question... the most intelligent, interesting and exciting offering provided at any time of the week on either channel', adding that 'A good deal of its charm, I suppose, derives from Mr Wheldon's personality, his rather offbeat good looks and his capacity for asking questions one would like to ask oneself... It warms the cockles of the aesthetic heart, this brave, sensible and intellectually snobbish programme.'[16]

Most vitally *Monitor* was respected by artists themselves. Marcel Duchamp, doubtless an artist too far for the likes of Driberg, set foot in a television studio for the first time for *Monitor*. So too Max Ernst. Duke Ellington appeared for the first time on British television on *Monitor*. EM Forster, Aaron

---

* Much was always made of Dad's appearance: 'Dark, lean, piquant, punctilious, and eager in profile like Punch', (Punch was constantly turning up) said *The Bulletin*. It was thought he could double for Trevor Howard, but Dad was leaner and darker and his nose was broken. Altogether craggier. Lots of people (I have mentioned David Attenborough) referred to him as tall, though he wasn't. (I remember him being accused of being Howard at, I think, the Royal Tournament, while ascending a ladder or perhaps stairs; on another occasion while on holiday in Wales we were pursued along the seafront at Criccieth by a woman who finally plucked up the courage to try to stop Dad in his tracks. 'I know who you are!' she screamed. 'No you don't', he said back, without breaking stride. 'Yes I do', she repeated, 'you're Derek Nimmo.')

Copland, Aldous Huxley had all featured on the programme even before Ken Russell arrived. Russell had himself watched John Berger on Russian art before his interview in Ealing with Dad.

Duchamp joined the ranks of Dad's heroes (Dad was big on heroes). He came hot on the heels of Orson Welles. Of the latter Dad said: 'He was full of tricks. He was mischievous and he liked behaving mischievously with life. He liked making life into a game, and he enjoyed himself, like Lloyd George. They were great people for enjoying themselves, these chaps.' Of Duchamp, he said:

> I think he was the cleverest man I ever met... I had the impression of a chap with a simply astounding intelligence, quite different from anyone I had ever met – with the possible exception of Mr Lloyd George – simply after hearing him speak five words. It was in his countenance, somehow in his eyes. It was like talking to a famous Chinese sage. He just seemed almost frighteningly clever... He had some mischief in him too, he was very keen on the game... he liked gamesmanry... he was ironic... I was more and more with him [as the film was being made] and by the end of the couple of weeks I really felt that I wished virtually to be his disciple... I don't know quite why, except for this mixture of extreme intelligence and irony.[17]

Dad was a celebrated raconteur – David Attenborough rated him the best in the land. Just about every assertion he made or idea he formulated was expressed or illustrated by a story. So it was with *Monitor*. 'I live with these stories in my mind for three weeks,' he said, speaking of each and every item in an edition. It allowed him to speak without notes or autocue. He was addressing his audience directly, that 'smallish majority' of, at its height, about three million viewers (not a lot then but now considerable): 'I will tell them what I don't know.' He adopted a *faux-naïf* style (maybe one of the conceits that Purser disliked) in order to ask direct questions. The idea was that he was finding out on the audience's behalf ('I want to annihilate the brows,' he told one interviewer). 'Why have you written so much?' he asked Darius Milhaud. 'Why do you take Indian music so seriously?' he asked Yehudi Menuhin. He promoted the right to fail: 'If it's a disaster,' he told Ken Russell before the new boy's first film, 'well, we can throw it away.' The enemy was mediocrity, the not trying; also to be avoided was the meretricious (one of his favourite words – I think he used it to mean self-regarding).

Team members had to work hard to get their ideas accepted. It took Ken Russell three years to do *Elgar*. Humphrey Burton wanted to do a film on the Allegri String Quartet. Dad thought it a bit on the dry side until Humphrey mentioned that the quartet was part of a family tradition. Therein, so far as Dad was concerned, lay the story. The film was a great success. 'Elaborate and witty,' said the *New Statesman*.

Every Tuesday morning ideas were discussed; there were always five or six features in the pipeline. The usual procedure with an item that he wasn't directly involved in was first to sell it to Dad, then to discuss the treatment, then to go away and make it. Dad would see nothing until the first rough cut. At that point he might completely restructure the film, and add his own commentary.

The medium suited Dad perfectly. 'On the whole,' 'by and large,' 'fundamentally' were all favourite phrases. Dad liked to generalise. Although *Monitor* was criticised by some for being too highbrow, most of the flak came from those who were offended by the obviousness of the questions ('ignore the obvious at your peril,' Dad used to warn me), but how about this for a rather wonderful exchange with the man considered by many to be the greatest sculptor of the twentieth century:

Wheldon: The King in your 'King and Queen' must be one of the few male figures that you've ever made.

Henry Moore: Yes, I think I've done about three or four male figures out of the hundreds and hundreds that I've done. And now you come to mention it, they practically all are women.[18]

Generalisation only works, however, if the story that carries it is well told. Dad told stories very well. Film-makers who worked with him, such as Ken Russell, attest that while he knew hardly anything, technically, about film-making, he knew a great deal about storytelling. I think that probably came from those preachers, from the Old Testament, that book of big myths. This is what he wrote about film-making:

The search (which begins before the shooting starts and sometimes long before) is for themes and subjects which carry overtones, which ideally are almost in the nature of parables, and which borrow meaning from their surroundings. This main search involves others. It involves a search for physical experience: for the movement of a hand, a piece of landscape, a note of music, or a footfall which will lend intimations to the themes, whether declared or implicit.[19]

The most celebrated film in the history of *Monitor* is that of the one hundredth programme, *Elgar.* I think it is worth reprinting Dad's story of how it was made, to give some indication of the way in which *Monitor* as a whole functioned. The following is from his Dimbleby Lecture, 'The British Experience in Television', which was televised live in 1976.

I personally had a curious experience in the matter of finding out what the story is about in making a programme. Three of us were very keen to make a programme about Elgar. I liked his music. I had two other colleagues who liked his music, and we all wished to make a programme about him. We felt he had been done down a bit, and there was a snobbish, peevish view about his music which needed knocking off its pedestal. So we set about trying to prepare a programme; and, of course, when you set off on a project of that kind there has to be a story.

Elgar's life was an interesting one. We had a research assistant called Anne James, who spent months, all over the place, seeing Mrs Elgar Blake and so on, and collecting material about his life until eventually there was a substantial file drawn from biographies and personal memories. He had had, after all, a very varied life.

Elgar, as you will remember, was very much Master of the King's Music; very much Edwardian England at its most majestic; very much a man of elegance and poise. He seemed to have something of the same quality as W.G. Grace or Rudyard Kipling, men of authority. And yet, Elgar's life had not been lived at all against the sort of background that you might read into that picture. He was born in Worcester, the son of a piano tuner, left school at 12, served in a shop in his teens, knew he was a musician, wished to compose, did compose for brass bands, never sold anything, went on composing in his 20s, never sold anything, set up as a piano tuner himself and as a music teacher and a bit of a fiddler, and married a General's daughter who was determined to make him a great composer and widely known. Even she was not able to do anything about it until at the age of 47 – I think I have the age right – he wrote the 'Enigma Variations' and sold them for the same price, I think, as Milton sold 'Paradise Lost'. He sold them for £7/10/0-, but there was a loophole in the contract which allowed the pianola rights to revert to the composer in the event of there being any such sales. And there were, and by the hundreds of thousands. He made a fortune out of the pianola sales and that was the beginning of his recognition. He brooded on suicide, he was given to fits of deep depression, he was neurotic, he was an extremely odd, talented genius. Clearly a story could be told; and the way we decided to tell the story was to get an actor and two or three actresses and without making them speak dialogue, get them to enact certain moments of his life. For example, we knew he courted the General's daughter. We knew various things about that courtship. We knew that he went to her house for tea, we knew they met on Tuesday evenings and went to church together in certain circumstances. There were several of 50 or more scenes we could have reconstructed simply to create the sequence of him courting the General's daughter.

I didn't like it, Burton didn't like it and Russell didn't like it, and we looked it up and down to know what was wrong with it because it was lifeless. It was Burton in the end who said one night, 'Our trouble here is that we are not telling the right story'. Russell and I knew this and we said, 'Of course.

But what is the right story?' He said, 'The right story after all must be something to do with his music, because he is of no interest except as a composer and the question is what is the story of the music.' Gradually we built up from that moment. Russell and I decided – Ken Russell was going to direct it – we decided the thing to do was listen to all the music very carefully. I did not do so, but Russell and Burton spent five days doing nothing but listening to Elgar's music. They found several things he had written for brass bands as a youth and so on; and out of all the music they listened to they eventually made up a soundtrack which consisted of short quotations from works Elgar had written from the beginning of his life to the end. Some were a minute long, some 3 minutes, some 12 seconds and some 5 minutes. It was not easy to make these quotations move smoothly one into the other, but one way and the other, they succeeded, and made a 50 minute soundtrack which consisted of quotations chosen in such a way as to provide a suggestion of the way in which Elgar's musical life had moved.

Now, with that soundtrack we then took all the biographical material and placed, according to the soundtrack, what seemed most appropriate to the music of any particular moment. When it came to a courtship sequence, for example (he had written 'Salut d'Amour' for his General's daughter when he was courting her – a lovely song), we could have shown him and his girl in all sorts of different situations because we knew, as I mentioned, 40 or 50 episodes of the courtship. The question was which situation went best with that melody. We decided that for them to walk through a field of waving corn (corny as it may sound) went best with that tune, and so we filmed the two actors walking through the precise field through which Elgar and his sweetheart had so often walked. In the same way for every bit of music there was, we chose the illustration available which seemed most appropriate to that piece of music.

In the end it was, to rationalize the matter, as if the music had suggested the pictures. The music was not simply an accompaniment. The music itself in a profound sense was what the whole thing after all was about. Later, we put on commentaries and so on and so forth. Ken Russell grew enormously excited at one time, I remember. 'I have found the lamp' – 'what lamp?' – 'the lamp under which he wrote the "Theme and Variations". I said, 'So what?' He said, 'Well, I have the table, I borrowed the cloth from Mrs Elgar Blake, and now I have got the lamp,' and I said, 'Nobody will notice it. It will make no difference, one way or another.' But, we did eventually film the lamp and it was the right lamp, and while I do not believe filming the right field and getting the right lamp and getting the composing of 'Enigma Variations' reconstructed in the actual house meant anything as far as viewers were concerned, in some curious way it provided confidence to people making the programme.

At the end of the day the programme may not have been that good, but it was a reasonable and honourable job, and was not simply a standard 'Biog' about a great Edwardian figure, but a programme about a great composer, which is, in fact, what Elgar was, and which was in the end the most important fact both about him and the programme we made about him. The problem was not how to tell the story, but how to tell the right story.

What Dad has left out of this story is the argument over the use of 'Land of Hope and Glory', which Humphrey Burton described in his 1991 Royal Television Society Huw Wheldon Memorial Lecture about *Monitor*:

> We argued in the canteen, we argued in the corridor outside the cutting room, and no doubt we argued on the iron staircase at the back of the studios, the only place one could smoke. We worked our way to a compromise. Huw found a way of keeping faith with Elgar's feelings but relating them to the world stage and the grander theme of the horror of war. His sense of the epic had prevailed.

The point that Russell and Burton had wanted to make was that Elgar was horrified that his music was being used as a kind of second national anthem against the country he loved, Germany. The problem was that this put the emphasis on Elgar's distress rather than the sufferings of those who fought or who had lost loved ones (what is more, the film was scheduled to go out on Armistice Day). In the 'compromise' both the composer's distress and the horror of war were demonstrated. Less a compromise than an improvement.

Dad stopped interviewing because, he said, he had interviewed everyone who interested him, but there was one subject he couldn't get: William Faulkner. In the summer of 1959, while on a busman's holiday in the USA, he had gone to Oxford in Mississippi to try to persuade Faulkner to do a *Monitor* interview. He wrote back to Mum:

> I did not see Falkner [*sic*] in the end, but only Mrs Falkner: but this was beyond all reasonable expectation. The

Connection is made, & if ever Falkner wants a platform, I think she'll fix it. But I don't suppose he ever will.

He has lived here all his life. The house is simply beautiful. White as usual, built of wood on Kentish ply-board lines, the usual tall wooden portico pillars, cedars surrounding. The tall, airy, high-ceiling-rooms and the slender wooden bannisters & the weathered timber floor all joined in a lovely unity. They were burning cedar in the fireplaces, & the aroma spread through the house.

Falkner stands for absolute negro equality, for the new South, for the American south in a way. Like an Irishman he savours and chews over the intolerable inescapable marvellous memories of his childhood & his past, but could not, I think, be called backward looking in any way. He is unsentimental, and is no longer fighting the civil war, as so many of them are in a fatuous Golf Club kind of way, claiming association and identity with virtues & graces they never had & never will have except by bogus proxy – and yet the picture over the sitting room fireplace in Falkner's house is the picture of Robert E. Lee...

Mrs Falkner, Mrs Estelle, is 58, delicate, survivor of two husbands, fragile, once a Southern Belle, and an absolute No 1 knock-out with more sex-appeal in pure concentrated quite irresistible form than all of Hollywood added together & multiplied by six. She was adorable, and, of course, quite impossible I suppose. She does not vote, ON PRINCIPLE: and what the principle is, as you watch her holding her cigarette between her fourth and little finger, her hands moving exquisitely on the fulcrums of her thin brown wrists, as you watch her alert, lovely head, and take in the lace and the fragrance, what the principle IS, who can tell?

I liked her. A knock-out. Once an alcoholic it seems, and her sister a crook. Oh Jay, you should have been here. To hell with California, interesting like Selfridges: but here, the interest is like Chartres or Dublin.

The success of *Monitor* was due primarily to the brilliance of the team that made it; but it owed its personality, its drive, its 'madness for truth', to my father. It may be thought a vulgar comparison, but I think of Alex Ferguson and Manchester United, Russell as Cantona or Ronaldo. Perhaps a more appropriate sporting analogy would be Carwyn James and the great Welsh rugby teams of the 1970s, Russell as Barry John or Phil Bennett (was there ever a better example of triumphant unpredictability than Bennett's ballet of sidesteps at the beginning of that Barbarians try against the All Blacks in 1973?). Humphrey Burton, in his Royal Television Society lecture, said that Dad 'identified passionately with everything he presented – he sought to get inside the subject and to find words which would reinforce its emotional charge'.

Dad regarded television not as a thing apart, but as straightforwardly another medium in which to tell stories: 'the word "television" is only like the word "print"'. In the letter he wrote to my mother after Dad's death, Tony Jay said that Dad 'never got broadcasting out of proportion. It was life that interested him – facts, ideas, arguments, creative imagination – and television was never more than a way of sharing these important things'. So he defended television against the ignorance of the cultural elites. I have mentioned his defence of Margaret Dale's *Ballet Class* (against Anthony Burgess's wholly positive review). In his 1964 lecture 'Television and the Arts', he took on first the celebrated American art critic Harold Rosenberg, and then the television critic of the *Times Educational Supplement*, who had unwisely used words such as 'stereotype' and 'pop-up' and 'run-of-the-mill' and 'manufactured' to describe a whole raft of television programmes. This, said Dad, was 'not a literate way in which to describe this body of programmes'. He listed then recent programmes about music: Tortelier Master Classes, programmes on Haydn and Paganini, transmission of the Ninth Symphony conducted by Klemperer, of Verdi's *Requiem* conducted by Giulini and Britten's *War Requiem*. He took the Beethoven symphony as an example of the skill required by the Director – Anthony Craxton – implying that the coverage itself was an act of art. Which it was and is.

> Perhaps the whole problem in this field is not so much that television reduces art, as that society... reduces television. That creative work has been, is being done, and will be done (and in passing, to a greater extent in this country than anywhere else in the world) is a fact of the greatest importance and not well enough recognized. Television needs the support and the help and co-operation, the involvement, of artists. It needs increasingly to be seen as a medium that has much to contribute. One method is to recognize its present virtues and future possibilities.

This very much sets the tone for what was to come in the following years, as Dad became, in the words of the *New Statesman*, 'the BBC's Horatio'.[20]

Monitor lasted seven years. During its seasons it was transmitted once a fortnight, on Sunday evenings, alternating with *Face to Face*.* 'Weeks without *Monitor* seemed dull ones,' wrote David Attenborough, years later,[21] although I've no doubt David enjoyed John Freeman.

Dad tried to persuade the director John Boorman to succeed him. Boorman later wrote, in his autobiography *Adventures of a Suburban Boy*:

> [Wheldon] took me under his wing, asked me to take over Monitor, that jewel I had admired for so long. I was too intimidated. Wheldon was an inspirational figure and a brilliant raconteur... I was always tongue-tied in front of Huw. I had a dream one night that he had painlessly extracted all my teeth and my gums were frozen.[22]

The final series was eventually edited and presented by Oxbridge man *par excellence* Jonathan Miller, whose keen desire to demonstrate his superior kind of seriousness rather alienated *Monitor*'s audience. 'Jonathan Miller has returned from the world of armpits and trousers lost on the underground to a more serious persona as the Huw Wheldon of the 'sixties,'[23] wrote the ever snarky Christopher Booker in *The Spectator*.

Monitor gave birth to any number of arts magazine shows, *Omnibus* and the *South Bank Show* among them, and its makers went on to success in television, film and theatre. Russell's and Schlesinger's careers are well known, as are Bragg's and Burton's. Patrick Garland went on to run the Chichester Festival, David

---

* John Freeman was to *Face to Face* as Dad was to *Monitor*. Among those he interviewed were Evelyn Waugh, Adam Faith, Lord Reith, Bertrand Russell, Jung, Martin Luther King and Danny Blanchflower. He notoriously reduced both Gilbert Harding and Tony Hancock to tears. He married Catherine Dove and later became British Ambassador to the USA.

Jones was a front line director at the Royal Shakespeare Company, before going to the USA, where he became a film director (making Pinter's *Betrayal* and *84 Charing Cross Road*); Nancy Thomas and Ann Turner both became senior producers at the BBC. Leslie Megahey, who edited both *Arena* and *Omnibus*, wrote that

> For us, the whole arts TV thing, the ethos, the methodology, the insistence on inventive storytelling and inventive (but precise, thought-through) image-making came from Huw, directly to Ken Russell and his generation, then inherited by us. Not that Huw might have approved of everything we did later in our storytelling, but he had pressed the 'on' button, and he left us to it, or left it to us.[24]

Monitor's influence was felt not merely in arts broadcasting. For example, while there had been many science programmes on the BBC before 1964, *Horizon* set out to be different. It took *Monitor* as its model. In so doing, the production team 'determined to make a programme that was focussed on the culture, ideas and personalities of science. They rejected being driven by the news agenda and they refused to be didactic.'[25]

Furthermore, *Monitor* contributed to the education of a whole generation of creative aspirants. In 2014 Sir Richard Eyre told Charlotte Higgins: 'As *You Like It* with Vanessa Redgrave was completely transformative; so was *Monitor* with Huw Wheldon... This was art that I hadn't dreamed existed. It was absolutely contagious and it changed my life. And it wouldn't have happened without the existence of the BBC.'[26]

Several of those involved in *Monitor* became family friends. Of course, with BBC Television being in west London, many staff lived there. Richmond, a little further out, officially both in Surrey and in Greater London, and at the end of the District line, was known in some quarters as media gulch. David Attenborough lived around the corner. Humphrey Burton and family moved onto Richmond Hill (Claire Burton, now Dibble, was one of Dad's godchildren), Melvyn and Lisa Bragg lived in Kew. We saw a good deal of both Humphrey and Melvyn. Melvyn's parallel career as a novelist meant that he had much in common not just with broadcaster Huw but also with novelist Jay. He wrote her obituary for the *Independent*. Sheila Allen and David Jones we saw some of: David with his saturnine baldness and serious voice was rather forbidding; Sheila was always interested in us all, and we liked her a lot. Patrick Garland I liked. He seemed quiet and bright. It was a shame not to see Ken Russell more often – not to get to know him, because of the affection Dad felt for him. I do remember him turning up at Kew on Dad's fiftieth birthday (May 1966). I was peering through the bannisters, a transfixed eight year old. As a gift Ken had brought a display case of pinned butterflies.

Earlier there had been John Berger (who said that Dad had taught him 'how to think while talking'), and his wife Anya, John in his leather-and-zips 'umm' jacket – named by me, in recognition of his tending to turn up by motorbike.* Another, non-television friend who lived in Kew was the American constitutional historian Robert Goldwin. Bob credited Mum with coining the phrase 'moral greed', an echo of Norman

---

* John Berger also provided the Wheldon family with a classic example of a Freudian slip. He had been at our house talking excitedly but anxiously about new techniques of painless childbirth when he received a phone call from his wife Anya to say that she had gone into labour. He picked up his crash helmet and dashed from the house, yelling out that he could not possibly miss his wife's 'childless painbirth'. My mother wrote the blurb for Berger's Booker Prize-winning novel G. It is perhaps the only example of the form that Frank Kermode, doyen of literary critics, ever singled out for praise.

Podhoretz's crediting Dad with the phrase 'spiritual illiteracy'. At Kew there were other visitors from America: Doris Blumenthal – who had been Mum's bridesmaid – and her husband Warren Wallace, a documentary maker; the Marcuses. Doris's sister, Gitta – married to the theatre director Peter Zadek – was also a friend. We had our first motor car accident with her, about which I remember nothing except her worry on our account. Her son and daughter – Simon and Michelle – were a little older than us, I think. Michelle was so beautiful I found it almost impossible to speak to her: difficulties with girls.

Melvyn and Humphrey have remained distant but true friends, and both have fought steadfastly for a maintenance of the broadcasting standards that my father embodied. Judging from *In Our Time*, Melvyn has an insatiable appetite for knowledge, and the rare ability to extract it from experts in such a way as to make it more or less comprehensible for the less expert among us. As Dad had with artists. It is not too fanciful to see *In Our Time* as the final hot ember of the conflagration that was *Monitor*.

Hitherto *Monitor* had been a Noble Cause, as war against the Nazis had not been (a waste of shame, rather), as perhaps even the Festival of Britain had not quite been. Now television itself, and the BBC in particular, was to become *the* Noble Cause.

From the fifth issue of Private Eye, *1962*

Like an admiral with a ship

CHAPTER 9

1963–1976: HORATIO

This is what I remember watching with Dad: *Morecambe and Wise*, *The Two Ronnies*, *Rowan and Martin's Laugh-in*, *Dad's Army*, *Monty Python*, David Attenborough's wildlife programmes, international rugby, occasional football, golf. And then there were the Big Series, like *Civilisation*, *The Ascent of Man*, *America*; Jack Pullman's brilliant adaptations of *War and Peace* and *I, Claudius*. Also movies: never did I see him laugh as hard (and I with him) as at a scene in *Les Vacances de Monsieur Hulot*, in which M. Hulot is desperately attempting to rid himself of a stoat or weasel (actually a stole) attached to the bottom of his trousers: 'How fatuous,' Dad squeezed out between the tears. Two films he particularly enjoyed were *True Grit*, with John Wayne, and *It's a Mad Mad, Mad, Mad World*, which starred, among many others, Spencer Tracy, whom he liked very much. The latter film, he claimed, he caused to have shown every Christmas. Another very different Spencer Tracy movie he liked was John Sturges's *Bad Day at Black Rock*. Oh, and like his mother-in-law and my sister Megan, he enjoyed *Kojak** (I think he had read Ross Macdonald's entire oeuvre and was keen too on Dick Francis).

I can remember two televisual events from our house in Kew, where we lived from 1960 to 1970. The first was learning that the racing driver Jim Clark had died. This was very shocking. Jim Clark was a hero of mine. I recall walking very solemnly from the study, where the TV was, to the kitchen, to inform my mother. I was ten years and two days old. Clark was the greatest driver of his day, and he drove a Lotus. Whenever I hear the word or see a Lotus, I think of Jim Clark's death. I have never wanted a Lotus, and yet I feel possessive about the marque. It is special to me. It brought me my first intimation of mortality.

For the moon landing on 20 July 1969 my mother put mattresses on the floor of the study (actually just the room with books in it – I'd happily played in there and still carry a scar on my shin from a miscalculated leap). It was exciting, like camping. The barf and blurp and *zzzjsh* of the TV pictures was tantalisingly mysterious. I have absolutely no idea whether I was awake for The Moment, but I remember it nonetheless. I'm fairly sure that my father had no particular interest. It was Mum who was intrigued.

---

* Dad met Telly Savalas on a trip to the USA and wrote home a postcard to Meg and Nanny, telling them so. Tremendous excitement all round. I was more impressed by having Francis Ford Coppola in the address book.

At Richmond we had two TVs and the regimen was different for each one. Downstairs, in the Green Room, a large room with a door into the garden inhabited three days a week by my grandmother (Nanny), the TV was pretty much ours. That's where we watched children's hour.

Upstairs, in the sitting room, was Dad's telly. Here we watched Particular Programmes. If we were going to watch something as a family, then we would have to have finished eating, and we would all have to be in our seats before the show started. When it was over the TV would go off. *The Ascent of Man*, then, became an event. We loved its author, Jacob Bronowski, with his too-big head, his unexpected wit, his sheer delight in what it was that he was saying with that extraordinary, lizard-slow delivery that made everything completely understandable.

The Ascent of Man was to science what *Civilisation* was to art. *America* was the third of the great triad that established a new genre of television programme (Carl Sagan's *Cosmos* being the most famous American version of 'the equivalent of a really important publication by a man who could approach a big subject with authority'[1]) and catapulted BBC television into the American public consciousness, and what's more ushered in great dollops of American money for co-productions, including David Attenborough's own incomparable contributions to the genre. Dad claimed credit for this invention; there is no reason to disbelieve him. He took television seriously as a medium, as serious a medium as print or radio.

We watched a lot of rugby. Dad had played outside half for London Welsh B, and he had stories from the army, of calling for 'Matthew' instead of 'Mark', of having to face real rugby players (among them, the great Haydn Tanner, a

Welsh Guardsman, British Lion and Welsh international, and regarded by those who saw both as a scrum half equal to if not better than Gareth Edwards). In 1974 Dad was invited to be the guest speaker at the Newport Rugby Club centenary dinner. He told me that he had addressed monarchs, heads of state, prime ministers, grandees of every persuasion, even a pope, but none of these occasions had caused such apprehension within him as did the prospect of addressing the members of Newport Rugby Club. This, he explained, was because the room would be full of gods.

The most divine of these entities, during my time certainly, was Gareth Edwards. Edwards was up there in the pantheon of my father's greats, as already listed. I was more a Barry John man. Another Welsh great was Cliff Morgan, who became a senior BBC executive – we would bump into him at the Proms, and one could feel the delight in the two Welshmen as they greeted one another in the great drum of Englishness that is the Royal Albert Hall, Morgan with his enormously wide smile, Dad with his enormous laugh.

Obviously Dad had to watch a lot of television at work, but I do not think that would have made very much difference to his viewing habits at home. He watched TV as people read books. There was nothing promiscuous about it. He would decide to watch a thing, watch it and switch it off. This was how he understood the medium to work – not as a twenty-four-hour companion. I suspect that was true of that entire first generation of TV watchers. Those famous documentary series came out of a desire to give TV the kind of authority that books have. Who knows the most about art, about America, about the rise of science? Find these people and let them make TV programmes with all the seriousness with which they would make books. The books that accompanied these series were just that – companion works. And although TV programmes must always lack the sophistication of books – books are made for individual readers who are in a position to go back over a paragraph, use a dictionary, and so on – television can tell stories just as well as books, and sometimes better, and stories are what give us the world. 'I fantasised this notion that if Freud and Marx had lived and Darwin had lived in the 1950s and 1960s instead of the 1850s and the 1860s that we would have had, as well as books from them, an occasional television series.'[2]

My father was in no doubt himself as to where British television's success, such as it was, came from:

> I believe that British television rests on specific British traditions, and in the first place, that it rests on the literary and dramatic genius of the British people and, secondly, on the sophistication in constitutional matters which you might expect from a country which has been talking itself in and out of trouble, and on the whole succeeding, for a long time.[3]

He made a distinction between entertainment and art.

> Preston Sturges, John Ford, Sam Goldwyn, William Powell, Myrna Loy, Spencer Tracy, Katharine Hepburn, Greta Garbo, these are resounding names and the films they made, or were in, or produced, reverberate in the mind... they were calculated, quite straightforwardly, to provide pleasure... to be inoffensive was not enough, they had positively to please. Nor is positively pleasing a disreputable tradition. It is a bit déclassé at the moment but there are great precedents. French cooking is a precedent, so is Chinese cooking, so are English gardens... and you can see this tradition at work in

some degree in American television... but you cannot see it in Fawlty Towers... whether you like it or not Fawlty Towers [is in] the tradition of British literary and dramatic art... the business of movies is pleasure, the business of literature and drama is... truth.[4]

And was it him or was it me who found in *Whatever Happened to the Likely Lads?* something more than the good though mere entertainment available in *The Dick Van Dyke Show?* Today, despite the current high standing of American television (in particular all those HBO series such as *The Sopranos* and *The Wire*) we can still see the differences if we set, say, *Extras* against *Scrubs* or *The Royle Family* against *Friends*. The former are written, the latter manufactured. It is not a question of better than; they serve different needs.

We were not encouraged to watch commercial television, but I think this was probably my mum rather than my dad at work. She had a sense of loyalty in these matters, and so we grew up never watching *Magpie*, the ITV version of *Blue Peter*. Nanny, however, would have none of that. She was a keen devotee of *Crossroads*. Nor do I remember it ever being suggested that things were inappropriate. Obviously parents have their own ways around these problems, but there were never any strictures on watching, for example, *Monty Python* (many of my sister Sian's friends were not allowed to watch *Python* – she herself was deeply disappointed, after watching it for the first time, to find that not only was it not a circus, but it had no flying in it either). Dad would sit and roar at the TV set. Actually, I say sit, but invariably he slipped down in the chair or on the sofa, until he was lying with his back supported but his bottom as it were suspended, his serious chin on his chest. Whether this was a function of friction-free cushions, chair design or physical temperament, I don't know, although I guess the last may be the most likely, as I find myself frequently adopting a similar position.

On holiday we never watched TV, because there wasn't one. However, on 30 July 1966 we arrived in Criccieth at around 3.45 pm, just in time to catch the second half of England's World Cup victory against West Germany on Dr Prydderch's poorly receiving set. We did not hear Kenneth Wolstenhome saying those famous lines, 'They think it's all over. It is now', because we couldn't pick up the BBC transmission. We watched it on ITV. At least the commentator, Hugh Johns, was Welsh.

Television politics never played much of a part in our lives. At Kew we lived next to Tom Sloane, Head of Light Entertainment, and the only man I ever remember knowing who wore a bowler hat; at Richmond we saw a lot of David Attenborough, who lived around the corner (David, rather exotically, wore braces and suede shoes). He and Dad, I daresay, had a lot to say to one another about the running of the service (in 1967 David was persuaded by Dad to run BBC2 and was responsible for talking Kenneth Clark into doing *Civilisation*, principally by thinking up the brilliant title), but we were much more interested in David's sensational mynah bird or his chameleon climbing with the calm though alert deliberation of a very good private secretary (or perhaps Jacob Bronowski) up and down the curtains. David – like Paul Wright – was also a wonderful pianist, able to translate a hum into a tune at once. He memorably played us The Scaffold's 'Lily the Pink', with fugue-like variations. He would return from his travels with little presents – purses and necklaces – for the girls, greeting each with a 'Hello gorgeous'. He once gave me a beautiful black scorpion pinned inside a Basildon

Bond box. For many years showing it was a party piece, until one day I showed it to a girlfriend, who screamed and sent the box flying and the scorpion was smithereened.

Although at the time much was made of Donald Baverstock's being overlooked for the job that Dad took as Controller of Programmes in the mid-1960s, Baverstock's son Glyn was my mother's godson,* and a properly attended-to one too before his tragic death in 1983. The point I am labouring to make is that television was one of a number of windows on the world. We watched, it must be said, very little pap.

Dad had left *Monitor* in 1963. To begin with he had continued to make programmes with Brian Horrocks (who refused to work with anyone other than 'my old maestro', as Horrocks called Dad in a letter on his retirement years later). Hilary Corke in *The Listener* reported that 'the highlight of a week in which I was sadly prevented from seeing Orson Welles in *Monitor* was Sir Brian Horrocks's last *Men of Action*'. Now Dad moved to become Head of Documentaries. At the same time Donald Baverstock of *Tonight* was made Controller of BBC1, and Michael Peacock of *Panorama*, Controller of BBC2 (not yet transmitting), under the Controller of Programmes, Stuart Hood.

Hugh Carleton Greene had become Director-General in 1960. He has been credited with much of the success the BBC had over the next few years, with turning it from 'Auntie' into

---

* And Enid Blyton's grandson. Oddly enough, while there was nothing we weren't allowed to watch, Enid Blyton's books were not allowed in the house. Whether this was quality control on my mother's part or loyalty to Blyton's daughter, Gillian – who'd had a hard childhood – I don't know. Perhaps a bit of both.

a progressive force. Mary Whitehouse, the puritanical gadfly of the 1960s and '70s, regarded Greene as 'more than anybody else... responsible for the moral collapse in this country.'*[5]

Dad respected Greene but felt that 'the young turks – Donald Baverstock and Michael Peacock and Dick Cawston and Dennis Mitchell and Dennis Vance and Troy Kennedy Martin'[6] – who had joined the Corporation after the war were unlikely to have been reined in anyway. Many were ex-servicemen with a lust for the life they had been deprived of by the six years of the war. 'Hugh Greene was a very good chief executive... but he was lucky in his time. He'd got good people.' These 'good people' replaced an older generation 'that did not take television seriously.'[7] Dad had by now already come to believe that it was not policy that made programmes but programmes that made policy, and it was 'very good programmes that broke their way through. *TW3* had not come about because Hugh Greene said [he] wanted satire.' Another reason given for the rejuvenation of BBC Television was the threat from commercial television, which started up in 1954. *The Times* wrote: '*Tonight* and *Monitor* came into being after the emergence of commercial television, and they have a youthful alertness which marks them off from programmes surviving from the monopolist era.'[8] Again, Dad's view was that it was the Corporation's producers who were responsible: 'people like Dennis Mitchell† and all the rest were not going to be kept down'[9].

One of the documentaries, made in 1964, under Dad's

---

* How she must be laughing in her grave as her eager puritanical successors seek to paint the BBC of the period as a hotbed of licentiousness and depravity.

† Mitchell was a highly regarded documentary maker, known for matching taped dialogue with non-synchronous visuals. He mentored succeeding talents such as Michael Apted and Mike Newell.

auspices, was *Culloden*, Peter Watkins's first film for television, and regarded as both brilliant and controversial.* His next project was to be even more so. Watkins had been handed on to Dad by Allan Tyrer, the film editor at *Monitor*. By most accounts a brilliant and committed film-maker, Watkins had already used questionable techniques – using film of one event as though it were of another (a technique employed also by Jeremy Isaacs in *The World at War*, of which I remember my mother disapproving) – but the results had been outstanding. *Culloden* was violent and expensive and used speaking actors (all amateurs) – something Dad had been loath to allow Ken Russell on *Monitor*. Dad gave Watkins his full support. Grace Wyndham Goldie congratulated him on backing 'a wildly impossible scheme'.[10] Richard Cawston, who succeeded Dad as Head of Documentaries, compared Watkins, who was still in his twenties, to Mozart.

Donald Baverstock† and Mike Peacock (having trouble with BBC2) did not rub along well. Baverstock was also having trouble with Sydney Newman (the Canadian Head of BBC Drama – an exotic creature. He was round and grizzled and had sideburns and wore one of those neck scarves with a ring around it, like a posh toggle – I liked the cut of his jib. He looked like a pirate.). Stuart Hood could not keep the peace, and it was he who left to join ITV, just six weeks before BBC2 was to go live. Hood was replaced by Dad, but only on condition that Peacock and Baverstock switch roles. (Dad wanted, he said, to be 'controller, not referee';[11] Hugh Greene

---

*   '*Culloden*... was quite brilliant and I got a lot of credit for it which I didn't deserve.' HPW to Gillard, BBC WAC R143/133/2.

†   Michael Leapman, in *The Last Days of the Beeb*, described Baverstock's style of leadership as being 'by irritation'.

told him: 'Kenneth [Adam – Director of Television] and I are quite clear that there is a great problem [about what] to do with Donald, and we expect you to solve it.'[12])

Baverstock, in high dudgeon, refused to be moved and resigned, having been o'erleapt by my father. Dad regretted the departure. He liked Baverstock, 'the Orde Wingate of the television service,'* who would have made something of BBC2, 'a place of great adventure'. Baverstock went North. I remember being excited by the fact that the Baverstocks lived on Ilkley Moor; we went to stay with them there. Donald was a hard-drinking South Walian who had retained his accent, and gave the impression of being something of a street-fighter, but actually he was Oxford-educated and did not speak Welsh.

"The one at the back looks like Donald Baverstock!"

Even before *Culloden*, Peter Watkins wanted to make *The War Game*. Dad had been so impressed by *Culloden* that he

---

* Orde Wingate was most famous for creating the Chindits, airborne deep-penetration troops trained to work behind enemy lines in the Far East campaigns against the Japanese during the Second World War.

thought Watkins should be allowed to go ahead. Nevertheless, this was a delicate and expensive subject – the devastation following a nuclear attack on the United Kingdom – and Dad referred upwards, bypassing (with her knowledge) Grace Wyndham Goldie, and going straight to Kenneth Adam, who in turn sent Dad straight to Hugh Greene. The budgetary concerns were one thing, but the more important point was that this was to be a film by a BBC staff member – not a commissioned work from John Osborne or David Mercer or Dennis Potter – and therefore might be taken as a statement by the Corporation. Nevertheless, Dad persuaded Greene to up the budget and proceed with the film.

Dad thought the rough cut was 'terrific'. He was 'very, very pleased'. But there were two things that bothered him. One was an Anglican bishop leaning into the camera and saying, 'We must learn to love the bomb'. Dad said to Gillard, years later: 'I didn't mind, it wasn't that it was insulting, simply fatuous'. In other words Dad didn't think it was believable. In fact he thought it was 'just cock'.

The second thing he disliked was the mercy killing scene in which policemen shoot the dying. Dad thought this equally unbelievable. If you were to have mercy killings, the last people a government would employ was the police. Dad thought this was 'a violation of the truth, truth about ourselves'. He insisted the scene be taken out. Watkins refused. Dad said if the scene came out then he wouldn't have to refer it up to the DG. He only had to refer things 'about which I am doubtful'.

Watkins refused. Up it went, to Greene, to Lord Normanbrook (Chairman of the Board of Governors), to Ministers. The Ministers handed it back to Normanbrook, who eventually decided that the film could not be shown. It was judged 'too horrifying for the medium of broadcasting'.[13]

Dad arranged for *The War Game* to have a cinematic showing at the British Film Institute, albeit to a select audience. The version shown contained the cuts he had recommended. The following year (1966) the film won the Oscar for Best Documentary. The BBC did not air it until 1985. Dad's disdain for the Governors could not have been diminished by this episode. And possibly their questioning of his judgement in it was to colour their debates as to who would become the next Director-General, a few years later. That he had been proven right probably didn't help.

Dad's disdain certainly wasn't dispelled the following year, when he almost resigned over a fuss made about the re-airing of Nell Dunn's play *Up the Junction*. He had not long been the first programme maker to be appointed Controller of Programmes, and my bet is that he wanted to make quite clear to those above him exactly what the borders were for their interference in his decision-making. The original showing of *Up the Junction* had caused controversy, meeting with an outcry from the censorious Mary Whitehouse brigade, 'because,' as Dad put it, 'the girls talked in a raffish fashion, like the title *Up the Junction*, but it didn't appear to me to be a violation of anything. I liked it.'[14] It was included in a selection of the best of *The Wednesday Play* (a slot invented by Sydney Newman, specifically for more 'advanced' contemporary drama), for re-broadcast. Normanbrook made it clear to Greene that the decision to do so should have been referred upwards. Greene passed this on to Dad, in the form of a 'reproof'.

Dad was not an easily reprooven sort of a chap. He spent two days writing a long minute demanding the reproof be withdrawn or he would have to resign. If his judgement in this matter was to be questioned then he had no choice. He sent the minute to Greene and was duly sent for.

Hugh and Huw didn't perhaps like each other. Greene was a Machiavellian news man; Dad was a straight-talking literary man. They talked around and around. Greene regarded it as trifling, Dad the opposite. Loggerheads.

Greene found out that the man between Dad and him in the Corporation's hierarchy – Kenneth Adam – had been away when the decision had been taken to show the repeats. Dad therefore might be said to have referred up to himself. 'Machiavellian nonsense', was Dad's view of this. If he rewrote the minute, Greene would be able to square it with the Governors. Dad 'despised it, at the same time thought that's what makes a powerful political figure'.[15] (I do wonder whether this was something Dad might have lacked as Director-General.) It was at this point that he found out that the Governors had not seen the play at all, and passed the information on. Greene was delighted: 'that makes all the difference'. In the event the play was not shown because the owners of the chocolate factory in which it was largely filmed threatened to sue the Corporation if the film were shown again.

To dwell on these crises is to distract from the extraordinary burgeoning of first class television that the BBC was responsible for in these years. Television Centre itself, completed in June 1960, was by some margin the largest such facility in the world. It might be argued that for a period the doughnut in White City in west London was the cultural hub of the nation, among the most culturally exciting and fertile addresses on Earth.

'All of us expected Wheldon to become DG when Sir Hugh Greene's term ended [in 1969]', wrote Leonard Miall. Politics, however, intruded. In order to rid himself of the troublesome DG Hugh Greene (administratively responsible, among other things, for *That Was The Week That Was*), Harold Wilson appointed Lord Hill, Chairman of ITV, to the Chair at the BBC, to replace Lord Normanbrook, who had died in office. It was a malicious act. Hill, who I suspect Dad regarded as a tad meretricious, had been Postmaster-General at some point, and one way or another had become a life peer, of a broadly conservative sort.* Hill was determined to be an executive Chairman. He therefore did not want too strong a personality as Director-General. In his memoirs he wrote: 'Would a gamble with Wheldon, "the last great actor-manager" as someone had called him, come off! I would have chanced it had there been some signs of support.'[16] He was being, to put it mildly, disingenuous. Choosing Wheldon would have meant sharing the limelight, indeed being quite 'overshadowed', as Bill Cotton, then Head of Light Entertainment, put it, something Hill, whose war service had seen him broadcasting as the BBC's radio doctor, had no intention of doing. 'He made sure Huw was passed over.'[17] Hill chose the intelligent bureaucrat Charles Curran.

Curran wasn't actually such a bad choice, although Robin Day disagreed:

The man who should have been appointed was Huw Wheldon... He had his shortcomings, like talking too much and enjoying being a personality too much. And his interest had always been much more in the arts than in politics. But Wheldon was a real, red-blooded man, not a faceless

---

* I think he thought himself an actual aristocrat. His indiscreet and self-regarding memoirs were not by 'Charles Hill', but by 'Lord Hill of Luton'. When Claus Moser suggested to Dad, after his retirement, that it was time for him to be raised to the peerage Dad replied that 'Lords have to have lands'.

bureaucrat. He was a man whose company was enjoyed by all those, especially politicians, who met him. He had presence, he had flair. He could speak in public. His eloquence was legendary,* as also was his robust good sense. Here is one Wheldon dictum which was loudly applauded by me: 'No real programme was ever made by a committee. You insure yourself against failure by having a committee, but you also insure against triumph.'

Wheldon was a man whom people were proud to look up to and follow. He had a huge sense of humour. He had been presented with his MC by Monty on the field of battle. He could use the language to persuade, to flatter, to cajole, to inspire. He was a leader. The failure to appoint this great broadcaster to be Director General was a major error by the Board of Governors.[18]

I think Mum was outraged, but I'm not sure Dad was that disappointed. I think he was happier being on the high seas, a Nelson rather than a First Lord. Hill was likely not alone in not wanting him as Director-General. It was my mother's view that the Governors were frightened of him, and that is probably the case to some extent. Dad preferred to keep his distance from them. They perhaps reminded him of the 'English half-men' of his war years; certainly he regarded them as ignorant when it came to television. So I think the new arrangement rather suited him: 'I was left extremely separate and untrammelled by Charles Curran... who was intelligent and brave... The qualification was News and Current Affairs. I

---

* 'I don't speak English very well, but I speak Welsh like a motor-bike,' he once declared, proving himself at least half-wrong.

left News and Current Affairs to Charles on the understanding that everything else was mine.'[19]

He missed making TV programmes.

> ... but I made an absolutely definite rule. The Chief Executive must release himself in such a way that the operation can run without him. At the same time he must then exercise a right of entry which is absolute... by virtue of my right of entry anywhere [I] got an enormous excitement and pleasure out of being mixed up with the service, so that I truly did feel like an Admiral with a ship. It did seem to me that this fleet did depend a fair amount on me and I was in a position to influence it and that gave me pleasure.[20]

He had first rate Captains in the form of David Attenborough (at BBC2) and Paul Fox (BBC1). Of the latter Dad said: 'Paul was terrific and he was big and patient and hard-working and elephantine of memory, cheerful, sardonic, loyal. I mean he was a very, very wonderful man.' Of the former: 'his strength was he was really marvellous at everything, he's a first rate human being.' These people liked, respected, and enjoyed each other. And with Joanna Spicer and Michael Checkland planning and accounting, it was a spectacularly talented crew. This is not to mention Humphrey Burton, Aubrey Singer and Bill Cotton, among others.

The 'right of entry' meant that he could pop up anywhere at any time, and he did. Some of his effect might be gleaned from the bumptious memoirs of Brian Blessed, who was playing police officer 'Fancy' Smith in Z Cars. 'His visits to the studios were eagerly awaited and left everyone feeling that they were part of The Team.'[21] Blessed goes on, in a chapter dedicated to Dad, to tell a story about attaching a condom to the penis of

Helios, the statue in the middle of Television Centre, my father holding the ladder by which Blessed gained access to the divine organ. I find it hard to believe, especially as the lovely chap was under the impression that Dad was Director-General in 1964.

Dad's edict was 'to make the good popular, and the popular good', and the titles of the programmes that spewed out of the BBC in these years still have a resonance: *Civilisation, America, Ascent of Man, Chronicle, One Pair of Eyes, Man Alive, Horizon, Dad's Army, Steptoe, Till Death Us Do Part, Search for the Nile, The Six Wives of Henry VIII, Monty Python, Elizabeth R, Take Three Girls, Cathy Come Home, The Two Ronnies, The Old Grey Whistle Test, Z Cars, Dr Who, Softly Softly, Troubleshooters, Dr Finlay*; adaptations of *Sense and Sensibility, Villette, The Tenant of Wildfell Hall, Daniel Deronda, Jude the Obscure, The Spoils of Poynton*, a thirteen part adaptation of Sartre's *The Roads to Freedom*; for children Dumas, *Little Women* and the *Last of the Mohicans* (how I do remember that); there were adaptations of stories by Somerset Maugham, *Play of the Month* featured work by Oscar Wilde, Sheridan, Chekhov, Ibsen, Rattigan and Shaw; *Play for Today* featured plays by Ingmar Bergman and Peter Nichols. Not forgetting Shakespeare.

In December 1970 he devoted an article in the *Sunday Times* almost entirely to a list of very good programmes broadcast by the Corporation that year, in response to a 'Master of a Cambridge college' who had said that 'the public laps up the junk that is offered because it is seldom offered anything less'. 'Let him look', wrote Dad. That Sunday evening, Dad finished, 'there is Christopher Morahan's production of *Uncle Vanya* on BBC1, *The World About Us*, a film about Stokowski, a new comedy series, and the Sartre serial on BBC2. They don't seem to me to be exactly slush or trivia or a mindless grab for the ratings.'

In June 1971 *24 Hours*, a current affairs documentary slot, broadcast a film by David Dimbleby entitled *Yesterday's Men*. It was about the unexpected defeat of the governing Labour Party in the previous year's General Election. It was not really a programme about politics, nor perhaps meant to be. I think it is what used to be called 'human interest'. The *Radio Times* promised viewers that the programme would reveal 'what it's like to be out of office and, in some cases, short of money, prestige, glamour and a chauffeur driven car'.[22] It was particularly interested in Harold Wilson's house-hunting. In the end, it seems that no one would have much noticed it, had it had a different title. Paul Fox said it was 'like making a programme about doctors and calling it *Quack Quack*' (Dad confessed to stealing this crack and making it his own).

Dad was fond of the story of *Yesterday's Men*, but the one he told had little to do with the politics involved or the consequences for the BBC. The story he told at the dinner that marked his retirement as president of the Royal Television Society – told 'in six chapters' – was concerned with the way in which life interferes. The controversies that surrounded the programme are long forgotten, but Dad's story itself bears retelling.

It plays with the facts and concertinas time, and it starts with himself and Charles Curran being called out of a fancy dinner with visiting Americans in order to attend a midnight meeting with Arnold Goodman, the Labour Party's solicitor. Dad's cigarette lighter came in handy as they attempted to find the right address in Cadogan Square. The meeting eventually took place and it was decided that Dad would prepare a press release for the following morning. But the following morning brought unexpected domestic problems at the Wheldon home. Megan (nine years old) had to be taken to hospital for some reason. Mum went with her. Dad had to prepare breakfast for me and Sian. Fine. I went off to school. Sian went off. Dad sat down to write the press release, which he had promised to deliver by 10.00 am. Within minutes Sian returned in floods of tears. She had come across the remains of our cat, Fluff, run over in the street. She had to be comforted but she also had to get to school. Mr Daniels, Dad's driver, came to the rescue. Dad sat down again. Presently he was aware of a little mewing sound. With great difficulty a kitten had made itself up the stairs. Dad phoned the vet. The kittens – there were three – had to be fed or they would die. Did he have a fountain pen? the vet asked. Yes. Well, the best way to feed them would be to fill a fountain pen with milk... At 10.00 am Lord Hill phoned wondering where the press release was. Dad had not written a word. He asked for the secretary to be put on so that he could dictate, and spoke off the cuff. When he had finished, the secretary asked, 'What was the word after "strong"?' Dad had absolutely no idea. The only word he could think of was 'reason'. Hill was listening in. 'Don't think it was "reason" – wasn't it "element"?' 'I do so beg your pardon,' said Dad, 'I can't read my own writing. Yes. "Element".'

Dad actually should have had little to do with *Yesterday's Men*, as politics and news were in the direct control of the DG, but Dad's standing as the BBC's Horatio[*] I suppose required his appearance. One consequence of the fuss was that a 'BBC Programmes Complaints Commission' was set up, though it was rarely to meet.

---

[*] 'Volatile, voluble, and still, 20 years after leaving the land of his fathers, distinctly Welsh, he is easily the least inhibited of the BBC's current crop of mandarins. Inevitably, therefore, it looks as if it will fall to him to make the argument against ITV getting the fourth channel.' (*New Statesman*, November 1971.) And of course they didn't. Channel 4 was born.

The following year, 1972, Dad caught pneumonia following a hot bath in his friend psychiatrist Tom Main's garden. What I remember about this was that it struck him while he was on a train to Manchester, sharing a compartment with Lord Longford. Dad didn't have much time for Longford, whom he regarded as a sanctimonious fusspot, and I can quite easily imagine Dad's fury at having to put up with his Lordship's well-meaning ministrations. Hitherto, over the last twelve years, he had taken five days off sick. I cannot imagine what they could have been for: Dad didn't really believe in illness. In order to get off school we children had to have a fairly serious temperature. On one occasion Sian, away on a cycling trip on the South Downs, phoned home to say she had had an accident and that the bicycle was a write-off. Dad's response to the news was 'terrific'. Morale was important, whether it was a company of soldiers, a corporation employing tens of thousands or a daughter.

In 1974 the Home Secretary, Roy Jenkins, announced that a committee was going to be set up to look into the future of broadcasting, under the chairmanship of Noel Annan (Norman Podhoretz's supervisor at Cambridge in the 1950s). It eventually reported in 1977. Dad wasn't impressed: 'I didn't quite trust the Annan Committee. I felt that Annan himself was a bit lightweight.'[23] And it is true that the members of the committee, with the exception of Tony Jay, were not broadcasters; nor were there any academic social scientists involved. It was Dad's feeling that the committee simply recorded opinion. Still, it made recommendations, two of which came to pass: an increase in the licence fee, and the birth of Channel 4. The latter began with much brio and panache and independent spirit, and has been allowed to run into mediocrity. The former was absolutely vital. By the time

Dad retired the BBC was seriously underfunded, despite the excellence of its programming.

'Huw Wheldon was clearly going to be prevented by age from achieving the Director-generalship he would have filled with such distinction... Following [him] was daunting. As one might expect of a man of such large and exuberant personality, Huw's style of leadership tended towards the flamboyant and inspirational.'[24] So wrote another quiet, intelligent man, Ian Trethowan, who succeeded Charles Curran, Dad having had to take compulsory retirement in 1975.

Dad wasn't really a manager. In a 1968 interview he described himself not as a 'planner' but as an 'Editor-in-chief'.* What he truly was, was *codwr canu*, a lifter of the song. 'It seemed to me that part of my business was constantly to teach people within the BBC about the BBC.' He told them stories – Churchill on Reith, that 'wuthering height', David Attenborough eating horses in South America (not actually, of course, but for the Accounts Department's benefit), Gilbert Harding responding to a question on the American visa form, 'Do you intend to undermine the constitution of the United States?', with the unarguable 'sole purpose of visit'. And in public and abroad he spoke up for the BBC as one of the great institutions of the Western world, and of the licence fee as an invention that allowed the Corporation to avoid, as best it could, the lures of both pap and propaganda. 'I wished to stand for the idea that the BBC could spread over a gigantic range and do well across the whole range.' Dad hated, saw no point in, 'doing things down'. And the BBC did do things well. It still does.

---

* 'The only person I'm afraid of is my accountant, Mr Kirshen.'

These years were the years of my childhood. I went to Colet Court, the prep school for St Paul's, where a second-rate teacher named Payne-Payne once told me that 'just because your parents wipe their arses with five pound notes doesn't mean to say that you can't do your French homework.' I didn't excel, and got into trouble for playing truant. The local policeman found me one day sitting on a low wall in the rain, near the potter Ruth Duckworth's studio in Kew. I claimed to be waiting for a friend and that we were going to go to Chessington Zoo together. PC Webb, a kindly man, suggested I return home, which I did, bursting into tears as I came through the front door and dashing upstairs to my bedroom. I think Mum and Dad had just got back from a trip to America. I have a vague memory of suitcases. The reason for my not going to school was two-fold: I hated swimming, and I hadn't done my maths. The swimming, I think, was understandable. Poor swimmers had to wear green trunks. Boys who could hardly swim at all were not permitted to wear trunks at all. My father's attitude to all this (the truancy rather than the nudity, which I never mentioned) was – well, I don't actually remember him having one. The headmaster was very cross. I don't remember Dad being cross at all.

What made him cross was his children making a noise when they should be in bed – his particular tread on the last flight of stairs was unmistakable. 'What the hell is this?' was his usual question, brandished like a whip, to which there was never any answer and obviously not requiring one. I may occasionally have tried a muted, muttered, pointless 'nothing'. And he never liked us being 'casual'. That was pretty much the worst thing you could be.

I recall two occasions of completely unjustified wrath: I once took a teabag out of my mug and put it into his. I had honestly thought that this might be a good way of making the tea a little stronger. He was extremely angry.

And then he got very cross with me for pronouncing Marseilles in the French manner, instead of as he thought it ought to be pronounced – Mar-sails. He thought me pretentious. But I had never heard Marseilles pronounced Mar-sails, not ever. I might perhaps have convinced him that I was right, but I was too astonished to speak, and I would have had to work very hard. 'You don't pronounce Paris "Paree", do you?' And no, we don't.

We went almost every summer of those years to Criccieth on the southern coast of the Llyn peninsula in North Wales. We looked out on Cardigan Bay from the window of the first floor flat at number 10 or 11 Marine Terrace, which Dad took for a month or so when we weren't staying at the Neptune Guest House. We went on holiday abroad once, in 1970. We loaded up the Mini – the gear on the roof doubled the height of the car – and set off. We went to Concarneau, where we would watch enormous tuna fish being unloaded from deeply unromantic fishing boats, and where I read my first Dickens, *David Copperfield*, and found an air-pistol. Sian woke on her tenth birthday and declared at breakfast that she was going to stop sucking her thumb. 'Why?' asked Dad, which discombobulated her.

It rained often in Wales, and then we might go for a walk along the so-called cliff path. There wasn't really a cliff at all; it was a narrow sandy track through blackberry briars, past fields in which sea scouts used to camp, down to a part of the beach where people didn't much go unless they wanted to gather driftwood and start a fire. We sizzled the odd sausage down there over the years.

In 1974 we went to Aspen, Colorado, all paid for by the

Aspen Institute for Humanistic Studies, of which Dad later became a Senior Fellow. I shook hands there with Lionel Trilling and Isaac Stern, with no real grasp of their standing. Trilling was dapper and Stern sweated (and unlike Stephen Spender's, with whom I shook hands once at the Proms, their grips were firm). I enjoyed Aspen, was told I sounded like Mick Jagger, got thrown off a horse.

But Wales was the home away from home. We climbed mountains, saw cousins, spent time with the Jonah Joneses, and built sandcastles.

Excellent work

CHAPTER 10

BUILDING A SANDCASTLE

It is a fine day, around the 70-degree mark. Marine Terrace, Criccieth, basks in the sun, which has risen from behind the great mound on which the castle sits, one of the oldest castles in Wales, a Welsh castle, indeed, not an English one. There is an anachronistic cannon up there, in the barrel of which Nanny, Mum's mum, likes to hide Opal Fruits or Milky Ways or Spangles for us to discover magically. Sheep graze on the hillside, impossibly retaining their balance on the steep lower slopes. *The mountain sheep are sweeter, / But the valley sheep are fatter; / We therefore deemed it meeter /*

To carry off the latter. As the old rhyme do zay (as the old Dad do zay most often).[*]

We are going today to Borth y Gest, or to Porth Neigwl – let's say the latter. We load up the Mini and drive out of Criccieth, westwards, through Llanystumdwy, where Lloyd George came from and returned to, through the tiny tight houses of Pwllheli, past Pontin's (or is it Butlin's?) and on out towards Aberdaron, where RS Thomas resides, howling white-haired against the sins of the world (or so I imagined once I had reached poet-knowing age). We park at the top of the cliff, at the bottom of Mynydd Rhiw, a long hump that stretches out to sea and into land, and on which my cousins' whitewashed *bwthyn* sits. It is a one up one down. The up is up a stepladder. It is cosy as hell. We never get to go there enough. Years later I will borrow the *bwthyn* for a long weekend, and write poems and a story. I will also entertain two Wolverhampton lads who have given me a lift there. They have come with tents and canoes and surfboards and cocaine and marijuana. Porth Neigwl – Hell's Mouth to the English tourists – is a surfer's paradise. We snort, we smoke, and I cook them a modest meal, and we drink cider and we laugh and they disappear into the night and I don't see them again. That is all in the future, though. Today we are on the beach. It's, say, August 1968. There are Soviet tanks in Prague. Leonard Cohen is being recorded for a BBC special.

To get to the beach we have to navigate a long zig-zagging path that clings to the side of the sandy cliff like ropey beading. We children take it at almost breakneck speed, going down and coming up like excited puppies. We carry buckets and

---

[*] Not an old rhyme at all actually, but the opening lines of Thomas Love Peacock's 'War Song of Dinas Vawr'.

spades. Dad appears to be carrying everything else. 'Clobber', he calls it. Mum is bringing up the rear (Nanny doesn't leave Criccieth). There may still be an au pair in tow – kind Linda (English) or lovely Meta (Danish) perhaps.

Porth Neigwl is as yet uncolonised by tourists or surfers. There is hardly anyone on this enormous beach. We are at the north west end. It bows away from us to the south, perhaps a mile (though to this ten year old it is a thousand miles) of uninterrupted sand. At the joint where the beach meets the cliff it is stonier and mucky with the detritus of the ocean. But we have no care for that. We are here for two things: to get knocked flat by enormous waves and to build a sandcastle. Mum will smoke cigarettes and read her book. It will probably be by Henry James.

First things first: the greasy kids' stuff – the suntan lotion. That is what we call it but it is made quite clear to us by Dad that its chief purpose is to stop us frying. He rubs it on us, one at a time. Somehow he has already managed to get his hands thoroughly gritty, and the experience is akin to having one's skin rubbed with light sandpaper. We are all of us thoroughly scrubbed with Nivea. Dad never puts the stuff on, and never burns. Mum puts lots on and always burns, painfully.

Sian (eight) and Meg (five) head straight for the waves. They have to swim every day on holiday. It becomes, over the years, a family tradition. They – and Dad – have to swim every day, come rain or shine. I – I take after my mother – do not have to partake in this particular rite. I have probably been so sour-faced about the whole business that my father has no interest in forcing me. Years later my mother tells me that she put my fear of the water down to my father's invariable method of plunging into 'the icy brine'. He employs it today. He strides backwards into the oncoming breakers, then turns and dives into an approaching wave. When very young I attempted to emulate this approach and suffered terribly for my devotion. There is, though, another reason why he might not feel like bullying me into the water. He had, after all, once tried to save a man from drowning, and had almost drowned himself. He knows the dangers of water, and he knows the fear it can instil. He probably won't make the connection (too like cod psychology) between that incident and his unwillingness to insist on my swimming, but it is not impossible that it exists.

On this occasion I am going to follow my sisters in. It is warm and the waves look fun. I am wearing my seriously cool trunks with the badges sewn on. The badges represent five castles: Criccieth, Caernarfon, Harlech, Conway, Beaumaris. The waves are long and strong and perfect for struggling against. We scream as we jump into them.

After we have finished and had a little jog along the beach to get ourselves dry it is time to build the sandcastle.

It begins with Dad scoring the lines of the preliminary dig in the perfectly consistent surface. That done, he slices into the sand with tremendous deliberation, and brings forth a neat rectangle which he equally deliberately places into the middle of the circle. And so it goes. I begin to help. The girls begin to help. Slowly the mound inside the circle rises. It isn't small, but it is not immoderate either. Years later, on a beach in Sussex I witness a man with an industrial-sized shovel almost shoulder deep in the sand, and reflect that Dad would never have considered undertaking such a thing. His final judgement, however, would have depended probably on the character of the man.

Time now alters. Or there is no time, there is now only the inexorable rising of the tide. That is how we will measure out our life over the next hour or so. We must build the castle and we must prepare to defend it. We begin the business of towers. Dad fills the buckets and then levels them off with his spade, with the scrape and slash of a bricklayer, and with a single hand from a considerable height – utilising gravity and assuring vertical integrity – plonks them down on their allotted spots. By now Mum has got up from her book and is bringing back odd bits of beachcombery with which to decorate various parts of the castle. Sian and Meg are returning with beautiful pebbles. Everything is offered and examined and passed by Dad. 'Excellent work – first rate.'

Now Dad has begun to refine the structure. Ill-looking walls are levelled and patted. And now he is using his hands. A profoundly impractical man – he cannot change a light bulb – he has a delicate, deliberate touch, fine hands. Fashioning an arch in the sand is anything but clawing, the opposite of clawing. He seems to get true sensuous pleasure in his excavating. He writes in the same way, as though the action gives him direct pleasure, always with the stub of a soft pencil, but held high up. When he writes it looks as though he is writing slowly. He seems to enjoy the physical sensation of what he is doing (he is an envelope user, or, when presented with a pad of paper, horribly promiscuous – sheets and sheets of writing surrounded in whiteness: the instinct of the poet).

The whole Wheldon family is whirring; and in comes the tide, slowly but surely. And now Dad and I have left the castle to be bedecked by the women folk and we are working like crazy designing 'waterworks' to divert the unstoppable ocean away from our magnificent construction. We dig deep trenches and put up massive walls. To no avail, of course, because dig as we might, shore up as best we can (and we do not stop until absolutely the last minute), the enemy is too dark, too wasteful, too wild. We stand and watch as the great walls dissolve, wave after wave, into a smooth nothingness, and the little decorative pebbles and shells resume their long-term plan to become sand. I love watching the demolition, the morphing of something laboured over into utter flatness. Suddenly there is nothing left. It is like a very good meal.

And so it is done. Dust to dust. The possibilities that lay within the sand have been realised and returned, a job has been done wholly and savoured. We have done our best, and what more can we ask of ourselves. It is time to rest. Or swim. And then it is time to go home.

New knight: Sir Huw with Mr Daniels*

CHAPTER 11

1976–1985: GREAT AND GOOD

Dad was elected Chairman of the Court of Governors of the London School of Economics in June 1975, and presided over the school as it settled down after the excitements of the 1960s. Relations with alumni were strengthened, and funds for the new library were successfully raised, new research centres established, and fundraising initiatives started. There were, as always, cuts in government expenditure. One academic described Dad's manner in meetings as 'conviviality with purpose'. Ralf Dahrendorf, Director of the School between

---

* It was a hoot going to the Palace. Dad was only allowed two guests, in addition to Mum, so we had to smuggle Megan in under some coats on the back seat.

1974 and 1984, described how his Chairman appealed for funds: "'Make no mistake," he would say to the head of a foundation or company, "what we are here for is one thing only, and that is, cash!'" Dad was nothing if not conscientious:

> I have to attend a lecture here [LSE] by Norman MacKenzie and then another one in a dinner jacket (at 8.00 pm) at the Savoy. This is what is known as Gluttony for Learning.[1]

In the early 1980s there was a BBC TV series entitled something like *Great Walks*, in which well-known people strolled their favourite walks in the company of a film crew. The producers approached Dad. He knew what they expected, which was much the same thing as what they wanted: they wanted him to describe the ascent of Cader Idris or the walk from Blaenau Ffestiniog to Croesor. But these were not his favourite walks. His favourite walk was from the London School of Economics to the Garrick Club (of which he was an enthusiastic member), from Portugal Street to Garrick Street. Actually it would have made a very good TV walk – the Aldwych, Fleet Street in spitting distance, with the Inns of Court, St Clement Danes, Bush House, Drury Lane, the Royal Opera House, Covent Garden market, Moss Bros, or perhaps by way of the Courtauld Institute and the Strand, or up Wellington Street, past the Lyceum. My father liked being in the city, in the midst of these great institutions. But it is less than a mile, this stroll, and possibly he felt the producers would think him facetious if he suggested it as a Great Walk. He declined the invitation.

Not that he didn't like proper striding, too, whether on a beach, up a mountain, on a golf course, along a terrace, in a park or through a gardens. He was not, however, a hiker, not as I knew him. I expect he would have regarded that as a little immoderate. He didn't buy special boots or heave heavy haversacks. He did it in a modest way. When he and I went up a mountain – let's say Cnicht (I think the English tourists in North Wales call it 'The Giant's Tooth') – he would take a small rucksack and put in it two apples, a pork pie and a bar of Bournville chocolate. He would have a map, though he liked to tell me how he had once led his battalion in entirely the wrong direction in Normandy.

Having said all that, he did, before the war, when he was about eighteen, walk alone from Munich to Venice. I believe it took him about ten days.

So it wasn't at all the case that he was against mountains.

It took me some time to recognise my father's interest in animal life. He may not have known it himself. His interest was not of a scientific kind; he was not curious about them in David Attenborough's way. I think, rather, that he was *taken* with them. They delighted him. His letters like to record the spotting of animals: 'Saw an owl.' He liked to relate the story of a live *Blue Peter* transmission in which a bird of prey and a mouse were presented as the best of friends, only for the viewing public to watch the bird majestically stretch out its 'crooked hand', grab the tiny mouse and eat it.

At Kew we had fed hedgehogs, but nothing had prepared us for the delight and tragedy of the chipmunks.

These had been recommended to us as a pet by David Attenborough. Uncle Harry – strictly speaking, my mother's uncle Harry, a craftsman in wood – built a large outdoor cage, and Sian's birthday present (perhaps eighth or ninth?), a pair of chipmunks, Muscadin (male) and Tammeus (female), were installed. Soon Tammeus was pregnant, and many were the children she gave birth to, apparently all male. One by one, as in some ghastly Greek tragedy, their father saw them off. Tammeus would sit in maternal plump stillness while havoc was wreaked around her. Sometimes quiet reigned. Dad liked to feed the chipmunks with Brussels sprouts, which they would peel in the belief that there was a kernel worth the eating within. No such luck. This is the only very remotely cruel thing I ever saw my father do. And they were not underfed. Eventually just the two remained, Muscadin with one eye, and scars all over him, like a long-serving pirate. I think David eventually removed them to Chessington, when that was still a proper zoo.

It is one of the sadnesses of my life that I did not go out running more often with my father. He asked me every time he went. I always found an excuse. Sometimes he would be markedly disappointed, sometimes cross that I never did any exercise, and sometimes he wouldn't mind in the least. He very much enjoyed this running (never 'jogging'), and he became very fond of Richmond Park. Characteristically, he got to know its history, to understand its governance, and to know who was and who was not allowed to forage for kindling and so on. He learned to recognise the trees, something he'd been meaning to do for a long time: 'I wish I had some book, in lieu of a knowledgeable companion, which could tell me what flowers were what and which architecture which and the names of cow-breeds – my place as 2iC B Coy means marching stolidly in the rear of the Coy, & day after day I am appalled and grief-stricken at my ignorance of these simplicities.'[2] He continued to be appalled and grief-stricken at his ignorance of the natural world. So in Richmond Park he made sure he knew what trees he was running under. He was particularly fond of hornbeams, but even fonder, I think, of knowing that they were hornbeams.

Here is Sian, my sister, on Dad, trees and illness:

Dad was hardly ever ill. On the extremely rare occasions when he was (I think I can only really remember one) he was a cheerful patient, relishing his time in bed and looking forward to trays of unexpected snacks and cups of tea. Pleased with the view from the bedroom window, pleased not to be allowed to do anything but read and listen to music.

But, when he had a major operation in 1976 to remove a cancer and quite a lot of his insides, he had to convalesce and take it easy for several weeks. This he did not relish to begin with (he was in the middle of filming Royal Heritage). He was sent to Osborne House on the Isle of Wight, where, actually, he was able to do some reading and research. Osborne, House and Grounds, was designed by Prince Albert, as a summer palace. Albert had a real knowledge of woodland and forestry, which Osborne gave him the opportunity to exercise. It seems likely that this contributed to Dad's decision to learn about trees during his enforced physical inactivity. I think that he had always liked trees but was unable to identify those beyond the common few. He admired Brian Murphy's wide easy knowledge of them. He sometimes remarked on his own lack of knowledge of the natural world, 'Goddammit why don't I know what those trees are?' He borrowed several books from the library in Osborne. For some time after his illness, tree books made a good birthday or Christmas present – something other than a box of 3 golf balls or sandalwood soap (both of which he was, however, always delighted with).

Dad learned about Britain's trees; where they came from;

where they grow; how they grow; the texture and pattern of their barks and the shape and nature of their leaves; the reasons for their planting, their uses, ornamental or practical. He was tremendously pleased by one particular writer, whose name escapes me, who referred to all ornamental maples as 'fancy trees' and Dad liked walking through a little glade in the Terrace Gardens, which was made up entirely of 'fancy trees', and passing this on to whoever he was walking with.

The short stretch of road from the Terrace to Richmond Park, past the Wick, was lined, as many London streets are, with London planes with their dappled scaly layered bark. He was enormously impressed by them, pleased that they actually thrived on pollution, that they were called London planes because the smoggy soot-filled air of Victorian London had made them the perfect big grand trees to line the city's streets, taking in the blackness and giving out oxygen. Also along the Terrace there were huge elms that were sadly killed off by Dutch Elm Disease, and he missed them when they were all cut down. I remember the seriousness and sadness with which he spoke of their disappearance from the landscape. He would be saddened now by the loss of so many ash trees.

After he came home from Osborne, he spent many Sunday walks in Richmond Park, or along the Thames towards Ham House or Kew Gardens, and sometimes in the Gardens themselves identifying individual trees and getting to know favourites. He was keen on many of them, hornbeams with their gnarled latticework trunks; Holm, or Jacob's Oak: an American evergreen variety – huge dense trees, dark-barked with thick deep green polished leaves; the two 'Redeyes' or red-candled Horse Chestnuts (smaller than their white-candled cousins) on the Terrace, as well as the Indian conkers growing there; of course the 'blasted' or lightning-struck oaks in Richmond Park, hardy survivors, growing on in gnarled forms after being struck down (oaks are often struck by lightning because of their immense height). Sweet chestnuts with their auburn swirling grained trunks and the huge smooth grey elephant legged beeches, small knotty hawthorns and blackthorns, the 'Locust Tree' (honey and locusts in the Bible) or False Acacia which grew at the end of our garden and which Megan did a school project on. He liked all those names – Jacob, Hornbeam, redeye, locust.

He would often spring a tree question during a walk and I would quite often get the answer right, which gave me great pleasure as I almost invariably got any classical music questions which came my way wrong. I can only have known from what he had told me, as I certainly did no independent tree study.

During his final illness I remember him telling me that while he, of course, gazed out over the glimmering Thames, he also could watch for a surprisingly long time two tall trees at the back of the house a few gardens away. They were pines of some sort, towering over smaller garden trees. They were growing right next to each other and might even have been joined at their base. They were, however, very distinctly two trees with two trunks, one slightly taller than the other. He liked the way they blew away from one another and then came back to lean their heads in together. He said that he felt that it was like watching a conversation, a marriage.

Bertrand Russell grew up at Petersham Lodge in Richmond Park, and suffered a childhood confusion wherein the future philosopher thought the aunts who brought him up were referring to the distant hills as 'the ups and downs' when in fact they were saying 'the Epsom Downs'. Dad was tickled by these sorts of detail.

He was proprietorial about the Terrace that runs along the top of Richmond Hill. He would explain to visitors that actually it was his and that he allowed people to use it without their even knowing that they were walking on private property.

He liked small things. He invariably wrote with very small soft pencils. He kept lots of little boxes. During the filming of *Royal Heritage*, he was quite enchanted by Queen Mary's Dolls' House, in which everything, on the insistence of its designer, Sir Edwin Lutyens, worked, including the lifts.

He liked the little streams that run through the Isabella Plantation in Richmond Park. The Isabella was something of a secret in those days (the 1970s); its spring and early summer glories were known only to a few. It was, I believe, instituted as a wildlife sanctuary. From outside it looked neglected, private. Inside was a paradise of azaleas and rhododendrons, all fed by rills and ponds. We walked out there one day with the American statesman Daniel Patrick Moynihan.[*] Moynihan's wife Elizabeth was an expert on gardens (while her husband had been US Ambassador to India, she had written a book on the gardens of the country, *Paradise as a Garden: In Persia and Mughal India*). Dad was no expert but he did love the Isabella Plantation. It is an unexpectedly

---

[*] Daniel Patrick Moynihan, a lifelong Democrat, was one of the big beasts of American politics. He pulled no punches as US Ambassador to the UN, and served as Senator for New York with great distinction.

beautiful place, and it is characteristic that Dad both loved it and thought of taking Moynihan out to inspect it. Moynihan was a big, florid man, and he wore a distinctive hat, a sort of huntsman's narrow brimmed tweed fedora with a feather. The two men enjoyed high banter. We children all thought Pat was a thoroughly Good Thing, as indeed he was. Dad liked the fact that the Isabella Plantation looked neglected, but this was not because he was jealous of its charms and wanted to avoid the hoi polloi. I think it was because he was attracted by the modesty and a kind of concomitant earnestness of the undertaking. At Kew Gardens, where he was on the Board, he argued for retaining a very low entrance fee on the grounds that the Royal Botanic Gardens was a scientific institution, first and foremost, and that if people were asked to pay more they would be entitled to expect more, and energy and focus would be shifted away from the science and on to the visitors. It is now very expensive to get into Kew, but once inside there is a wide variety of cafeterias and shops where you can spend still more money.

Dad liked a bit of weather. He and I were once surprised by fog at the top of the Glyders (I forget whether *fach* or *fawr*), peaks that face Snowdon across the Llanberis Pass. It is a very desolate place, a moonscape of splintered rocks, and the silence and claustrophobia that fog brings made it weirder still. We found a bit of shelter and finished the Bournville. I don't recall being at all anxious. This is almost certainly because Dad would have expressed our plight as being 'rather good'. He was very much of the opinion that all experience was good for you, as long as it didn't actually kill or disable you.

In the chapter on Dad in *The Gallipoli Diary*, trying to capture the mood and substance of his conversation, Jonah Jones wrote:

Once we all climbed Manod Mawr near Ffestiniog. It began to rain stair-rods and we descended in a hurry, soaked to the skin, crowded like sardines into the Mini and in no time the little car was steaming like a laundry and smelling worse. 'Frightfully foetid in here, don't you think,' said Huw, 'in fact, a quite considerable fet.' A fet henceforth entered the family vocabulary.[3]

I remember it well. It got to a point when we were so wet that trying to keep dry ceased to have purpose. Dad thoroughly enjoyed the drama of the thing. He taught me to relax my limbs, accept that I was soaking, and enjoy the experience. He took Mum up mountains. 'Body off the rock!' he'd advise. Or he'd encourage: 'Green fields ahead!' I think Mum enjoyed being bullied by Dad. This was maybe not because she liked keeping her body off the rock or coming upon green (well, greenish) fields, but because she loved him. I'm not entirely sure she liked mountains, except that she was curious about everything.

Of golf Mark Twain (or perhaps Bernard Shaw) declared: 'A good walk ruined.' Dad liked to speak of 'playing exceedingly bad golf with exceedingly good chaps', and the Royal Mid-Surrey in Richmond was one more institution that he loved. He enjoyed losing to 'friends with missing limbs' such as the one-armed television critic Peter Black (who was later to write that 'Huw Wheldon... was perhaps the finest man I ever knew') and Jacky Droogleever. And I loved going to the Royal Mid-Surrey too. I liked the smell of the changing rooms. It wasn't pungent with Algipan as a rugby changing room is, but rather of soil, of leather, of wood, of metal, all seasoned with a cocktail of Imperial Leather, other man-soaps and discreet aftershaves. I liked the way the men bantered with each other, and how the banter echoed around the wooden-lockered rooms. I liked Dad's locker. I liked it having bits and pieces in it. At home, Dad's dressing room was a rare extravagance but one he absolutely adored – most people would have turned the room into an en suite bathroom: there was a bidet and a sink, a wardrobe and a chest of drawers; it was dark and smelled of lavender and sandalwood (Sian made bags of lavender for him to store among his clothes – 'he always smelled nice,' she says) and it was serious and leathery, a place of mystery, full of his boxes and miniature drawers, and, well, *things*. We didn't go there unless bidden. It was Dad's sort of *sanctum sanctorum*. There is a lot to be said for having such a place.*

Although I liked the golf club, I only really liked it when I was with Dad. He knew everyone, and everyone always was glad to see him. I became a junior member, but I was not clubbable, and what is more I was soon losing to – and not driving as far as – children shorter and younger than me, which is a hopeless situation for a twelve year old. What is more, lacking my father's thoroughly egalitarian soul, I didn't much like the junior members. They seemed a bit flash to me, a bit vulgar. They were too sure of themselves and I suspected that they had more money than I did. They certainly had flashier clubs and golf gear. Dad himself used to wear a moth-eaten blue sweater and a pair of nondescript grey trousers. What I best recall him wielding a club in was waterproofs.

Although I liked the RMS as a course, I loved Criccieth. Criccieth golf course is on a hill above the town. It is spotted with sheep and their pellet-like droppings. The final hole (it is a nine-hole course) started at the top of a steep escarpment,

---

* Before moving to Richmond Dad had seethed with envy of Uncle Dai's dressing room at Abercothi House, even being somewhat scathing.

and ended at the bottom. The distance to the hole was, I think, around 96 yards. I very nearly scored a hole in one. Succeeding must have been fairly common, but I can still see that ball not quite dropping. After we had finished there was a utilitarian club house where I would have half a bitter shandy and listen to Dad speaking Welsh with the locals.

Golf was important to my father because it let him into the society of those not involved in the world of television and all the worlds that television touches. Occasionally he played with colleagues, such as Alasdair Milne ('hits the ball incredibly hard in the wrong direction'), but I think what he truly liked was the company of men, as he had enjoyed it in the army. With Uncle Dai, with whom he had competed – and lost – at reading during the invasion of Europe (*Moby Dick* was preceded by Gibbon), he had ferociously competitive games. They loved beating each other. Funnily enough, the only scorecard I have records them both as having taken 84 shots, at Carmarthen, which isn't at all bad. And his most treasured award, with the exception perhaps of his *Monty Python* Huw Wheldon Award for Being the Best Huw Wheldon, was a trophy he won at Gleneagles, while taking part in a BBC Club golf tournament. He really was very proud of that. He also once beat James Bond: Sean Connery, another big-hitting, multi-directional Scotsman.

Golf remains a remarkably courteous, if crusty, sport. One Sunday morning, on the first green on the ladies' course, I missed a relatively easy putt and walked away, muttering. My back was turned to the green, and to Dad, who was putting. Before doing so he took note of me not taking note of him, and he admonished me: 'You'd never see Nicklaus doing that.' Manners maketh man. A final word on golf (and walking): he never used a trolley. Golf was a form of walking and walking was an exercise for the building up of moral fibre. Trolleys were a drain on moral fibre. (I worry here that this might be taken too literally. My father's mode was gently ironic. He meant what he said, but he liked to overstate it. He found all sorts of things inexplicably amusing. As I have said before, people who did not know him occasionally thought he was drunk. I have the same difficulty: my children's friends suspect me of dipsomaniacal tendencies. So, yes, walking was good for the moral fibre – as it indeed is, isn't it? – but then many things were good for the moral fibre: waking up early to go to the airport, taking the cat to the vet, eating spaghetti with butter because he had burnt the bolognaise...)

One last story about Dad that I think illustrates many sides of his character. My sister Sian again:

It was Mum's birthday morning, I was about twelve or thirteen, and I had forgotten to get Mum a present. Dad was furious with me with a towering and terrifying anger; selfishness and thoughtlessness were apt to make him especially cross and I can remember other times when they did. He banished me to school and told me to make Mum a card.

At some point, in the middle of an interminable lesson, during a long and unhappy school morning, something unexpected and unheard of happened; I was summonsed to the bursar's office for a phone call. Dad was on the phone, cheerful now, sorry for his temper and with a plan. I was to meet Mr Daniels, his driver, outside the school gates at 12.15. Mr Daniels would drive me somewhere and on the way we would stop and buy some flowers.

So at 12.15 I went to the school gates where Mr Daniels was waiting, rosy and beaming. I got into the smart black BBC car and we whizzed off. Armed by now with a bunch of flowers and a card I got out of the car at what turned out to be Bentley's oyster bar in Swallow Street, just off Piccadilly. I walked into the darkness and was directed towards the polish and gleam of the bar, and there were Mum and Dad. Dad was beaming and Mum was speechless and overcome. She told me she had been delighted to find herself at Bentley's on a weekday lunchtime, but intensely irritated when told by Dad that he had invited a special guest. She didn't want anyone else to join them. Dad told her that she would be pleased when the guest arrived. She flatly refused to believe him, and remained put out until I walked through the door. Her surprise and pleasure were real and visible and absolutely equal to mine. We all ate oysters (I for the first time) and had an extremely memorable and cheerful lunch; it might have been the only time that I ever went out with both Mum and Dad on my own. Mr Daniels then whizzed me back to school, where I spent a pleasingly short afternoon, day-dreamy and forgiven.

A few days afterwards Dad took great pleasure in telling me about the outrage expressed in a letter from the headmistress about my leaving the school premises without prior arrangement, and the swift effectiveness with which he had responded. I don't remember what that response was, but I have heard that one of his favourite pieces of advice (not for his offspring's ears, of course) was: 'Don't ask permission. Ask forgiveness.'[4]

Here then is the furious temper, and its characteristic

reasons. He used to like to say that he was 'well known for my tremendous insensitivity', but he wasn't at all insensitive: when he was critical it was because he had listened. Here is his trust in his lieutenant Mr Daniels and his slight contempt and impatience with the arbitrary authority of school; here is a plan well worked out, the coup de grâce perfected; here is total forgiveness and reparation; here is flair; and here is the delight in his own delight and the delight in the delight of those he loved.

Dad never gave the impression that he missed the BBC, but he must have done. There was a compulsory retirement age of sixty, and he stood down accordingly, remaining in an advisory role for a while. He conducted a review of the regions. It was in that period probably that he was given the manuscript of Alan Bleasdale's *Boys from the Blackstuff* (or possibly the original *Play for Today*, *The Black Stuff*) to read. BBC managers wanted his advice. For its time its language was rough, it was full of contention and anger. The broadcasters were nervous. Dad was tremendously taken by it. I recall sitting on the arm of the sofa as he enthused about 'real writing'. I was later to meet Bleasdale, for whose series *GBH* my wife made the title sequence. He was a man fully himself, a force, nothing sham or sanctimonious about him; Dad would have recognised him at once as 'big'.

'Real writing' is hard to find. I have myself read scores of proposed film scripts over the years and very few have the tang of truth about them. Occasionally they are well crafted, and likely to please, and perhaps that is all one should ask a film to do, but British cinema has always occupied a curious place in between the giving of pleasure and the discovering of truth. Shakespeare lurks.

On leaving the Corporation, Dad started work on *Royal Heritage*, a ten hour history of Britain, told through the artefacts of the Royal Collection and produced by the stupendous Michael Gill of *Civilisation* and *America* fame. It was a kind of history of Britain in a thousand objects, ranging from castles and effigies and barges to sculptures and paintings and dolls' houses. It was co-written with JH ('Jack') Plumb, a man unlike Dad in very many respects. Plumb was small, neat, plumpish, precise, academic and greedy.* He very much liked the good things in life; he 'kept a fine table', as they say. I suspect Plumb, Master of Christ's College, Cambridge, initially distrusted a man he probably saw as a vulgar populariser. They argued and hit it off, bringing two different kinds of expertise together in a winning compromise.

This wasn't quite the case with the Duke of Edinburgh. The Duke was under the impression that making television was a straightforward business, always an assumption that infuriated Dad. Dad couldn't hide his irritation from us but he remained discreet about the details of their disagreements. The series, broadcast during the Jubilee year of 1977, was immensely popular. Simon Schama was one of Plumb's celebrated pupils, and perhaps *Royal Heritage*, which I think was grievously under-marketed by the BBC, provided a kind of model for Schama's own whiggish BBC *History of Britain* (although it rather lacked the vim and dash of its predecessor). It is pleasing to note that Schama, as Dad did, reveres

---

* On one occasion the two men had entered expenses chits for precisely the same outing. Plumb's was four times Dad's, and he was questioned by the BBC accounts people as a consequence. He was furious with Dad.

Rembrandt perhaps above all other painters.* As a book *Royal Heritage* sold 250,000 copies, which even a historian as fastidious as the self-proclaimedly *haute bourgeois* Jack Plumb must have enjoyed. He claimed sole authorship, though in truth the book was as much my father's as it was Plumb's, and it was Dad's name and presentation that produced the sales. *The Observer* called it 'a remarkable tour de force', and reckoned it '*the* book of Jubilee year'. The programme itself received very good audience figures and an exceptionally high popularity rating. It was successful in the United States too. At some promotional dinner, Dad told me in a letter, he 'sat between Jacqueline Onassis, who is absolutely Queen-like, & a person called Este [*sic*] Lauder, who is a kind of Empress in the Fashion World'.

Royal Heritage, being popular with the unwashed masses, was, of course, unpopular with the Oxbridge wits. The permanently sour Richard Ingrams, who is seldom as funny as he thinks he is, complained that 'Sir Huw belongs to the "Er" school of commentators, that is those who believe that the word "er"' should be inserted at regular intervals in their commentary'. (Christopher Booker, another *Private Eye* misanthrope, had years before written of 'the Wheldon approach to modern culture – that the offbeat, the trivial, the gimmicky must always be preferred, in any field, to the Real Thing'.)

Dad remained busy, working in an advisory role for the Corporation, as Chairman at the LSE and the Royal Television

---

* Schama gave the 2006 Royal Television Society Huw Wheldon Memorial Lecture on 'Art and the Art of Television', a title of which Dad would have approved. My mother was keen on Schama. She devoured *Citizens*, his book on the French Revolution; her (now my) copy is full of her marginalia.

Society, and in a host of other roles. He had a very simple but useful set of criteria for accepting invitations: they had to provide either cash, or glory, or to satisfy the demands of piety. One of his favourite excuses for not being able to attend a function was that he was 'visiting a submarine'. He thought that was more or less ungainsayable. For cash, for example, he went for a short trip to advise in a not-to-be named Middle Eastern country, where he found that 'What they like best on television is All In Wrestling, & what they like least is readings from the Koran'.[5]

He didn't stop making programmes either, or making friends. Through the filming of an enormously long documentary, *The Library of Congress* (with which he was not very happy), he became close to the librarian and historian Daniel Boorstin and his wife Ruth. Boorstin was one of those immensely gentlemanly, worldly, humorous and educated Americans who give their country a good name. He wore a bow tie, had a sophisticated sense of humour and got on with Dad like a house on fire. His name lives on in books of quotations for his remark that a celebrity is 'a person known for his well-knownness' or, as it is better remembered, 'famous for being famous'.

Dad also made a documentary to mark the fortieth anniversary of D-Day, *Destination D-Day*, which was principally about the deception plans that convinced the Germans the landings would be at Calais, but it also featured a short passage in which Dad described his own landing in Normandy by glider. Of it, he wrote (to me): 'D-Day thing... neither good nor disastrous, but rather ordinary with a few interesting moments and insights.'

So perhaps Dad didn't miss the BBC and we were never overwhelmed by television politics and we didn't watch too much of the stuff, but I continue to feel proprietorial about the BBC. I care about it. I care what people say about it. I don't like to hear it criticised, unless it is by myself or by some former employee. Of course, it has gone to the dogs, just as everything, continually, goes to the dogs, and in many respects it has, actually, gone to the dogs. I think that the Corporation relies more than it knows on the reputation for ethical trustworthiness established first by radio during the Second World War and then by television in the 1960s and '70s: despite all the pap, all the mediocrity, it is still perceived to be a great and benevolent organisation, pursuing excellence – and truth – in its programming. Nor do I believe that the BBC makes fewer good programmes than it used to. It is simply that it makes more bad ones. The air has to be filled.

The writer Marghanita Laski (niece of that same Harold Laski who had discovered my mother) once declared that the BBC was the greatest single influence for good upon the life of the nation since the decline of the Churches.[6] He may not have gone quite so far, but I think, fundamentally, Dad would have agreed.

Meanwhile, I was seeing Led Zeppelin from a lighting gantry at Earls Court (ignorant of Dad's fame as Jimmy Page's first interviewer), and Bruce Springsteen at Hammersmith Odeon (both 1975), gaining a scholarship to Oxford (1976), about which Dad was markedly unimpressed, getting fired from the *Wokingham Times* for being 'a woozy lad' (1977), spending five nights before 'Mods' exams seeing Dylan, again at Earls Court, and subsequently losing my scholarship (1978), seeing The Clash at Acklam Hall (Boxing Day, 1979), discovering that I loved Brahms, reading the complete works of David Lodge, going to Israel (1980), meeting my future wife (1981), working in a bookshop, fighting CND with Tom Stoppard, snorting cocaine in the 'john' at the Institute for Policy Studies in Washington DC (it seemed *de rigueur*), and promoting exchange in the arts between the USA and the UK. At some point I lost my virginity to a lovely girl (the scorpion destroyer), who abandoned me for Scientology. I drank and smoked and laughed. A lot.

CHAPTER 12

1985–1986: FINAL DAYS

In the late summer or early autumn of 1985, Mum took me to lunch on a boat at Charing Cross, called, I think, the *Queen Elizabeth*. She was not a great taker-to-lunch; she preferred coffee bars on her own with a cigarette and something to read. I am much the same. How she came to choose a floating restaurant I don't know. It was very uncharacteristic. Looking back, however, it was perhaps entirely characteristic. She needed a particular place to tell me that Dad was going to die. Or perhaps she felt that I needed a particular place in which to be told. A place I would remember. It was certainly the kind of detail she would have thought about.

The food wasn't very good, I remember, and I think I

remember being very calm as she told me what to expect. She was business-like, as I suppose one has to be in this kind of situation, and she spoke deliberately, so that I knew she had thought about what and how she was going to tell me. This deliberate tone of voice, again rare, was usually irritating, in the sense that she was taking on a manner: it was easy to feel patronised, while at the same time finding her not entirely serious. On this occasion, however, I felt neither patronised nor condescended to. I think I understood that now was the time for all good men, and so forth.

I do not know precisely what my father died of: it was lung cancer of a complicated sort, or with complications. Nor do I know how long it was before he died that Mum took me to lunch. I occasionally think I ought to know, but I think, like my father, I do not have very much time for that kind of detail. My ear and eye are not very journalistic. I am more interested in the tale. Dad deteriorated quite quickly. I think too – and I find this much more shaming than my vagueness about dates – that he had tried to tell me himself that he was grievously ill.

Some time before the floating lunch, he had taken me to a favourite restaurant of his, Luigi's in Covent Garden, a popular hangout of actors from the Strand and the Aldwych theatres (my brother-in-law, the theatre director Lindsay Posner, occasionally lunched there with Harold Pinter*). We sat in a corner table in an upstairs room, with a window

---

* The Pinters lived in Kew when we were growing up there, and I spent many afternoons playing with their son Daniel in their flat on North Road. For a couple of Whitsuns we went to their flat in Worthing. Pinter was another one of the exotics – dressed all in black with black sideburns and thick curly black hair and spectacles that were black at the top but transparent on the bottom. He had a wonderful voice. To hear Dad and Harold laughing together was to be spoilt in the way of laughter. Mrs Pinter – Vivien Merchant – had a lovely face. Mum had a couple of stories about Harold's treatment of Vivien. After their divorce and her suicide we saw no more of Harold Pinter.

looking out towards the Lyceum and Waterloo Bridge, and naturally received excellent service. Towards the end of the meal he made me a proposition. He said he would give me a certain amount of capital towards a flat on condition that I promise to look after Mum after he died. Furthermore, he wanted me to undertake, should he be reduced to a state in which he could not make his own decisions, to make sure that any medical care he had was not a financial burden on my mother. One would have thought that this kind of talk might alarm me. I remember, however, merely laughing and assuring him that of course I would look after Mum – not, in other words, accepting the gambit that would have allowed him to tell me that he was dying.

'I'm well known for my terrific insensitivity,' my father was fond of declaring, but there at Luigi's I simply did not hear what his words meant. I have a kind of dimness in this respect, which annoys the hell out of me so that I find myself reconstructing conversations long after they have been had, in order to understand what it is I have been told. But that is the only occasion on which I regret not having been brighter. Maybe his death was simply inconceivable; his mortality had not intimated itself to me.

Sian (a couple of years my junior) was told at about the same time as I was. With Sian Mum was again characteristic/ uncharacteristic. She said: 'Your father won't make old bones,' and Sian had to ask for an explanation, never having heard the phrase before. Megan (five years younger, but still a woman of twenty-three) was not told until much later, on the grounds, I think, that she was too passionate. I am sure it was my father's decision not to tell her, and I am sure, too, that although he might not have admitted it, the idea of inflicting pain on her was more than he could have borne. It was a mistake, I believe, for it excluded her, and made her loss a lonelier one to deal with.

She could hardly have failed to recognise that he was very ill.

The chronology of events leading to his death is a blur, and I can recall only incidents and images without the benefit of any order. He wanted the illness kept secret, and so it was, 'with knobs on'. He continued to accept engagements although he was in considerable pain. He gave a tour de force address to the Royal Television Society, in November 1985, in which he told the story of *Yesterday's Men* in 'seven chapters'. And he insisted that the Christmas Party, always held at home on the Sunday before Christmas and involving around 100 guests, should go ahead. Upstairs we had to put 'No Smoking' signs, and I remember cigar-toting Ronnie Harwood letting out an anguished, unbelieving yell as he spotted one on the sitting room door: 'Oh, no, not you too, Huw!' He assumed that the Wheldons (champion smokers all at some point in our lives) had succumbed to the rising trend. I longed to tell him the truth, but he was likely to have guessed it as soon as he saw Dad.

We had had a Christmas Party for as long as I could remember. At Kew we had had a Christmas Party. At Richmond, with its stupendous view over the Thames towards Windsor and the Epsom Downs, the party grew more expansive still.

It would start at noon with coffee in the kitchen and wine in the sitting room – Valpolicella, Muscadet and Hock, unswervingly. Kingsley Amis and my godmother Babs Wright were allowed scotch, which it was my job to dispense. Kingsley always brought a bottle (I think Talisker), from which his drink would usually be poured the following year. We would then proceed downstairs at about 1.30 to the dining room where Mum had laid out the spread: tongue, ham, chicken, hot pies, pork pies, her famous sausage-and-apple, peas, cheesy potatoes, salads, cheese, creations made of fruit and florally decorated by Sian and Meg, mince pies, cream, brandy butter, and so on. Mum usually prepared this all on her own, although we would muck in in various ways (I did a lot of furniture moving). When it came to the day itself my function was to keep people's glasses filled. This both suited me and didn't. It meant I couldn't have a proper conversation with anyone, but it also meant I didn't have to have a proper conversation with anyone.

I suppose a good half of those who came regularly were what the gossip columnists (or hack biographers) would have called TV folk: the Attenboroughs, the Braggs, the Foxes, the Milnes, the Peacocks, Aubrey Singer (usually with a couple of pheasants hanging in hand and a bottle of Balvenie, none of which would be eaten or drunk), Ken and Shirley Russell, the Cottons, the Burtons, David Jones and Sheila Allen, Michael and Isabel Charlton, Peter Black; there were also literary friends, such as Fred Warburg and Pamela du Bayou, Dan and Margaret Jacobson, Dannie and Joan Abse (almost always with a delicious book of theirs as a gift), Colin Spencer and Bob Swash, Kingsley Amis; LSE friends Claus and Mary Moser, Ken Minogue, the Morris Joneses; Bill and Jackie Thomson; William Mars-Jones and Kenneth Bradshaw, clubland friends; theatrical folk such as Harwood and Tom Courtenay and the inimitable Kenneth Griffith; and family friends of course: the Murphys, Ivor and Hilary Rees-Roberts, Ernst and Klary Friedl, the Fletchers; and our (the children's) friends too, maybe a couple each: Robin Herbert (whose paternal grandfather APH had sat on the Board of the Festival of Britain with my own grandfather, and whose maternal grandfather was General Horrocks), Pom Hoare, Francesca Brill, Polly Wickham, Michelle Arthur, Melanie Thaw, all artists and actors.

Over the years I managed the odd conversation. Fred Warburg's wife, Pamela du Bayou, told me my father had done exactly the right thing by not marrying before he was forty. She also told me that Proust was much better in English than French. She wore wonderful hats and make-up and was an accomplished painter. Dannie Abse was always very interested and interesting, but a little intimidating too in his intelligence and expectation. Not half so intimidating, however, as Claus Moser, who would ask difficult direct and yet ironically intended questions that I laughed at and ran away from. I tried to spend as much time as possible in Kingsley's company because he was very funny. He would always sit down. He was not one of those people who ever had to wander. He was like strawberry jam. People were attracted to him. He was a kind man, too, without affectation (well, no – he tended to affect the opposite).

Despite the distinguished cast, the Christmas Party was not remotely grand. There was never a maid in black frock and white pinafore offering finger food, there were no handsome young men in starched shirts and Brylcreemed hair holding trays of drinks. These people were all, absolutely and without question, good friends, and I liked almost all of them, and wish I had known them better. It was always enjoyable, and Dad was tremendously himself. He was very life and he was very soul. The 'No Smoking' of the 1985 party was the only compromise I ever remember. And Dad knew that this was likely to be the last time he saw many of these friends.

One of the last engagements he accepted was an address – the Elsie Fogerty Memorial Lecture – to the staff and students of the Central School of Speech and Drama in Swiss Cottage. 'Serving the Text' was the title of the lecture. I am moved still by the memory of the courage Dad showed that day.

For some reason or another Sian and Meg and Mum and

I had arrived separately from Dad. He was going to come with Isabel Charlton, who was supposed to pick him up at Richmond Hill. For some unfortunate reason, she was late in doing so, and they then found themselves in unmoving traffic at the Regent's Park end of Avenue Road, a mile or so short of the school. I can imagine Dad's anger and frustration, and I can imagine poor Isabel's plight. Frustrated anger was my father's worst vice. He got out of the car, intending to walk. It was a preposterous idea for a man in his condition. Indeed it shouldn't have been possible. Inside the theatre we began to be concerned. Dad was never late for anything. I went to wait outside. Eventually he heaved into sight. I ran to him. He was furious and struggling very hard to breathe. Poor Isabel, who had parked the car, trailed behind.

He was ushered into a little office. I wanted to call a doctor. I didn't think there was any way in which he could speak for fifty minutes, standing up, projecting. I didn't think even five minutes was on the cards. He asked for a glass of water, drank it, and rose from the chair and made his way to the auditorium and proceeded to make his address. It was, as ever, engaging, serious, humorous and successful. I remember his reciting of a lovely Arthur Waley translation from the Chinese poet (and sixth emperor of the Han dynasty) Wu-Ti:

The sound of her silk skirt has stopped.
On the marble pavement dust grows.
Her empty room is cold and still,
Fallen leaves are piled against the doors.
Longing for that lovely lady
How can I bring my aching heart to rest?

Some years before he had recited this – and a passage

from Beckett's *Murphy*, one of his favourite novels – at the Festival Hall in a poetry gala. Other speakers included Diana Rigg, Sylvia Syms, Vivien Merchant and Patrick Wymark, but according to one somewhat surprised reviewer 'Huw Wheldon was much the best thing in the whole evening'. Dad had a beautiful voice and read very well. His narration on *Elgar* is exemplary.

At home, a chair lift was installed. It ran from the bedroom to the sitting room. Dad made a great deal of this, to the extent that when he was high on painkillers he would travel up and down on it making absurd child-like remarks, which we found not remotely embarrassing or pathetic, but rather very funny. Even out of his mind he was still himself.

Other images impress: a particular beaker into which he spat the gunge he dredged up from his poor chest – we threw the beaker away afterwards; Sian, Meg, me, Mum sitting around the kitchen table, smoking, not being upstairs, Dad being alone upstairs, talking deep into the night, as though now licensed; my saying, for one reason or another, that I was an idiot and Dad saying quietly, 'No, you're not that, you're not that'; the tape machine I set up in his bedroom, and the Bach (David Attenborough brought the B Minor Mass) and the Poulenc and the Mozart that issued from it; Michael Peacock bringing Johnson's *A Journey to the Western Islands of Scotland*; Mum trying to persuade Dad to take homeopathic remedies and his breaking her heart by rejecting her ministrations. My mother went very deep – characteristically – into the question of complementary medicines, sending Sian into the depths of Southall to consult with various gurus. It was, I suppose, something to do. She had a certain arrogance, my mother, and she loved my father profoundly, and it is possible that she thought she could save him.

There weren't any priests about. Norman Podhoretz has suggested that Bach fulfilled this role. During the war, music, and especially Bach, had been consoling:

> Earlier this evening, as I was battling, not very successfully, with the supply of petrol in the field, I heard very smoothly played Bach drifting over the lawns. So I crossed the courtyard to a bare room where I know there is a piano & there playing it in a grey light under a great mullioned window was a vast Canadian major with a sweaty teutonic face, bald, steel glasses: a singularly impassive chap attached in some way to the Staff. Still otherwise immobile, 250 pounds of solid flesh and a shining pate, there he was playing Bach for dear life, with a certainty of touch which made my heart ache.[1]

Music made Dad's heart ache. But of the priestliness I really don't know. Everything that happened was prosaic; there was no religiose heightening of the senses. Ten years earlier he had nearly died from cancer of the gut; a brand new treatment had worked. He had considered the following ten years a kind of bonus – 'ten years buckshee'. He told Sian that he was 'quite interested' in the process of dying. Sian now considers this to have been a straightforward act of kindness towards her. But, as I say, there were no priests running across the field; no incense was lit, there were no prayers.

And yet. The day before my father died I left work early. I was fortunate enough to be employed by a woman called Jennifer Williams, who ran an outfit called the British American Arts Association, promoting exchange in the arts between the USA and the UK. Humane and funny and affectionate, she could have done with a more zealous, certainly a more organised, Information Officer, but she liked having me about, I think. Anyway, I left early perhaps because I had promised Mum I would do a chore of some sort. The BAAA office was in Wellington Street (almost opposite Luigi's restaurant), and so my way home was over Waterloo Bridge to the railway station. It was a fine March day, with a bit of breeze and lots of blue sky. Halfway across the bridge I stopped and looked into the sky above the Royal Festival Hall. There was a large cottage-loaf-shaped cloud, and beyond it there was the flawless blue empyrean. I was glued to the spot, staring. I knew then that Dad was going to die very soon and that it would be good that he should do so, that his death would make him happy. I smiled up into the sky. It felt like a moment of grace. It was certainly emphatic.

I lived at that time with Ute Arnold in the self-contained flat in the basement of the house on Richmond Hill. On 14 March 1986 Ute shook me awake, saying that my mother was calling me. I went out into the passage between the staircase and the kitchen. I don't know what she said. Perhaps she said nothing. We hugged each other for a long time, and then I got dressed and began to go about my duties. It was my sister Megan's twenty-third birthday. Halley's Comet had passed the night before.

I saw my father's dead body once, that morning. Or rather I saw his head and his feet. I had helped lift his skimbleshank bones in and out of bed, and had become used to the shock of its deterioration, but I did not want to see the corpse, because of course it was not merely a corpse, however much I would try to convince myself it was. But I knew I ought to see death. I knew I should not make Mum suggest it. So I went, and I looked and I saw a dead, dead thing, quite unlike what my father had been. Dai, however, who had arrived from Carmarthen within hours, saw his friend. I watched at the bedroom door as he pulled up the sheet at the foot of the bed, and took hold of Dad's toes. He spoke some words of Welsh, soft, endearing, affectionate, words of friendship and love, and I felt powerfully for him. The touching of the feet was a lovely last connection, and somehow holy. My chest still hollows a little thinking of it.

The days that followed I enjoyed: not the ecstatic joy of pleasure, of course, but the deep joy of a sense of duty being fulfilled. I made myself strong and executive, damned if I was going to let Dad or myself down. There was a good deal of press attention, and a seemingly endless number of friends and admirers on the telephone and at the door. (The first was Roy Davies, whom neither Mum nor I had ever met, a fellow Welshman who had produced *Destination D-Day*. Roy was Head of History at the BBC. Because he was unknown to me, his sadness touched me tremendously.)

There was, of course, the funeral to arrange, and the wake afterwards at home. There were the Americans to book hotel rooms for; there seemed, all in all, a great deal to do, and this was of benefit to me. It kept me from being too much acquainted with grief.

Not so for the women. Chaucer describes women's grief disturbing Theseus' homecoming in *The Knight's Tale*.

swich a cry and swich a wo they make
That in this world nys creature lyvynge
That herde swich another waymentynge

Sian and Meg and Mum were, to lesser and greater degrees, unable to stop sobbing for any period of time. Megan especially was distraught. There is no consolation for the death of someone so wholly loved. All one can do is be on their side. For myself I remember one moment of pulverising sorrow. It was a fine day, some time after the funeral. I put on the CD player a piece by Haydn, pretty loud. There hadn't been any music in the house since Dad had died. The CD player was in a room we called the Red Room (actually it was blue – only the curtains were red) and the speakers themselves in the sitting room. I stood for a moment in the doorway between the two rooms, looking out to that peerless view over the Thames. Mum appeared at the door that led from the sitting room to the stairs. I walked to the window, and then broke down, and turned, and Mum was weeping too, and we knew it was too soon for Haydn. I turned off the CD. I had put it on in an act of defiance, or rather as a gesture of which I hoped Dad would approve: the glorification of Life. But the glory was too much to bear.

The day of the funeral was a grand March day, all sun and leonine gale. It seemed right. The sun sliced in through the stained glass of Richmond Parish Church, illuminating the coffin. I read 'Death be not proud'. We sang 'Come Down O Love Divine' and 'Bread of Heaven', or tried to, and then we went on to the crematorium.

Two months later, on what would have been Dad's seventieth birthday, a memorial service was held at Westminster Abbey. Humphrey Burton helped us arrange it. Sir Paul Fox (of the BBC), Sir Ralf Dahrendorf (of the LSE) and Sir Robin Cooke (of the New Zealand judiciary) gave eulogies. The BBC Chorus sang Handel's 'Zadok the Priest', I insisted on Poulenc's 'Agnus Dei' from the Mass in G, a piece Dad was very fond of late in life, and the marvellous Jessye Norman sang 'Dido's Lament' by Purcell:

> When I am laid in earth, may my wrongs create
> No trouble, no trouble in thy breast;
> Remember me, but ah! forget my fate

Mum spent a long time wondering where to place the ashes. On the one hand there was Wales; on the other there was London. She made the right decision, and a good time after he died we sprinkled them around the Liquidambar sapling a couple of hundred yards inside the Victoria gate to Kew Gardens.

Seven years later we sprinkled Mum's ashes there too. They are both remembered in the graveyard of the cold low little church nestled on the flank of Snowdon at Nant Peris where other older Wheldons are buried. Jonah Jones carved their names in slate, and slate is hard and not easy to erode, and is beautiful, as were my mother and father both.

I have attempted in the foregoing to describe the values that my father lived his life by, where those values came from, and how he applied them, with some reference to my own experience. I have touched upon their application in his professional life, but others are in a better position to judge his success in that realm.

My father hit me once. I must have been seventeen or eighteen. I pushed him back. I think I was shocked more by my own action than by his. I do not remember anything else about the row, except that it had spilled from the house onto the road. Eventually, I had left. Sian had been a witness. This is her account:

> I have a feeling that Wynn was still in bed, at, say, midday. Dad exploded into a wild rage; he demanded to know why Wynn didn't have a bloody job to go to. Wynn moved fast, up and dressed and trying to hold his own against this towering and terrifying inferno (what I was still doing there I cannot imagine – too scared to run maybe). Wynn made

it to the front door, down the steps and had almost made it
to the gate, when Dad picked up a flower pot from the top
step and flung it at him with tremendous force. It smashed
on the gate post, hit Wynn (with no ill effect) and landed
broken on the ground. Wynn was gone. Dad was still raging
– I had never seen him use physical force before (or after).
He was shaking and bubbling and boiling: 'I was in the
bloody army by the time I was his age... I was a (Captain
/ lieutenant / whatever) by the time I was his bloody age,
I was...' Then suddenly his full rushing torrent of fury
seemed to smash into an unbidden memory, stopping
him in his tracks. 'No... actually... I wasn't, no, I wasn't...
not actually at his age (he seemed to do a quick mental
calculation)... no...'

I ventured to say something mild in Wynn's defence like 'He's
good, though, he will be fine, it is the holidays.' Dad, suddenly
affectionate and instantly truly sorry, was friendly, put his
hand on my shoulder and said, 'Yes, I know he is, I know he
will, I know, I know.' His fury had left him sorry, reflective,
calm and kind again. Memories of my own arguments with
Dad all include full unreserved and real apologies from him,
never any little fragments of rancour left over.[2]

Peter Black, a friend but not an intimate, wrote that Dad 'had
a generous optimism about people. Absolutely lacking in
malice or pettiness himself, he was always flummoxed to find
them in others.'

So far as I am concerned, he was a Good father; according
to my mother, he was a Good husband; judging from the
nature of the correspondence with his father, he was a Good
son. According to professional colleagues he was not only

greatly admired and respected but, by many of them, loved. He was a Good Man, a Great Man.

There were many obituaries and remembrances. 'I don't think I have ever known anyone who gave so much pleasure and reassurance, marvellous feeling, to his friends,' wrote Kingsley Amis. 'He was the idiom, the dialect of a whole territory,' wrote Robert Robinson. Tony Jay wrote: 'One of the things I loved most was that underneath all the ebullience and pleasure he took – and had every right to take – at holding the centre of the stage, he had a genuine humility. I'm sure that he honestly never believed he was the great man the rest of us knew him to be.' And Stephen Hearst's 'the most life-enhancing friend it has been my good fortune to make' was echoed and reiterated in letter after letter. The most touching note came from Dan Jacobson, perhaps because it recorded something intimately recognisable to myself: 'I shall never forget Huw kneeling down with tiny Jess [Jacobson's daughter] to do a charade of Jack and the Beanstalk, in the garden of Jonah Jones' house, above that estuary in Wales. All of him was there.'

Of the publicly published eulogies, the most heartfelt, the one that moved me most, came from Norman Podhoretz, written for the *Washington Post*, and read into the US Congressional Record by Pat Moynihan. These are the final paragraphs:

Serving God as my friend came to understand it translated into devoting oneself to something greater than self – in his own case it was a great national institution, but almost anything large would do – and praising God translated into praising life.

Although hymns and hosannas were certainly necessary to glorify what deserved to be glorified, one was not mainly supposed to praise life by verbal affirmation. Mainly one praised it through a readiness to enjoy what there was to be enjoyed, to relish what there was to relish, to savor what there was to be savored, and most especially to accept every invitation to a good laugh that the world had to offer.

All this my friend did, and more. Like Falstaff, he was not only witty in himself, but 'the cause that wit was in other men'. And even more than wit, he was the cause that laughter was in other men. His own laugh was so loud and boisterous that – I do not exaggerate – it became famous from one end of England to the other. Nor do I exaggerate when I say that his entry into a room invariably made everyone smile, in happy anticipation of the laughter he was sure to bring.

That such a man – a man so alive that thinking of him dead seems a contradiction in terms – should rage against death is not surprising. But why should such a man torment himself over dying in a state of rage.

He hinted at the answer in telling me that one day, when his physical pain was at its most unbearable, he turned in desperate search for help to a cantata about dying by Johann Sebastian Bach, Ich habe genug – 'I have had enough'. And he asked himself: 'If Bach can say it, why can't I?' He meant that if Bach, in his eyes perhaps the greatest of all men, was permitted to yearn for death as an escape from the awful miseries of this life, why should he, an ordinary mortal, be required to go on raging?

But of course, he knew why. Bach, who believed in an afterlife, was permitted to serve God and praise him by welcoming death as a deliverance into the arms of his savior. My friend could only serve God and praise Him by cherishing life on this earth to the very end, and by refusing to curse it.

And so even, or rather especially, in the extremity of his suffering, he did not curse life – neither with the words of his mouth, nor, I feel sure, in the meditations of his heart. Least of all did he curse it as so many do nowadays when they declare that life is worth having only when it is good and, worse yet, when they act on that satanic idea.

My friend's name was Huw Wheldon. Though he would have accused me of blasphemy for saying so, he taught everyone who was given the great and blessed gift of knowing him – including, I suspect, people who knew him only from the television screen – how, in what he himself called these spiritually illiterate times, when it is so hard to die with the peaceful resignation of a true believer, it is still possible to live a truly godly life.

There were many flowers at the crematorium in Mortlake. We strolled by them, reading the inscriptions. One bouquet bore the inscription: '*...he loved chivalrie, Trouthe and honour, fredom and curteisie...*'[3] It was unsigned, but we knew it was from Mum. My mother gave her life for his. In doing so perhaps she had deprived the world of her own talents, but then that genius had already discovered for itself the simple old New Testament truth, that God is Love and Love God, and I think she observed that belief with devotion, even piety.

She knew she had been fortunate: she had loved and been loved by a *parfit gentil knight*.

He was thought unintellectual but he could recite Rilke in German and had taught Plato. Others thought he must be public school and Oxbridge. He was grammar school and LSE. People thought he was tall. He was under six foot. Almost everyone thinks he was the Director-General of the BBC. He was a much more complicated individual than was perhaps commonly thought. At the same time, several people, in print, called him the finest man they had known.

Did Dad die disappointed? I don't know. Had he stayed in the army it is impossible not to imagine him becoming very senior indeed. Had he stayed with the Arts Council he would at the very least have become Director, and then what beyond? That he did not become Director-General of the BBC, and thereby cement himself into history, like an archbishop, I don't think especially upset him. He never complained about it, and was delighted that Charles Curran was there as a barrier between him and 'the sodding Governors'. I think his readiness to laugh, to be 'convivial with purpose', disguised the real, the important, intellectual heft he brought to running BBC Television, and I honestly believe that his ability as a leader – an Admiral – is something the Corporation has lacked in the decades since his departure.

Had he been 'aflame, mad for the truth, drunken with the wine of a noble aim?' I think he is likely to have thought that he'd had his moments, and that one cannot, perhaps should not, ask very much more of oneself.

* * *

'Shall we kick the bar?' asks Dad.

It's a phrase well known in Wales, associated with the university seaside town of Aberystwyth. The origins are unclear, but it is agreed that the 'bar' is the lower railing at the northern end of the promenade.

Dad is just back from work and there is no time before supper for a run or even a walk round the block. There is a terrace that runs past our house which overlooks a view of the Thames – loved by all who have seen it, from Constable to Kandinsky. The dusk-dark river bends with an inimitable curve (actually, I can draw it with my eyes shut). The sky burns on the horizon.

We walk out on to the terrace and stroll first to the Terrace Gardens end. We kick the bar, the lower horizontal bar of the iron railing that encloses the terrace. We stroll back, past the house, towards The Wick end. We kick the bar. We go back to the house.

Perhaps he has told me of his day. Perhaps he has asked after mine. Perhaps we have said nothing. Perhaps he bade 'good evening' to neighbours. It is a 300-yard constitutional. It is cheerful because he is usually cheerful. I am cheerful because I know we like each other and because it is a short walk and I do not have to feel guilty about not accompanying him into the park for a run. But it is not a pointless meander. There is a target, something achieved. Together, we have kicked the bar.

HPW off to play 'exceedingly bad golf with exceedingly good chaps'.
Pencil and ink sketch by Sian Wheldon

NOTES

ABBREVIATIONS

HPWP = Papers (uncatalogued) of Huw Wheldon (held by Bangor University)
WPWP = Papers (uncatalogued) of Wynn Wheldon (the author)
JMWP = Papers (uncatalogued) of Jacqueline Wheldon (privately held)
HPW Dimbleby = The British Experience in Television, BBC 1976
HPW = Huw Wheldon

NOTE: My father's letters almost always start *in medias res*, without a greeting, so it is not always clear whom he is addressing.

Introduction

1   Edmund Gosse, *Father and Son* (London: Heinemann, 1907).

Chapter 1

1   Dr D Martyn Lloyd-Jones, 'William Williams and Welsh Calvinistic Methodism', in *The Puritans: Their Origins and Successors* (Edinburgh: Banner of Truth Trust, 1987), pp. 191–214.

2   DD Williams, *Cofiant Thomas Jones Wheldon* (Caernarfon: 1925), p. 114.

3   Emyr Humphreys, 'A Lost Leader?', *Planet 83*, October/ November 1990, p. 3.

4   Kenneth O. Morgan, *Rebirth of a Nation, Wales 1880–1980* (Oxford: Oxford University Press, 1981), p. 65. Published by permission of Oxford University Press.

5   *Welsh Outlook*, September 1925.

6   'Reminiscence of the United Free Church Assembly of 1902, Glasgow', Miscellaneous papers, HPWP.

7   Miscellaneous papers, HPWP.

8   Letter to *Liverpool Daily Post*, 9 July 1968.

9   Morgan, p. 105. Published by permission of Oxford University Press.

10 Jonah Jones, *The Gallipoli Diary* (Bridgend: Seren, 1989), p. 69. Published by permission of the Estate of Jonah Jones.

11 Thomas Jones Wheldon to Wynn Powell Wheldon, undated, HPWP.

12 Miscellaneous papers, HPWP.

13 Humphreys, p. 5.

14 Morgan, p. 123. Published by permission of Oxford University Press.

15 Ibid.

16 Miscellaneous papers, HPWP.

17 *The Ladies Field*, [?] August 1915, press cutting in HPWP.

18 Morgan, p. 203. Published by permission of Oxford University Press.

19 Miscellaneous papers, HPWP.

20 *Bangor: The Touring Centre for North Wales*, Issued under the Auspices of the City Council by the Bangor Traders Association.

21 JA Hoare, 'Sir Huw Wheldon, A Public Man' (unpublished typescript), p. 6, HPWP.

22 Miscellaneous papers, HPWP.

23 *The Western Mail*, press cutting in HPWP.

24   Hoare, p. 3.
25   Norman Podhoretz, 'On the Death of a Friend', *The Times*, 22 March 1986.

Chapter 2
1   Report by the Vocational Guidance Department of the National Institute of Industrial Psychology, 10 August 1932, WPWP.
2   HPW to Mair, 11 May 1934, HPWP.
3   Hoare, p.4.
4   Hoare, p.2.
5   Paul Ferris, *Sir Huge: The Life of Huw Wheldon* (London: Michael Joseph, 1990), p. 15.
6   Letter from HPW to his father, Wynn Wheldon (WW), 1938, HPWP.
7   HPW to Desmond Leeper (DL), [?] 1938, HPWP.
8   HPW to DL, April 1940, HPWP.
9   HPW to DL, 21 February 1939, HPWP.
10   HPW to DL, 15 March 1939, HPWP.
11   HPW to DL, March 1940, HPWP.

Chapter 3
1   Letter from HPW to WW, June 1940, HPWP.
2   Letter from HPW to his mother, Megan Wheldon (MW), June 1940, HPWP.
3   Miscellaneous papers, HPWP.
4   HPW to WW, 9 July 1940, HPWP.
5   HPW to WW, September 1940, HPWP.
6   HPW to DL, 18 September 1940, HPWP.
7   HPW to DL, 3 October 1940, HPWP.
8   Ibid.
9   HPW Dimbleby.

10 HPW to Ben Leeper (BL), 15 December 1940, HPWP.

11 HPW to WW, 9 January 1941, HPWP.

12 Ibid.

13 HPW to DL, September 1941, HPWP.

14 HPW to MW, November 1940, HPWP.

15 HPW to DL, 17 November 1940, HPWP.

16 HPW, 'Television and the Arts', BBC 1964.

17 HPW to WW and MW, 20 September 1941, HPWP.

18 HPW to MW, February 1941, HPWP.

19 HPW, *The Achievement of Television* (BBC 1975).

20 HPW to DL, April 1941, HPWP.

21 HPW, *The Achievement of Television.*

22 HPW to WW, 9 June 1941, HPWP.

23 HPW to DL, April 1941, HPWP.

24 HPW to WW, July 1941, HPWP.

25 HPW to family, June 1941, HPWP.

26 HPW to WW, 20 September 1941, HPWP.

27 HPW Dimbleby.

28 HPW to WW, March 1942, HPWP.

29 HPW to WW, April 1942, HPWP.

30 Hoare, p. 4.

31 HPW to DL, September 1938, HPWP.

32 HPW to WW, February 1942, HPWP.

33 HPW to MW, 1942, HPWP.

34 Richard Rees, 'Memoirs of an Infantry Medical Officer, 1942–1945', unpublished memoir.

Chapter 4

1 HPW to WW, June 1942, HPWP.

2 HPW to WW, 7 July 1942, HPWP.

3 Ibid.

4 HPW to WW, summer 1942, HPWP.

5   HPW to DL, November 1942, HPWP.

6   HPW to DL, spring 1943, HPWP.

7   HPW to WW [?], 13 December 1943, HPWP.

8   HPW to WW, early spring 1944 [?], HPWP.

9   HPW to WW [?], March 1944, HPWP.

10 HPW to DL, mid-April 1944, HPWP.

11 HPW to MW, April 1944, HPWP.

12 HPW to BL, April 1944, HPWP.

13 HPW to WW, May 1944, HPWP.

14 Ibid.

15 HPW to WW and MW, June 1944, HPWP.

16 HPW, *Red Berets into Normandy* (Norwich: Jarrold & Co, 1982), pp. 15–16.

17 HPW to WW, 29 August 1944, HPWP.

18 David Orr and David Truesdale, *The Rifles Are There* (Barnsley: Pen and Sword Military, 2005), p. 125.

19 Rees.

20 HPW to MW, 4 July 1944, HPWP.

21 HPW to DL, 16 July 1944, HPWP.

22 HPW to MW [?], 2 August 1944, HPWP.

23 Evelyn Waugh, *Sword of Honour* (London: Penguin, 1999 edition), p. 144.

24 HPW to WW, 6 August 1944, HPWP.

25 REH Sheridan, 'Recollections of a V.O.P', unpublished memoir.

26 HPW to WW, 29 August 1944, HPWP.

27 Rees.

28 HPW to Leepers, January 1945, HPWP.

29 HPW to WW, January 1945, HPWP.

30 HPW to WW, 21 January 1945, HPWP.

31 HPW to WW, 5 February 1945, HPWP.

32 Ibid.

33 HPW to WW, 3 April 1945, HPWP.
34 Rees.
35 HPW to WW, May 1945, HPWP.
36 Orr and Truesdale, picture section.
37 Jones, p. 69. Published by permission of the Estate of Jonah Jones.

Chapter 5
1 Miscellaneous papers, HPWP.
2 Ibid.
3 ACGB Archives, EL 6/1.
4 Paul Wright, *A Brittle Glory* (London: Weidenfeld & Nicolson, 1986), p. 34.
5 Ibid, pp. 34–5.
6 © Copyright Michael Frayn 1963, 2009. This is an extract from an essay entitled 'Rainbow over the Thames' included in *Travels with a Typewriter* published by Faber and Faber, 2009.
7 Sir Paul Wright to JMW, April 1986.

Chapter 6
1 John Grist, *Grace Wyndham Goldie* (London: New Generation Publishing, 2006), p. 66.
2 Grist, p. 67.
3 Grist, p. 68.
4 Leonard Miall, 'Huw Wheldon', *Inside the BBC* (London: Weidenfeld & Nicolson, 1994), p. 190.
5 WE Williams to George Barnes, BBC WAC L2/242/1.
6 Interview with Frank Gillard, BBC WAC R143/133/2.
7 BBC Radio Wales interview, 1980.
8 Gillard, BBC WAC R143/133/2.
9 WE Williams to George Barnes, BBC WAC L2/242/1.

10 Gillard, BBC WAC R143/133/2.
11 *Daily Mail*, October 1952.
12 Peter Black, *The Mirror in the Corner* (London: Hutchinson, 1972), p. 20.
13 Lia Low, *Look and Listen*, June 1955, p. 10.
14 TV Talk by Eleanor Wintour, *Tribune*, 28 October 1955.
15 Miall, p. 194.
16 David Attenborough, *Life on Air* (London: BBC, 2002, 2013), p. 14.
17 Grist, p. 5.
18 HPW to WW, 15 January 1955, HPWP.
19 Gillard, BBC WAC R143/133/2.
20 Grace Wyndham Goldie, *Facing the Nation* (London: Bodley Head, 1977), p. 171.
21 Gillard, BBC WAC R143/133/2.
22 Michael Cockerell, *Live from Number 10* (London: Faber & Faber, 1988), p. 55.

Chapter 7

1 Ferris, p. 117.
2 HPW to DL, autumn 1938 [?], HPW.
3 *The Times* obituary by Dan Jacobson, 29 June 1993.
4 Jacqueline Wheldon, *My LSE*, ed. Joan Abse (London: Robson, 1977), p. 131.
5 Ibid, p. 134.
6 Ibid.
7 *Clare Market Review*, quoted in *My LSE*.
8 *My LSE*, p. 143.
9 Letter from Professor Smellie, JMWP.
10 *Daily Mail*, 9 February 1966.
11 Thomas L. Jeffers, *Norman Podhoretz, A Biography* (New York: Cambridge University Press, 2010), pp. 44–5.

12 HPW to JMW, 22 March 1955, WPWP.

13 HPW to Co-op Bank manager, 9 March 1955, WPWP.

14 Sian Wheldon, in a written note to the author, March 2008.

15 *The Times* obituary, 29 June 1993.

16 Introduction to unpublished anthology.

17 *Daily Telegraph* obituary, 1 July 1993.

18 *Daily Mail*, 9 February 1966.

19 *The Times* obituary, 29 June 1993.

20 *Independent* obituary, 28 June 1993.

21 Norman Podhoretz, letter to the author.

22 HPW to JMW, October 1959, WPWP.

Chapter 8

1 Ken Russell, *A British Picture* (London: Heinemann, 1989), pp. 15–23.

2 K Adam to Leonard Miall, 'New Magazine Programme', 19 March 1957 (T32/937/12).

3 Gillard, BBC WAC R143/133/2.

4 HPW, letter to Jean Anouilh, 1958 (T32/933/1).

5 Grist, p. 173.

6 Gillard, BBC WAC R143/133/2.

7 John Schlesinger, *Omnibus: Huw Wheldon by His Friends* (BBC TV, 1986).

8 John Baxter, *An Appalling Talent* (London: Michael Joseph, 1973), pp. 118–19.

9 Baxter, p. 113.

10 John Betjeman to Nancy Thomas, quoted in Paul Sutton, *Becoming Ken Russell* (Cambridge: Bear Claw, 2012), p. 194.

11 HPW to John Betjeman, quoted in Sutton, p. 194.

12 Huw Wheldon, Introduction, *Monitor* (London:

Macdonald, 1962), pp. 12–13.

13 HPW, 'Television and the Arts', BBC 1964.

14 Jeremy Brooks, *The Spectator*, 21 December 1962.

15 Oscar Turnill, *Sunday Times*, 11 November 1962.

16 *Time & Tide*, 31 January 1959.

17 Hoare, p. 8.

18 HPW, *Monitor*, p. 19.

19 HPW, *Monitor*, p. 11.

20 'Wheldon, the BBC's Horatio', *New Statesman*, December 1971.

21 Attenborough, p. 199.

22 John Boorman, *Adventures of a Suburban Boy* (London: Faber & Faber, 2003), p. 102.

23 http://archive.spectator.co.uk/article/28th-may-1965/9/the-satirists-move-o.

24 Email to the author, 8 April 2015.

25 Tim Boon and Jean-Baptiste Gouyon, 'Horizon at 50', http://www.bbc.co.uk/historyofthebbc/resources/horizon50/tim-boo.

26 Charlotte Higgins, *This New Noise* (London: Guardian and Faber & Faber, 2015), p. 63.

Chapter 9

1 Gillard, BBC WAC R143/133/.

2 Ibid.

3 HPW Dimbleby.

4 Ibid.

5 http://www.theguardian.com/media/2001/nov/24/guardianobituaries.obituaries.

6 Gillard, BBC WAC R143/133/2.

7 Ibid.

8 *The Times*, 25 May 1959.

9 Gillard, BBC WAC R143/133/2.

10 Ferris, p. 171.

11 Ferris, p. 175, absolute control memo, HPW to Kenneth Adam, 2 February 1965.

12 Gillard, BBC WAC R143/133/2.

13 Asa Briggs, *The History of Broadcasting in the United Kingdom*, Volume 5: Competition, 1955–1974 (Oxford: Oxford University Press, 1995), p. 534.

14 Gillard, BBC WAC R143/133/2.

15 Ibid.

16 Lord Hill of Luton, *Behind the Screen* (London: Sidgwick & Jackson, 1974), p. 104.

17 Bill Cotton, *Double Bill* (London: 4th Estate, 2000), p. 156.

18 Robin Day, *Grand Inquisitor* (London: Weidenfeld & Nicolson, 1989), p. 175.

19 Gillard, BBC WAC R143/133/2.

20 Ibid.

21 Brian Blessed, *Nothing's Impossible* (London: Simon & Schuster, 1994), p. 7.

22 Quoted in Briggs, p. 897.

23 Gillard, BBC WAC R143/133/2.

24 Ian Trethowan, *Split Screen* (London: Hamish Hamilton, 1984), p. 145.

Chapter 11

1 HPW to the author, May 1978, WPWP.

2 HPW to WW, summer 1944, HPWP.

3 Jones, pp. 71–2. Published by permission of the Estate of Jonah Jones.

4 Sian Wheldon, in a written note to the author, May 2008.

5 HPW to the author, 15 February 1978, WPWP.

6   Peter Black, *The Biggest Aspidistra in the World* (London: BBC, 1972), p. 231.

Chapter 12

1   HPW to DL, March 1942, HPWP.
2   Sian Wheldon, in a written note to the author, May 2008.
3   Chaucer's Prologue to *The Canterbury Tales*.

INDEX OF PERSONS

SUPPORTERS

Unbound is a new kind of publishing house. Our books are funded directly by readers. This was a very popular idea during the late eighteenth and early nineteenth centuries. Now we have revived it for the internet age. It allows authors to write the books they really want to write and readers to support the writing they would most like to see published. The names listed below are of readers who have pledged their support and made this book happen. If you'd like to join them, visit: www.unbound.co.uk.

Alice Adams
Jennifer and
   Matteo Adinolfi
Bill Akass
Jonathan Alwyn
Marilyn Anderson
Melanie Arnold
Miranda Arnold
Nora Arnold
Thomas Arnold
Ute Arnold
Sam Arnold-Forster
Val Arnold-Forster
Michelle Arthur
Michael Attenborough
Byron Baber
David Barlow
Julie Bartle
Philippa Barton
Susanne Bast
Luke Beauchamp
Zalie Benda
Ros and Andy Birkby
Evanthe Blandy
Amanda Bloore
Mark Bottomley
Christopher Bowen

Francesca Brill
Lindsey Brodie
Humphrey Burton
Matt Burton
Simon Callow
Tom Cash
Bill Chamberlain
Kathy Chamberlain
Hugo Chapman
Mathew Claridge
Kenneth Clarke
Alastair Conway
Lou Coulson
Paul Crabtree
George Craig
Tom Cullen
Elinor Davies
Gareth Davies
Rhodri Davies
Clare Dibble
Amanda Dickinson
Suzie Doscher
Roger Dowling
Ursula & Ian Drummond
Michael Duff
Peter Dumont
Robert Eardley

Donald Earl
Judy Easter
Antony Easton
Mark Ellingham
Michael Fairbairn
Karen Falkner
Dave Fawbert
Jane Fehler
Piers Feltham
Ginny Felton
Victoria and
   Dudley Fishburn
Sion Fletcher-Rees
James Forbes
Sir Paul Fox
Isobel Frankish
Lesley Frazer
Michael & Pamela Frazer
Susan Gafsen
Vic Galler
Marguerite Galloway
Kate Garrett
Amro Gebreel
Sean Glynn
Andy Goldberg
Elizabeth Goodman
Ben Graham

Stephen & Teresa Graham
Tahlia Granger
Kathryn Gregory
Simon Griffith
Stephanie Harvey
John Hayes
Iain Hepburn
Mitch Herbert
Robin Herbert
Paul Herzberg
Mark Honigsbaum
Lucy Hooberman
Matthew Hooberman
Cressida Hudson
Alistair Humphrey
Marcus Hutton
Andrew Jacob
Anne James
Thomas Jeffers
David Townsend Jones
Peter T Jones
Gerry Judah
Adam Kean
Claire Kean
Rick Kemp
Tarka Kings
Wendy Knox
Neal Kozodoy
Peter Kravitz
Jeff Krolik
Nicolas Kullmann
Martin Lambach
Katie Lassman
Jimmy Leach
Mabel Lee
Karen Lewis
Terri Lichstein
Will Liddell
Caitlin Line
Helena Line
Jason Line
Jill Line
Kit Line
Matthew Line

Molly Line
Nick Lipley
Carol Long
DeAndra Lupu
Jutta Lutgen
Patrick Macaskie
Ben Macintyre
Alexander Mackay
Selina Macnair
Ian McBain
Mary McCormack
Robert McCrum
Sam & Linda McKee
Colin McLean
Emma Medd
Leslie Megahey
Amelia and Neil Mendoza
Debby Mendoza
Gillian Mendoza
Valerie Mendoza
Julia Middleton
Sarah Middleton
Alex Moghissi
Keyvan Moghissi
Annabel Moorsom
Jane Morris
Trevor Morris
Keith Moss
Alan Munden
Alla Murphy
Charles Murphy
Carlo Navato
Stephen O'Brien
Emma O'Bryen
Giles O'Bryen
Brendan O'Hea
Judith Paisner
Sirpa Pajunen-Moghissi
Peter Palumbo
Stephen Paul
Michael Peacock
Roland Philipps
Ed Pilkington
John Podhoretz

Norman Podhoretz
Justin Pollard
Lindsay Posner
James Postgate
Edward Powell
Prolebooks
Mel Pryor
Celia Purcell
Qona Rankin
James Reader
Griff Rees
Jill Rees
Mair Rees
Stephan Rees
Wynn Rees
Janet Rees and
    Andrew Williams
D & T Rodzianko
Danny Rosenbaum
Judy Ross
Rupert Rumney
Victoria Salmon
Chrys Salt
Christoph Sander
Janet Sayers
Matthias Schwaab
Sheila Sheehan
William Sieghart
David Skynner
Susan Sluglett
Phil Smith
Anthony Stobart
Apple Stuart
Gordon & Mair Stuart
Malcolm & Fiona Stuart
Kate Summerscale
Gavin Sutherland
Jonathan Tafler
Andrew Taylor
Jay Taylor
Steve Tello
Chris Tennant
Melanie Thaw
Andrew Thompson

Barnaby Thompson
Piers Thompson
Sally Thompson
Eliana Tomkins
Jody Tresidder
Naomi Trodden
Craig Van Straten
Ros Van Straten
Mark Waites
Rupert Walters
Catherine Warner

Luke Weston
Caleb Wheldon
Jacob Wheldon
Megan Wheldon
Nans Wheldon
Sara Wheldon
Sian Wheldon
Sion Wheldon
Merle Wheldon-Posner
Sue Whitmore
Polly Wickham

Andrew Wiggins
John Wiggins
Gareth Wheldon Williams
Islwyn Williams
Meriel Brooke Withnell
Nick Would
Hazel Wright
Will Wyatt
Victorria Wytcherley
Rachel Yorke
Louisa Young